Opportunity in Adversity

———⌇———

*How Colleges
Can Succeed
in Hard Times*

Janice S. Green
Arthur Levine
and Associates

Opportunity in Adversity

How Colleges Can Succeed in Hard Times

 Jossey-Bass Publishers

San Francisco • London • 1985

OPPORTUNITY IN ADVERSITY
How Colleges Can Succeed in Hard Times
        by Janice S. Green, Arthur Levine, and Associates

Copyright © 1985 by: Jossey-Bass Inc., Publishers
                        433 California Street
                        San Francisco, California 94104
                                    &
                        Jossey-Bass Limited
                        28 Banner Street
                        London EC1Y 8QE

Library of Congress Cataloging-in-Publication Data
Main entry under title:

Opportunity in adversity.

    (The Jossey-Bass higher education series)
    Includes bibliographies and index.
    1. Universities and colleges—United States—Adminis-
tration. 2. Universities and colleges—United States—
Administration—Case studies. I. Green, Janice S.
(date). II. Levine, Arthur (date).
III. Series.
LB2341.067 1985   378.73   85-45062
ISBN 0-87589-663-4 (alk. paper)

Manufactured in the United States of America

The paper in this book meets the guidelines for
permanence and durability of the Committee on
Production Guidelines for Book Longevity of the
Council on Library Resources.

JACKET DESIGN BY WILLI BAUM

FIRST EDITION

Code 8538

The Jossey-Bass
Higher Education Series

*This book is dedicated
to the faculty, staff, and trustees
of Bradford College for
proving that there is opportunity in adversity.*

Preface

Recently, one of the editors attended a meeting on the future of American higher education. As the gathering of policy makers, administrators, scholars, and industrialists drew to a close, an auto industry executive said he had been to lots of meetings like this and offered these chilling remarks:

> A few years ago we used to have them in Detroit all the time. We sensed something was wrong but never identified the problems. I think higher education may be doing the same thing today. I would say colleges have fundamental problems that go far beyond the shrinking budgets and declining numbers of young people that so deeply concern higher education today. The problems seem terribly familiar. They undid the auto industry, and they could do the same thing to American higher education.

In *The Decline of the American Automobile Industry,* Brock Yates cites eleven problems that contributed to the fall:

1. Leaders of broad vision gave way to managers whose concern was the bottom line.
2. The industry emphasis shifted from product quality to finance and marketing.
3. Cost cutting took precedence over product improvement, updating, and development.

4. Form (for example, glitter, chrome, and size) was exalted over substance (for example, maintenance, mileage, and safety).

5. In bad times, the focus was on "quick fixes" rather than on long-term solutions.

6. The industry became increasingly self-absorbed and isolated.

7. There was a tendency to live in the past: Major social and economic changes were not recognized; declining public confidence and satisfaction were not perceived.

8. New competitors (car companies from abroad) were ignored.

9. The industry failed to keep up with new technologies.

10. A history of success was transformed into complacency and ultimately lethargy.

11. Work force solidarity declined. Alienation and atomization grew. Self-concern rose. A mood of "look out for number one" came to prevail.

This is a good news–bad news story for higher education. The bad news is that this list sounds familiar. Each of the eleven problems exists to some extent in America's colleges and universities today. In fact, some are rather widespread. In this sense the auto executive may have offered higher education a vision of "the ghost of Christmas future."

The good news is that there are auto companies, like Chrysler, that have made dramatic turnarounds. They recognized the problems facing them, responded directly and boldly, and are now thriving. Several hundred colleges across the country have experienced the same phenomenon according to research conducted by the Consortium for the Advancement of Private Higher Education.

Over the past several years, higher education has heard more of the bad than of the good news. A mood of doom and gloom has fallen over much of the profession. Stories of decline, retrenchment, and closure dominate higher education news reporting. Rumors of colleges in trouble, sometimes correct but often not, fly thick and fast. Conversations among college ad-

ministrators focus too often on enrollments (bodies) and finances (bucks) rather than on education. For some colleges and
universities a sense of crisis exists, a growing belief that decline
is inevitable.

This is one future. But there is also another that is more
inviting and more hopeful. The Chinese word for crisis consists
of two characters: one stands for danger, the other for opportunity.

Opportunity is implicit in adversity. Hard times have produced some of higher education's greatest success stories. The
1840s and 1850s, an era of declining enrollments and diminishing resources, an era not unlike the present, brought forth bold
and excellent new programs that made the names of institutions
as varied as Brown University, the University of Michigan, the
University of Vermont, and Union College in Schenectady, New
York. The depression years saw precisely the same phenomenon
at the University of Chicago and at St. John's in Annapolis.

Good times have meant business as usual for higher education, continuing growth achieved largely by adding the new to
what already existed. In contrast, hard times have necessitated
cutbacks and reappraisals. They have forced some institutions
to develop new visions to guide their futures. In the past, a
number of hard-pressed colleges with thoughtful approaches to
education have thrived. This volume is concerned with how
some colleges are doing this again today.

Organization of This Book

Opportunity in Adversity is divided into three parts. Part
One, "Thriving in Periods of Decline," looks at past and present
periods of adversity. The first chapter, by Michael O'Keefe, describes the social and economic forces that will affect higher
education during the next decade. It goes far beyond the familiar recital of demographic and fiscal woes. O'Keefe cites technological advances; the shift from a production to a service
economy; the emerging role of industry in pure research and in
education; political and social conservatism; a student body
characterized by diversity, materialism, and inadequate prepara-

tion; institutions facing ever-increasing expenditures for salaries, maintenance, and capital improvements; aging, research-oriented faculties; lack of opportunity for younger academics; overspecialized and value-free curricula; institutional fragmentation; and many other factors. The world he describes is profoundly changed, and the changes are both recent and powerful. But he concludes that "leadership, dedication, and the wisdom to know the changing world and to evaluate one's own response to it can alter those trends or harness them to positive effect."

In the second chapter, Frederick Rudolph provides the historical context for O'Keefe's observations. He reminds us that hard times like the present are not new. Since the founding of Harvard College, "adversity and sluggishness" have been more prevalent than "dynamic growth and success." And, examples of institutional achievement and courageous innovation can be identified in even the most confused and adverse periods of American history. Indeed, many of our most prestigious and unique colleges and universities emerged as creative responses to new social and economic pressures. The most successful institutions cited by Rudolph showed these characteristics: a fundamental commitment to educational mission and purpose and a refusal to abandon quality for expediency.

Part Two, "What Colleges Need to Succeed," focuses on those elements that have proven critical for institutional success in hard times. In Chapter Three, Warren Bryan Martin writes about the foundation for success—institutional mission. He explains that a mission enables a college to identify and build on its unique characteristics, those qualities that set the college apart and make it distinctive. A clear definition of mission provides a firm base for developing curriculum and nurturing institutional culture. The optimum mission, Martin believes, is multidimensional, influencing all aspects of a college's programs and activities and permitting the rise of a college culture. Indeed, at the point where culture and mission become synonymous, the college will have consciously achieved a distinctiveness and character that will ensure long-term success and stability.

But this most difficult of all tasks requires a particular brand and caliber of leadership, a sound understanding, not only of the presidential role, but of the qualities and talents inherent in a successful presidency. These topics are addressed first by David Riesman and Sharon Elliott Fuller in Chapter Four and then, from a more personal perspective, by Leon Botstein in Chapter Five. Although the college presidency has become an increasingly transitory, difficult, and beleaguered position, institutional success is directly linked to presidential effectiveness and potency. Similarly linked are leadership style and institutional culture, characteristics, and needs. A particular presidential style and personality may work miracles at one college or university and fail dismally at another. According to these authors, however, we can identify a number of qualities common to those presidents "who have made a difference." They are highly energetic, hardworking, entrepreneurial men and women who know when to speak out and when to listen. By nature they are creative and are frequently risk takers. They can set a respectable intellectual and academic agenda and effectively move their institution, whether by persuasion, charisma, or the earned respect of campus members, toward well-established goals. They are good managers but exemplify the principle that management skills unaccompanied by intellectual vision, sensitivity to campus dynamics, and tireless effort will produce only transitory results. They are, finally, resilient and convincing.

Leon Botstein states that the president is perceived today as a figure engaged primarily in projecting a positive institutional image to external forces and in fund raising. The fact is that both of these activities will be unsuccessful unless founded upon valid, coherent educational purposes and programs.

This is affirmed by Arthur Levine in Chapter Six, where he writes that "the best solutions to today's demographic, financial, and political problems are educational." Levine warns, however, that no single educational model or curricular panacea will translate into institutional success. On the contrary, the best program is one that closely conforms to a college's mission, student body, faculty, resources, and history. Curricular quality and effectiveness can only be assessed within the context of institutional circumstances and purpose. Yet today's educational scene is dominated by programmatic bloat and confusion—"the junkyard curriculum" as Levine calls it—that reflects a survival mentality. In the desperate scramble to attract students and dollars, we may lose sight of educational values, forgetting that institutional success and quality are products of curricular vision, not of expediency or the "quick fix."

The educational vision provided by good leadership can be translated into programmatic reality only by the faculty. Yet, as Jerry G. Gaff notes, in Chapter Seven, today's faculties are largely unprepared to take on that challenging task. The key to successfully changing the curriculum as well as to maximizing faculty effectiveness and flexibility is keeping a faculty vibrant and vital. Gaff describes an emerging agenda that "relies on the generic qualities of development activities but applies them to serve the particular needs of the institution." This approach aims at a simultaneous renewal of faculty and institution based on mutuality of need and purpose. In effect, the specific developmental initiatives proposed by Gaff will result not only in better teaching and learning but in a stronger academic community and more broadly based collegiality.

The successful institution will invest time and resources in establishing a multifaceted program of faculty development that supports curricular change, faculty renewal, and student demands. But how best to attract students to our campuses in this era of intense competition and mounting consumer sophistication? In Chapter Eight, Richard Moll identifies the major obstacle to successful student recruitment: inconsistency between self-perceived mission and external image. Although institutional image is the overriding factor in recruitment, many colleges fail to promote a valid and representative image in marketable terms. Often the public perception of an institution is twenty years or more out of date. Change has occurred, but an updated message has not reached the public. At other campuses, the mission may be so unclear and ill-defined that the projected image is muddied and therefore unappealing. Recruitment, says Moll, must involve all constituencies in a "self-conscious, ambitious, well-organized" campaign. Once recruited, however, the student must be the target of careful, personalized advising aimed at assisting the individual through change and growth. The student who falls through the cracks of the advising system will soon be asking for a transfer recommendation.

Any discussion of institutional success or failure must inevitably lead to the topic of resource management, the focus of Chapter Nine by Robert H. Atwell and Madeleine F. Green. They offer a scenario based on sound decision making and recognition of trade-offs resulting from resource allocations. Once again the emphasis is placed on two key factors: mission and leadership. Successful management of shrinking resources is propelled by the demands of institutional mission and culture and directed by purposeful, decisive, yet collegial leadership. Colleges are not businesses, warn Atwell and Green, and they must beware of entrepreneurship that diverts attention from educational purpose. Nevertheless, certain strategies can be borrowed from the business world with positive results.

Part Three, "Five Success Stories," offers five case studies of very different colleges and universities: Alverno College, Birmingham-Southern College, Bradford College, Brooklyn College, and Hood College. The five chapters in this section tell the stories of institutions that faced the challenges that plague all of higher education today and thrived by applying the strategies discussed in Part Two. Each of the five institutions arrived at a clear statement of its mission and purpose that accorded with a particular collegiate tradition, culture, and set of circumstances. Each has enjoyed a brand of leadership marked by an ability to achieve consensus and a recognition of the appropriate and necessary. The curriculum of each institution reflects its declared mission and purpose, as does the ongoing or proposed program development. Time and resources have been committed to faculty development initiatives designed to promote programmatic objectives and campus goals. Recruitment efforts convey an accurate picture of mission and culture. Resources are managed and allocated so as to serve targeted goals and purposes within the constraints affecting all institutions today. With the exception of Bradford, these chapters were written by the presidents responsible for turning their colleges around.

In the Epilogue, Janice S. Green considers the mistakes

that colleges make in responding to the challenges facing higher education and the ways they can thrive in the years ahead.

For us, this volume has been a labor of love. Neither of us is a Pollyanna. We both believe the next few years will be very difficult for higher education as a whole, perhaps the most challenging years since the great depression. But we are convinced that most *individual* institutions have a chance to excel during the decade ahead.

The present is a time of flux for higher education. Colleges are looking for models of institutional success. New flagships are likely to emerge in the next decade; some familiar and established, others less well known and still developing. The point is that colleges can make great strides in this period of transition, particularly if they recognize the challenges they face and respond to them boldly and directly. The opportunity has never been greater.

Acknowledgments

A great many people are responsible for this volume. Edited volumes are supposed to be hellish affairs; the war stories are not for the fainthearted. Fortunately, this has not been our experience. The contributors, for the most part old friends, were marvelous. JB Lon Hefferlin, one of American higher education's great resources, gave us invaluable advice and counsel. And Eileen Welch, along with Jody Zafris Robidoux and Diane Boardman, of Bradford College held this project together and turned it into a manuscript. We are very grateful to all of them.

Bradford College   Janice S. Green
August 1985   Arthur Levine

Contents

The Authors

Janice S. Green has served as vice-president and academic dean of Bradford College since 1981. She holds a B.A. degree (1962) from Boston University and M.A. (1964) and Ph.D. (1970) degrees from Tufts University in French with a specialization in Renaissance and nineteenth-century literature. Prior to coming to Bradford, she taught at Tufts University and then served for five years with the Massachusetts Board of Higher Education and the Massachusetts Board of Regents for Higher Education.

Green has published numerous articles and a French language textbook. She regularly chairs evaluation teams for the New England Association of Schools and Colleges and is a member of the Association's appeals board. She is also a member of the Executive Council of the Association of General and Liberal Studies and serves as director of major projects funded by the National Endowment for the Humanities, the Exxon Foundation, and the Fund for the Improvement of Postsecondary Education.

Arthur Levine was appointed president of Bradford College in 1982. He received a B.A. degree (1970) from Brandeis University in biology and a Ph.D. degree (1976) from the State University of New York at Buffalo in sociology and higher education. Prior to coming to Bradford, Levine served as senior fellow at the Carnegie Foundation for the Advancement of Teaching in Washington, D.C., and senior fellow at the Carnegie Council on Policy Studies in Higher Education in Berkeley, California. He has taught at both the University of Maryland and the State University of New York at Buffalo. He has also taught at the elementary and secondary school levels.

Levine is the author of dozens of articles and reviews. His previous books include *When Dreams and Heroes Died: A Portrait of Today's College Student* (1980), *Why Innovation Fails* (1980), *Handbook on Undergraduate Curriculum* (1978), and *Quest for Common Learning: The Aims of General Education* (1981, coauthored with Ernest Boyer). A 1982 Guggenheim Fellowship winner, Levine's other awards include the American Council of Education Book of the Year award for *Reform of Undergraduate Education* (1973, coauthored with John Weingart) and the Education Press Association of America's award for best article in 1981.

Robert H. Atwell, president, American Council on Education

Neal R. Berte, president, Birmingham-Southern College

Leon Botstein, president, Bard College and Simon's Rock Early College

Martha E. Church, president, Hood College

Sharon Elliott Fuller, research associate, Harvard University

Jerry G. Gaff, dean, College of Liberal Arts, Hamline University

Madeleine F. Green, director, Center for Leadership Development, American Council on Education

David Charles Haselkorn, assistant to the president, Bradford College

Robert L. Hess, president, Brooklyn College of the City University of New York

Warren Bryan Martin, scholar in residence and senior program officer, Carnegie Foundation for the Advancement of Teaching

Richard Moll, dean of admissions, University of California, Santa Cruz

Michael O'Keefe, president, Consortium for the Advancement of Private Higher Education

Paul Byers Ranslow, dean of admissions, Pitzer College

Sister Joel Read, president, Alverno College

David Riesman, Henry Ford II Professor of the Social Sciences emeritus, Harvard University

Frederick Rudolph, professor of history emeritus, Williams College

Stephen R. Sharkey, associate professor of sociology, Alverno College

Philip A. Shirley, director of public information, Birmingham-Southern College

Opportunity in Adversity

*How Colleges
Can Succeed
in Hard Times*

1

Emerging Challenges to Higher Education

Michael O'Keefe

Few faculty members or administrators are unaware of the diverse pressures now coming to bear on our colleges and universities. American society, slowly emerging from a serious recession, has become increasingly preoccupied with creating jobs and beating back foreign competition. The decline in the traditional college age population is just beginning to affect higher education. Not only are there fewer young people, but their values and interests are quite different from those of a decade ago. They are also less well prepared than were their predecessors of decades past. Colleges and universities, following thirty years of heady expansion, are themselves struggling with the prospect of limited or even declining resources, increased competition for both students and funding, and increasing signs of bureaucratic middle age within their own ivy-covered walls.

This chapter will address the forces likely to affect higher education in the next five to ten years. Most if not all are already well known to the reader of this volume. The intent, therefore, is not to explore in detail each of the many crosscurrents of a complex, changing, and often unpredictable society. Rather it is to reflect on the aggregate impact that these forces are likely to have on higher education.

1

What will be argued is that the prospect of enrollment declines, though admittedly a serious problem, is not the greatest challenge facing our colleges and universities. Far more serious is the prospect that higher education will find itself increasingly out of step with the changing needs of both society and the students whose values and concerns are rooted in that society. How, and to what extent, higher education should trim its sails to meet those changing needs are the central questions.

In the broadest sense, pushes and pulls on higher education come from three directions: society, students, and colleges and universities themselves. Changes in society are often faithfully mirrored in the concerns of students, faculty, and administrators. Changes within academe can also affect the broader society, although that influence is not as great today as it was in the late 1960s and early 1970s. Frequently, an emerging trend in one sector creates an opposing reaction in the other. However they interact, they are closely linked, sometimes to positive effect, other times with unfortunate results. The challenges to administrators in this decade of change are (1) to understand the changes taking place around them, (2) to assess which responses in their own institutions are healthy and which are not, and (3) to develop strategies to enhance the former and neutralize the latter.

Changes in Society

Consult almost any poll, man-on-the-street interview, political advertisement, or popular magazine and you will find, not surprisingly, that the deepest concerns of most citizens are for a strong economy and job security. If there is a single focal point of concern in our society today, it is probably for the economic future of the nation. On first impression, the character of our economy seems encouraging for higher education. During the past half century, the economy has undergone profound structural changes, most of which have enhanced the importance of education. Indeed, some of these changes are in part the result of the successes of education. Many of today's trends look as though they will continue, suggesting that higher education will play an even more critical role in the years ahead.

One major change of the last fifty years has been the shift from the production of goods as the nation's major economic activity to the provision of services—services increasingly based on information and aided by technology. In 1935, 45 percent of the work force was involved in obtaining or processing raw materials, manufacturing, or distributing finished goods. By 1980, this had dropped to 32 percent. During the same period, the service sector grew from 55 to 68 percent of the economy, most of this growth coming in the postwar period. In the last decade, the collecting, analyzing, and managing of information, along with the design and production of the tools needed for these tasks, have enjoyed explosive growth. The critical fuel for this major shift has been human capital. E. F. Dennison estimates that about two-thirds of the growth in the economy between 1948 and 1973 can be attributed to the increased educational level of the work force and to the availability of new knowledge.

A glance at a shopping center parking lot or a stroll through a consumer electronics store will demonstrate the second major change in our economy since the Second World War. It has become far more international. Between 1950 and 1980, imports and exports combined grew from less than 7 percent of our gross national product to more than 15 percent. An estimated 70 percent of domestically manufactured goods now faces competition from imports as compared with only 25 percent two decades ago. We presently export over $200 billion in goods and services per year.

Increased dependence on the rest of the world became far more than a matter of dry statistics in the winter of 1973–1974, when Americans rudely learned that the oil ministers of a few sparsely populated countries around the Persian Gulf could force them to wait in long lines for gas and to shiver in their homes and workplaces. Perhaps even more serious, what had been the backbone of our economy, the automobile industry, suddenly found itself outdesigned and outmarketed by a former and supposedly vanquished foe. The resulting decade of hard times, in which unemployment touched 10 percent and interest rates made a mockery of usury laws, has left the nation with an abiding anxiety and xenophobic conservatism about jobs and the economy. The evidence is on all sides. The United

Auto Workers Union launches a well-financed public relations campaign to "keep jobs in America." Import quotas are imposed on foreign competitors. Domestic content legislation gains supporters. Prosperity is no longer assumed as every American's birthright. Competition is back in style. The bottom line is what counts; and technology, computers, and improved management are viewed as the magic carpets that will put America in the lead again.

At first glance, this looks to be exceptionally good news for higher education. The emphasis on human capital means that education will be at the heart of any strategy to strengthen the economy. Shortages of engineers, computer programmers, and other specialists mean fuller classrooms and laboratories. Continuing growth in technology, health care, the information business, and the ranks of middle management presumably will translate into an expanding demand for college graduates strong in analytic and communication skills. Further, universities are sure to receive a sizable share of new federal, state, and private industry spending on research and development. The aggregate result might well be an unprecedented expansion and revitalization of higher education.

On closer examination, however, this profile of the emerging economy may not mean as much for higher education as at first appears. Yes, future demand for highly trained technical manpower is impressive when measured as the percentage increase in the number of jobs to be filled. In absolute numbers, however, the need is in all likelihood small enough to be met by existing programs with only modest enrollment increases. Further, in some areas of growth, the argument can be made that there will be little, if any, increase in the role played by colleges and universities. Consider the demand for college-educated graduates as a result of expanded and new high-technology industries. In today's economy, these industries account for about 6 percent of all jobs. Relatively few of these jobs, however, require the higher level skills associated with postsecondary education. For example, computer and data-processing companies typically have only one-fourth of their labor forces in technologically oriented jobs. Manufacturers of electronic components have even less, about 15 percent. Factories and businesses in high-tech fields typically require small numbers of very creative and highly trained specialists who perform design work and large numbers of workers who must precisely follow the resulting specifications.

There is little reason to believe that either the proportion of all jobs that are in high technology or the job mix within high technology will change. The U.S. Bureau of Labor Statistics estimates that between now and 1995 about twenty-three to twenty-eight million new jobs will be created in the entire economy. An estimated one and a half million of these new jobs are expected to be in high-technology industries, about the same relative proportion as in today's economy. Openings for technicians or equipment operators are expected to make up a sizable fraction of the new jobs. These will require very limited training, and it will bear little resemblance to the kind of education received in a traditional baccalaureate program.

Why, then, all the talk about dramatic increases in demand for engineers, computer scientists, life and physical scientists, and technicians? Because, according to the Bureau of Labor Statistics, these occupations are expected to grow at twice the rate of all occupations between now and 1995. For example, the number of computer systems analysts will grow by 85 percent and the number of programmers by 77 percent. Demand for computer service technicians will almost double. The drama, unfortunately, is again in the percentages. The total increase in demand for computer programmers, for example, is projected to be slightly over 200,000 jobs, less than 1 percent of total employment growth over the ten-year period in question. While more impressive than job growth for lawyers and short-order cooks, this is only a fraction of the new openings that will be available for building custodians (780,000), secretaries (720,000), or even teachers (510,000).

But what about the impact of high technology on other more traditional industries? Commentators have suggested that our older industries will become competitive in the world economy only if technology can be used to increase productivity and thus enable us to compete with Third World countries whose labor costs are far lower than ours. So, will this not increase the demand for better-educated workers? Probably not. Studies have found that changes in "old" industries have two effects: Some workers are replaced, and the average skill level of those that remain is lowered, not raised. These effects are hardly surprising. After all, a new capital investment is justified only if it pays for itself (and more) by reducing labor costs. This means either fewer or less well-paid workers.

What about the increasing importance of research and development? Again, caution is advised in concluding that growth in overall investment in research and development by the American society will be of any sizable benefit to colleges and universities. Over the last five years, higher education has been gradually losing its share of the basic research dollar. Only about a third of the new dollars spent on basic research during this period has gone to colleges and universities. Instead, support has shifted to federally supported research and development centers and to industry. In recent years, industry has not only increased expenditures for its own basic research but has also captured an increasing share of federal research support.

Another reason for caution derives from the character of the new knowledge needed by a more competitive economy. A case can be made that our economy in recent years has not suffered because of any significant loss of edge in basic research. Rather, in the past decade we have had inadequate transfer of the results of research into marketable technology. The transistor and the integrated circuit were invented in the United States. Cutting-edge research in semiconductors continues to thrive here. Yet, it is the Japanese who have most successfully exploited these discoveries to tap a huge American (and international) market for state-of-the-art television sets, Walkmans, and videocassette recorders. Higher education plays a limited role in technology transfer and practically none in product development and marketing. If these are the greatest needs of the economy, then higher education will have a smaller rather than larger share of future growth in this arena.

An important trend in the corporate world should also be noted. Companies are themselves providing increasing amounts of training and education for their employees, in many instances bypassing more traditional providers of such services. While accurate figures are difficult to come by, education and training by business and industry are now estimated at more than $80 billion per year. Compare this with the $85 billion expended in traditional higher education. Much of this instruction by business and industry deals with content that colleges and universities are neither able nor willing to offer. Some of it, however, is directly competitive with what higher education does for a living. Further, those familiar with education in the corporate sector have observed that the volume of instruction duplicating that offered by colleges and universities appears to be on the rise. One reason may be the inefficiencies, in time and dollars, associated with traditional credit-based instruction. Another reason, especially evident in the rapidly changing world of high technology, is that state-of-the-art expertise is increasingly as available among corporate personnel as among the faculties of our universities.

The underlying conservatism of this intensified concern for the nation's economic strength is reflected in today's views on social issues. The 1960s and 1970s were a time of rapid social change—the civil rights movement, student demonstrations, conflicts between police and demonstrators that often led to violence, and assassinations of political leaders. In contrast, the majority of people today seem to want to slow down, consolidate gains, correct excesses. Busing schoolchildren to achieve integration and hiring quotas for minorities are under attack, even from some groups that might benefit from them. Abortion, prayer in schools, and the role of religion in politics have become respectable public policy issues. Federal domestic programs, most of them created in the 1960s and expanded rapidly in the 1970s, have been cut by nearly 40 percent in the last five years. Many social action programs have been eliminated altogether or reduced by 60 or 70 percent. In contrast, spending on military and space programs increased by over 20 percent during the same period.

The shift in values reflected in these changes is evident on campuses across the country. Access and equal opportunity are no longer as important as they were a decade ago. Merit scholarships and standards of progress have become fashionable again. A recent study found that over 80 percent of colleges surveyed give "no-need" scholarships. A new "get-tough" competitive spirit is coming to the fore. High schools boost graduation requirements. States require graduation tests for the high school diploma. Colleges demand tighter standards even as they worry about how to maintain enrollments. Competency tests for freshmen become a new tool in determining course assignments. The aggregate effect is an emphasis on rote learning of facts, concepts, and skills that can be measured on computer-scored multiple-choice tests.

In summary, colleges and universities exist in a society that has become decidedly more conservative than it was a decade ago. Concern about the strength of our economy, especially relative to that of other nations, has intensified emphasis on human capital, technology, and the information services as sources of future growth. Each seems to hold promises for increased demand for higher education. Yet, in each case, demand for the services of colleges and universities may be less than we would hope. Ours is also a society less willing than formerly to make social investments unless they yield clear economic dividends. We are increasingly distrustful of our own institutions. Accountability is emphasized, and there is a greater willingness to turn to alternative providers if traditional sources cannot deliver.

Changes in Students

Mention students and the instinctive response of most administrators and faculty members is: "fewer." Can there be a Rip Van Winkle who has not heard of the impending decline in the number of college age people? Warning flags have been flying for well over a decade now. In 1979, there were over four million eighteen-year-olds in the United States, the largest number in our history. By 1992, there will be one million fewer, a decrease of more than 25 percent in a thirteen-year period. This demographic portent has occupied—some would say has preoccupied—discussions of higher education for more than a decade. There are, however, other changes in the occupants of our classrooms that are likely to have an even greater impact on education than will the decline in their numbers. One such change is the deteriorating level of preparation that they bring to their freshman classes. Numerous negative indicators are painfully familiar to everyone in higher education: the steady decline in Scholastic Aptitude Test scores from 1963 through 1980; the discouraging evidence of the National Assessment of Educational Progress; the increase in remedial courses on college campuses; and the rising complaints of businessmen and military leaders about the incompetence of college graduates. (Ironically, as these various indicators of academic accomplishment have drifted downward, average high school grades have moved in the opposite direction. In the 1960s, more than two students had a *C* average for every one with an *A* average. By the end of the 1970s, however, *A*-average students had come to outnumber those with *C* averages.)

But, fortunately, this long deterioration in student preparation is one trend that shows strong signs of bottoming out. Test scores have stabilized. Since about 1980, the number of years of study of academic subjects by entering college freshmen has risen sharply, with substantial increases in mathematics and physical sciences. The recent burst of concern about school reform efforts will undoubtedly have further positive impact. And the expanded interest in cooperation between high schools and colleges should improve the fit between student achievement and college entrance requirements.

Another change is that the pool from which future freshmen will be drawn will be blacker and browner than it is today. Minority populations in this country are growing more rapidly than the white majority. Between 1975 and 1980, for example, the white population aged eighteen through twenty-four grew by 5.6 percent, while the same age group of blacks grew by 10.6 percent and of Hispanics by 35 percent. As these figures suggest, the highest growth rate is among Hispanics. (If current birthrates continue, Hispanic Americans will outnumber blacks early in the twenty-first century.) This shift in the

composition of the college age population has several implications for higher education. Students entering colleges and universities will have, on average, lower family incomes and less impressive academic records than their present-day counterparts.
Financial aid will become more important as will the need for
special academic programs. Further, unless there are changes in
college-going behaviors, particularly among blacks and Hispanics, the rate of participation in higher education is likely to
fall. About 26 percent of whites in the eighteen-to-twenty-four-
year-old group are now enrolled in college, but only 19 percent
of blacks and 16 percent of Hispanics in the same age group.

On the one hand, the overall impact of these changes on
total enrollments is likely to be modest. Hispanics now make up
only 8 percent of the total population between eighteen and
twenty-four, while blacks make up 10.6 percent. On the other
hand, however, the regional impact will be substantial. Half of
all black students now attend colleges in southern and border
states. Hispanic students are even more concentrated; excluding
Puerto Rico, a mere twenty-one colleges enroll 24 percent of
all Hispanic college students.

The values and attitudes of students are also changing,
as any counselor or freshman instructor will testify. Today's
college student has a quite different view of the world from that
of his or her older sibling. Changes in what students expect
from college increase the need for faculty retraining and for the
reallocation of faculty positions, as demand for specific courses
and curricula alter. They also pose a special challenge to the traditional values of the liberal arts. Not surprisingly, the shifting
values of students mirror the anxieties of the broader society.
Compared to those who were in college as recently as a decade
ago, today's young people are decidedly less altruistic, more
concerned about self, and more anxious about the future. There
is increased interest in landing a high-paying job, gaining public
recognition as an authority in one's chosen field, and being able
to supervise other people. There is less interest in environmental
issues, racial understanding, and public affairs in general.

The most dramatic shift has been in the goals that students indicate they are pursuing. According to an annual UCLA

survey of the nation's entering freshmen, the percentage of freshmen who selected "developing a meaningful philosophy of life" as an important or very important objective has steadily dropped from over 80 percent in 1967 to less than 45 percent in 1983. In contrast, the percentage who chose "being well-off financially" rose from 40 percent to 70 percent. The increasing pragmatism that this trend suggests is reinforced by the students' changing political views. The number of freshmen who consider themselves "liberal" in their political views has declined steadily from 40 percent in 1971 to slightly over 20 percent in 1983. Those identifying themselves as "middle of the road" increased from 44 percent to 60 percent in that same period.

These shifting values have had a direct impact on college campuses, particularly in the choice of majors. Since the late 1960s, there has been a sharp decline in freshmen intending to major in English, languages, philosophy, history, and mathematics. At that time, the arts, humanities, and social sciences accounted for one-third of all majors. Today, these fields combined account for less than one in ten majors. Business, engineering, computer science, the professions (medicine and law) are the fields of interest. Together, these now account for over 56 percent of the declared career intentions of students. Demand has become so strong for some fields that administrators are worrying about the resulting distortion in the academic program. At the Massachusetts Institute of Technology recently, over a third of the seniors were pursuing majors in computer science or engineering. The resulting overcrowding has led the faculty to seriously consider limiting enrollments in these fields.

Concern for a college degree that provides easy job entry and security is likely to endure or even increase. Its roots go deep. Partly, this concern is a reflection of the present economic anxiety of the whole society. But it also flows from a distinctive and enduring characteristic of the group of young people now entering college. They, and those who will enroll over the next decade, follow in the wake of the largest cohorts in our history. For well over a decade, we have had a surplus of young people relative to the number and quality of jobs avail-

able in the economy. The number of women entering the labor
force has also increased dramatically in recent years, further increasing competition for jobs. The result is that the pipeline
ahead is badly clogged. Entry-level salaries for college graduates
are now lower than they were a decade ago when adjusted for
inflation. There is also no longer the same prospect for the rapid
future salary increases enjoyed by earlier generations. The climb
up the career and salary ladder will take longer because the
higher positions will be occupied for many years by people only
slightly older than those still on their way up. Already, in recent
years, the baccalaureate degree has lost nearly half its lifetime
economic advantage over the high school diploma.

The lesson of all this is not lost on today's students. If
both the job market and opportunities for promotion have become much more problematic, then making sure one earns an
eminently "marketable" degree becomes a shrewd strategy to
gain an edge in that competition. Engineering, computer science, medicine, law, business—any field in which shortages are
reported—become roads to economic security in anxious and
competitive times.

Changes in Higher Education

What about colleges and universities themselves? How
prepared are they to respond to these changes in society and in
the students who come knocking on their doors? Are they
healthy organizations, ready to respond to challenges, or do
they approach the future with serious handicaps? Generalizations are risky. In spite of substantial homogenizing influences,
American higher education remains quite diverse. Public and
private institutions face dissimilar prospects for the future. The
likely impact of the trends discussed earlier varies according to
the size of the institution, its geographic location, the character of its existing academic program, and its underlying financial strength.

Our colleges and universities possess many strengths. As
a sprawling, uncoordinated enterprise, American postsecondary
education serves a multitude of needs for society and individ-

uals. The scholars and teachers who form its vital core comprise a historically unprecedented pool of talented, trained, and dedicated people. For sheer quantity—and probably quality—it is unmatched anywhere else in the world.

However, all is not well. There are ominous signs of internal weaknesses and rigidities that may well compromise the capacity of many institutions to adapt to the changes that are surely at hand. One of the struggles of the next decade will be to recognize and address the challenges that lie within, not just those that threaten from without. Among the more sobering of these challenges, given the prospect of a declining clientele, is upward pressure on costs. Faculty salaries will be one area of increasing costs. The average cost per faculty member will rise as the average age of faculty members increases. Further, over the last decade, academic salary levels have slowly slipped relative to those of other white-collar workers. Boards and presidents are likely to encounter strong pressures to make up for that relative loss.

Increasing costs will also result from the need on many campuses for extensive maintenance and capital improvements. Recent studies suggest that the walls of academe are crumbling, in need of improvements that in the aggregate will cost as much as $50 billion. Much of the physical infrastructure of the nation's campuses was built or updated during the years of rapid enrollment increases. Due to the passage of time, many physical components—roofs, wiring, plumbing, heating systems—are near the end of their useful lives. Further, over the past decade, administrators frequently coped with inflation through cutbacks in maintenance and capital improvements as they strained to allocate as much money as possible for faculty salary increases. In many ways, this was a sensible strategy. After all, the fundamental strength and vitality of an educational institution depend primarily on the quality and dedication of its people. However, the maintenance work that was postponed remains to be done. The problem is not only bricks and mortar and steam pipes. Laboratories and libraries also require substantial investments if the scholarship and education they support are to remain of the highest quality.

In the midst of many worrisome conditions, however, this may actually be a bright spot. The capital needs of higher education appear to be eliciting a response from society. Fundraising campaigns, whether for additions to endowment or for new capital expenditures, are setting records both for the speed with which goals are met and for the extent to which they exceed those goals.

The most well-known characteristic of faculty members as a group is their gradually increasing average age. As with the prospect of declining enrollments, however, other characteristics may be more significant to a college's capability to respond to change. Stabilizing or declining enrollments have reduced faculty mobility from one institution to another within all but the most selective sectors of higher education. As a result, many faculty have come to feel trapped, seeing few possibilities for career growth or escape from unhappy work environments. Lagging salary increases, the shadow of possible cutbacks due to enrollment decline, and the scarcity of career alternatives make many faculty particularly anxious about the future. In response, they tend to increase their participation in governance, especially where budgetary matters, academic program changes, or reallocation of faculty positions are concerned. Many campuses now have a number of faculty members, tenured and with limited teaching loads, who have become as expert in the arcane details of the institution's fiscal affairs as most administrators. Increasing concern about job security and salaries also reduces the openness and frankness with which the problems of the institution can be aired. Many presidents, sometimes against substantial evidence, refuse to admit aloud the possibility that their institution will suffer an enrollment decline. One reason for this seems to be their unwillingness to play Cassandra before their own faculties.

One group of faculty members is in particularly difficult straits: those young scholars who made up the great Ph.D. boom of the 1960s and early 1970s. The more fortunate of these managed to land academic jobs when tenure was still available. When the market became more crowded, however, others found themselves accepting positions at institutions of lesser academic quality or commitment to research than they would have liked. Products of top research universities, many of these scholars feel deeply that, had demographic fate not intervened, they would occupy distinguished chairs at prestigious institutions. Instead, they find themselves on the faculties of a former teacher's college or a community college, expected to teach struggling undergraduates in what are in truth remedial courses. Those young Ph.D.'s who graduated even later have become the gypsy scholars of the twentieth century. Now in their thirties and early forties, they spend six years at an institution, fail to be promoted, then move on to another institution to repeat the cycle. Whatever the variety of experience, the result is erosion of self-confidence, cynicism, and—mirroring the new generation of students—paramount concern about job security.

A side effect of the tremendous growth of the 1950s and 1960s is that much of higher education has come to be dominated by a single definition of academic quality, one that is most purely represented in the highly selective research institution. The most noble calling for an academic is to engage in cutting-edge research, to advise graduate students, and occasionally to teach an upper-division or graduate-level course. Journal articles and presentations at scholarly gatherings become the measure of faculty quality, not teaching or service to the community. Not only does teaching lose importance, but the whole manner and content of that teaching become dominated by the values of the research model. The preparation of candidates for graduate study has increasingly come to be the purpose of any self-respecting undergraduate curriculum. As a result, the undergraduate experience becomes one of being force-fed the "basics." Information, definitions, and fundamental concepts are emphasized. Broader insights and most of the exciting and unresolved research questions of a given field are postponed until graduate school.

A related characteristic of academe is its fragmentation, first, into various disciplines and, then, into the innumerable specialties within those disciplines. The isolation that results is exacerbated by tight enrollments and dollars. Most budgeting systems used by state legislatures for public institutions, as well

well as those used within campuses, set department against department in an open competition for students and for the dollars linked to enrollments. The intellectual enterprise is fractured into its smallest pieces and so is the organizational and bureaucratic structure of the campus.

The overloading of undergraduate courses with information, as well as the emphasis on academic specialization, works against integrated curricula that emphasize the broader concepts and skills needed by the well-educated person. Our colleges themselves often play right into the hands of students who clamor for highly specialized training rather than a broad liberal education. Many educators are also uncomfortable dealing with either intellectual values or the broader political and moral values of concern to society. Some professors still carry the wounds of the 1960s and 1970s when many campus communities became large-scale encounter groups open to explorations of the feelings and idiosyncratic views of students and faculty members alike. This reluctance to deal with values also flows from the efforts of many disciplines to mimic the physical sciences by becoming as quantitative as possible. Qualitative and value-oriented modes of inquiry are less in fashion now than they were twenty years ago. The dominance of symbolic logic in philosophy and the mathematicizing of economics and sociology are examples of the trend toward a more "scientific" and less value-based approach to many subjects.

The overall effect of these changes is a decided mismatch between the changing needs of society and students and the character of colleges and universities. On the one hand, society clearly needs individuals who are analytic and independent and have the creative streak necessary to compete in an increasingly aggressive environment. But on the other hand, the large corporate and governmental structures within which much of modern work takes place require individuals who can work in groups toward a common goal. Yet much of American higher education is didactic, is fraught with detail, and emphasizes competition rather than cooperation. Colleges have become increasingly fragmented. Society has problems; colleges have departments. There is discomfort in dealing with values; a scientific distance from such questions is the preferred stance. In many institutions, the size and organizational structure frustrate rather than enhance interaction among disciplines and individuals. Often, little time is available for the crosscutting intellectual explorations clearly needed to prepare people for the changing world they will enter as graduates.

Generalizations are especially risky when one is reflecting on three worlds as complex as society, contemporary students, and higher education. The analysis laid out in this chapter cannot be wholly reflective of any one group, area, or institution. Within society at large, among students, and among our institutions, there are many exceptions to the portrait sketched here. Nor are the broad trends and forces now present in our society and at work within our institutions inevitable. Leadership, dedication, and the wisdom to understand the changing world and to evaluate one's own response to it can alter those trends or harness them to positive effect. Challenges can, indeed, become opportunities, as the succeeding chapters in this volume so well illustrate.

Bibliography

American Council on Education. *The American Freshman: National Norms for Fall.* Los Angeles: Cooperative Institutional Research Program, University of California, 1975–1984.

Astin, A. W. *Four Critical Years: Effects of College on Beliefs, Attitudes and Knowledge.* San Francisco: Jossey-Bass, 1978.

Botkin, J., Dimancescu, D., and Stata, R. *Global Stakes: The Future of High Technology in America.* Cambridge, Mass.: Ballinger, 1982.

Bureau of the Census. *Current Population Reports,* Series P-25. Washington, D.C.: U.S. Government Printing Office.

Committee for Economic Development. *Stimulating Technological Progress.* New York: Committee for Economic Development, 1980.

Etzioni, A. *An Immodest Agenda: Rebuilding America Before The Twenty-First Century.* New York: McGraw-Hill, 1983.

Frances, C. *College Enrollment Trends: Testing the Conven-*

tional Wisdom Against the Facts. Washington, D.C.: Association Council for Policy Analysis and Research, 1980.

Froomkin, J. (ed.). *The Crisis in Higher Education.* Proceedings of the annual meeting of the Academy of Political Science, vol. 35. New York: Academy of Political Science, 1983.

Ginzberg, E., and Vojta, G. J. "The Service Sector of the U.S. Economy." *Scientific American,* Mar. 1981, pp. 48–55.

International Monetary Fund. *World Economic Outlook.* Washington, D.C.: International Monetary Fund, 1983, 1984.

Keene, K. "American Values: Change and Stability." *Public Opinion,* Dec./Jan. 1984, pp. 2–8.

Levin, H. M., and Rumberger, R. *The Educational Implications of High Technology,* Project Report No. 83-A4. Palo Alto, Calif.: Stanford University, 1983.

Lynton, E. A. "The Economic Impact of Higher Education." *Journal of Higher Education,* 1983, *54* (6), 693–708.

Naisbitt, J. *Megatrends: Ten New Directions Transforming Our Lives.* New York: Warner Books, 1982.

National Center for Education Statistics. *Digest of Education Statistics 1983-1984.* Washington, D.C.: U.S. Government Printing Office, 1984.

National Governors' Association. *Final Report: Technology and Growth: State Initiatives in Technological Innovation.* Washington, D.C.: National Governors' Association, 1983.

National Science Foundation. *Detailed Historical Tables, FY 1967-1983.* Washington, D.C.: National Science Foundation, 1984.

Organization for Economic Cooperation and Development. *Economic Outlook.* Paris: Organization for Economic Cooperation and Development, 1984.

2

A Historical Look
at Institutional Success
in Hard Times

Frederick Rudolph

Harvard College, like hundreds of colleges that came later, was
founded before there was a clientele adequate to its aspirations.
Changing the name of the Massachusetts Bay village of New-
towne to Cambridge did not bring forth a university. That took
time. In fact, from one perspective the history of American
higher education is an account of empty dormitories, half-filled
classrooms, and underpaid professors. Selectivity in admissions,
a questionable index to academic health, is a recent phenomenon, first practiced early in the twentieth century by the older
universities and colleges of the East as a device for keeping out
Jews and since the Second World War as a means of dealing with
an unexpected and unprecedented wave of applications (Wechsler, 1977). The American style in higher education from the
very beginning has been: VACANCY.

Higher education has of course had its good times, and in
any given period there have been institutions of solid achievement. Most colleges, if not all, however, have experienced more
adversity and sluggishness than dynamic growth and success.

Harvard was more than two hundred years old before it graduated a class of 100. By then, according to one calculation, over
700 colleges had opened and closed in the United States. Moreover, until after the Civil War there was no significant difference
between institutions that called themselves universities and
those that were comfortable being known as colleges.

The temptation to define institutional success and academic hard times by some absolute measure and set of standards is difficult to resist. But to impose such measures is to
make the same sort of mistake often made by students of comparative culture. What is considered violent behavior in one
culture may be judged quite differently in another, just as conformity in one society may be seen as social responsibility in
another. Nuances of time and place must enter into any consideration of whether a college or university is successful and
whether higher education as a whole should be understood as
experiencing good times or bad times, fortune or adversity. The
low enrollments and endowments in the first half of the nineteenth century were signs of adversity, but the high enrollments
and endowments of the first half of the twentieth century were
not necessarily signs of institutional health.

In the decades before the Civil War, society demonstrated
its hostility to colleges in many ways, even as many colleges
gathered sufficient support to fulfill their mission as beacons of
learning and piety and as neighborhood and regional centers of
nurture for aspirants to the governing class. Surviving a period
of adversity, however, is not a demonstration of institutional
success. Mark Hopkins was a superb classroom teacher, but at
the time of his retirement from the presidency of Williams College in 1872 the enrollment had fallen to what it had been in
the year of his inauguration in 1836, his faculty was uneasy
with his leadership, and an element among the alumni was won-
dering if the college's problems could not be solved by admitting women.

Institutional success requires a degree of vibrancy, a direct challenge to the special conditions defining adversity at the
time, as well as a public response that suggests, for awhile at
least, that the challenge works. It calls on resources of leader-

ship and imagination in the best of times and on the kind of boldness that disarms skeptics in the worst of times.

A Time of Adversity: 1828-1868

Probably no period in the history of American higher education presents so dreary a picture as the years between the unleashing of the egalitarian impulses of Jacksonian democracy in the 1830s and the opening of Cornell University in 1868. From colonial times into the 1830s there was widespread public acknowledgment that the American liberal arts college imparted a quality of moral and intellectual authority to its graduates, that is, to those young men who would assume positions of leadership in the professions and society.

Equalitarianism, always a force to be reckoned with in the New World, experienced an especially powerful upsurge in the United States about the time that Andrew Jackson entered the White House. Unlettered Methodist and Baptist clergymen now surpassed in numbers the college-educated clergymen who ministered to Anglicans, Congregationalists, and Presbyterians. State laws giving medical societies and bar associations the right to examine and license candidates were repealed. Thus, the constitution of Indiana provided that "every person of good moral character who is a voter is entitled to practice law in any of the courts of the state" (Rudolph, 1984, p. 14.)

This disestablishment of the professions robbed the liberal arts colleges of students and public support. Even in New England, college enrollments decreased in both number and proportion to the population. Henceforth the colleges, vulnerable to accusations of being centers of privilege and purveyors of useless learning, entered upon a long period when coherence in the course of study and clarity of mission began to escape their grasp. For the fifty years after 1830 American higher education was on the defensive and no longer vitally connected with society, as the professions became debased and the status value of a bachelor's degree declined. In these years, torn between allegiance to the classical course of studies and demands that it be made more practical, the colleges allowed themselves a bit of curricular tinkering. Until after the Civil War, however, with certain notable exceptions, the colleges were for the most part intellectually immobilized—captives of their past, spurned by a suddenly and aggressively mobile society, vulnerable to whatever movement or idea that held out the promise of renewing their contract with society and their faith in themselves.

Adversity appeared in many guises. Philanthropists gave their money to academies, libraries, and workingmen's institutes, which had become more popular expressions of civic need than colleges. Amherst College, desperately seeking funds, offered its name twice to potential benefactors only to be twice denied. Lafayette and Marietta colleges unsuccessfully tried to coax income out of mulberry trees and silkworms. Sectarian rivalries and the founding of new colleges as expressions of those rivalries led state legislatures to shy away from the kind of support that had been so important to the survival of Harvard. Complicated devices for luring students to the colleges essentially meant that students were being subsidized by underpaid professors and by the uncertain mortgaged future of the institutions themselves.

Yet, in a world that was being shaped by the likes of John Jacob Astor and Cornelius Vanderbilt, an analysis of the colleges' difficulties offered by one of their friends in 1851 was persuasive: "The commercial spirit of our country, and the many avenues of wealth which are opened before enterprise, create a distaste for study deeply inimical to education. The manufacturer, the merchant, the gold-digger, will not pause in their career to gain intellectual accomplishments. While gaining knowledge, they are losing the opportunity to gain money" (Rudolph, 1962, 219–220.) It was an open secret: Opportunity in America did not require a college education. The word *credential* had not yet been applied to a college degree. Careers in engineering, merchandising, manufacturing, the merchant marine, and railroads—not to mention the possibilities offered by the nation's rich natural resources—were available to young men in a hurry. And hurry, not contemplation and wisdom, was the style with which Americans took possession of their country. In 1846 the population of New York City was 500,000; the enrollments in the city's colleges totaled 247.

Even in adversity, however, there were indications that institutions that understood themselves, their strengths and weaknesses, could become islands of reliability and academic stability. Times as uncertain as these, however, were capable of inspiring academic gestures that were either premature or wildly out of character with the real world. Such were Thomas Jefferson's blueprint for the University of Virginia and Philip Lindsley's for the University of Nashville, the efforts to create a graduate university in New York in 1832 and again in the 1850s, Henry Philip Tappan's ambitious plan to infuse the University of Michigan with the scholarly ideal of the German universities, and Francis Wayland's brave but flawed democratic program for obliterating or overhauling all the inherited practices and curricular certainties of the past at Brown in the 1850s. Each of these reforms reached beyond the understanding and needs of their publics. They did little or nothing to relieve the depressed condition of higher education. Indeed, their failures and difficulties seemed only to accentuate the troubles.

Where was the good news to be found? One place certainly was in all those steady colleges that held to their last and simply refused to give up belief in themselves and their mission: They chose to keep on doing what they did as well as they knew how. Columbia College in New York was certainly not among such places. In 1830, while not abandoning its traditional mission of training society's leaders, Columbia College offered a course full of so many options that it was clearly pandering to all those elements of the population, including factory superintendents, for whom Columbia had made no difference that mattered. Columbia's enrollments nonetheless continued to decline. At the same time, scattered around the country were self-contained small colleges of sure moral purpose, held together by underpaid but dedicated faculties and attended by boisterous but ambitious young men intent on making something of themselves. In many ways it is easy to fault those little provincial colleges; but to the degree that they refused to panic in the face of demands that they be popular and practical and to the degree that they held to their priorities and purposes, they delivered a coherent education at a very low price. These colleges were not hunkering down: They flew their banners without embarrassment. With only experience and tradition to guide them and with very little support from federal or state governments, boards of trustees, confirmed in their authority by the Dartmouth College case of 1819, were managing enterprises that provided more or less the same educational experience throughout the country.

Efforts to move higher education in dramatic new directions were on the whole thwarted and premature, as a whole array of reformers from Jefferson to Wayland learned; but experimentation was not prohibited, and diversity and flexibility were not wholly absent. The American college was evolving, in substance and style, as a creature of the society it served. It would not be rushed, but neither would it be held back, not even by those dismal fundamentalist colleges that were as hostile to life as they were to learning or by those essentially superfluous colleges that overestimated the potential call on their services and ended up collapsing as a result of trying to be all things to all men.

In a sense there were more colleges than could be adequately supported but probably not many more than were necessary to give vitality to the Jeffersonian ideal of educational accessibility. It must be remembered that the pre–Civil War college antedated the development of academic disciplines and professional academicians, that it was just becoming aware of the challenge of an undeveloped continent to the potentialities of applied science, and that it regarded traditional ethical and religious values as beyond challenge. Given these conditions, large libraries and generously equipped laboratories were not necessary. The equipment and staffing at many colleges were, if not optimal, as good as they needed to be.

The colleges judged themselves by the quality of their graduates as human beings. They knew that very few people went to college, that it was possible to be elected to high office by appealing to the passions rather than to the intelligence of the people, and that a great deal of money could be made and was being made by ambitious and often crude young men who, spurning both a secondary and a collegiate education, were eager to transform the natural resources of an unexploited continent into personal fortunes. But just because all that was so, the colleges saw their particular function as cautionary, diluting, admonishing. They regarded themselves as preparing the clergymen, the judges, the teachers, and the men who occupied the best houses in town to carry the burdens of community leadership.

If the exit standards varied from college to college, there was no question about the preeminence of Harvard, Yale, and Princeton. If state institutions were neglected, the numerous little denominational colleges provided an expanding country with determined echoes of the East. If the course of study was being challenged, as it surely was, by those who would make it more relevant and practical, new subjects and extracurricular enthusiasms provided a great deal of evidence that the colleges were not standing still. If the arrangements that passed as a "system" of collegiate preparation could at best be described as chaotic, the colleges were doing as well as that chaos permitted them to do.

It was no blemish on Abraham Lincoln's record that he had not gone to college. However, in the cabinet that took office with him in 1860, the two most important positions, that of secretary of state and secretary of the treasury, were held by graduates of Union and Dartmouth. Union College, alma mater of Secretary of State William H. Seward, was one of two especially exemplary and, although in different ways, successful collegiate institutions of the pre–Civil War years. (The other was Harvard.) Under the driving presence of Eliphalet Nott, who presided over the destiny of the college in Schenectady, New York, for an unparalleled sixty-two years, from 1804 to 1866, Union was unique in arriving early and successfully at a workable course of study, one that neither jettisoned the old course of study with its aim of training leaders nor denied the legitimacy of new subjects in a changing world. Nott understood his age. He even invented a coal-burning stove that handsomely enriched his college. He welcomed the Greek-letter fraternity movement to his campus and had no qualms about encouraging as transfer students young men who had experienced disciplinary collisions at other colleges. Contrary to some expectations, this policy did not turn Union into a refuge for rascals so much as a school for success in nineteenth-century America (Hislop, 1971).

The respectable and worthy colleges that held to their standards and purposes while resisting more change than was appropriate to their own comfort and style adhered to the famous 1828 report of the Yale faculty, which advanced a notable rationale for the traditional liberal arts college. The same year, however, Union fell dramatically out of step with most American colleges by arranging its course of study so "as to afford a choice between the branches abstract and scientific and branches practical and particular" (Rudolph, 1977, p. 86).

Union College was ready for the reform. Over the years Nott had assigned significant portions of the college's income to the purchase of scientific apparatus; he had been careful in his appointment of professors; and he himself fully embraced the optimistic materialism of the age. In an 1824 address at the college, Nott invited his audience to join in a great Christian-scientific assault on nature, an assertion of man's dominion over nature through science in order to achieve moral and material perfection.

Union's new scientific course provided freshmen with a greater concentration of Latin and Greek than was customary in the traditional classical course, but omitted these subjects altogether after that. The remaining three years were divided equally among science, mathematics, and a group of studies that included modern languages, social studies, law, English composition, and oratory. An ornament of the Union experience since 1804 had been senior year in moral philosophy with President Nott, and it continued to be exactly that in both the traditional course and in the new scientific course. The most symbolic evidence of Union's belief in what it was doing was its decision to award the bachelor of arts degree to graduates of both programs. Nothing there about the integrity of the bachelor of arts degree, no implication of second-rateness for the scientific course, no apologies. When Harvard and Yale in the 1850s created scientific programs, they created new degrees (bachelor of science and bachelor of philosophy) to go along with them; and at Yale the students pursuing the scientific course were separated in chapel from candidates for the more prestigious bachelor of arts degree.

Union was not alone in developing a parallel or scientific-literary course, as it was sometimes called, but where others failed Union flourished. Columbia's comparable program reached an enrollment of zero in 1843 and was abolished. Union apparently benefited from notoriety. The opposition to Union's four-year scientific course and the college's insistence on not differentiating it from its classical course in the awarding of degrees blew up a storm that drew attention to Union as a place where a liberal education with practical applications was available. The enrollment went merrily up. In 1830 Union graduated ninety-six seniors to Yale's seventy-one, Harvard's forty-eight, and Princeton's eighty. As late as 1861 its graduating class was the third largest in the country. About a third of the students in each class were enrolled in the scientific course; these were young men on their way to careers in engineering, railroading, medicine, law, and mining. Union under Nott had designed a course of study that was sensitive to the shift that had been taking place in the way young men looked at themselves. Once they had asked, "How can I be saved?" Now they asked, "How can I be successful?" On the eve of the Civil War the American college with the largest endowment was Union.

A somewhat different road to academic good health was taken at Harvard under the cautious but determined presidency of Josiah Quincy. He discovered soon after taking office in 1829 that he was on a ruinous path in following the lead of Yale in adhering to a more demanding classical course at a time when Harvard was being pressed to be more utilitarian and democratic. Quincy's efforts to make Harvard, like Yale, a model classical college so adversely affected enrollments that by 1835 a solution to the problem of numbers had to be found in the recruiting of special students, probationary admissions, and remedial sections. Refusing to put Harvard permanently on the road to utter utilitarianism as a means of overcoming the unpopularity of its classical course, Quincy chose to envision Harvard as a college from which a university might one day emerge (McCaughey, 1974).

Eschewing numbers, he opted for quality—a decision that

surely was easier to make in Puritan Cambridge than on the American frontier. Earlier efforts to incorporate the curricular practices of the German universities into the Harvard course of study had failed, but in 1825 one of them—the creation of academic departments charged with the responsibility of nominating professors and supervising and controlling instruction—edged Harvard in a direction that would facilitate Quincy's intentions. These departments of instruction, which were the first to be established in any American college, placed the Harvard faculty in a position of effective control over the curriculum.

For five or six years after 1835, at the instigation of German-trained professors who did not want to teach lazy or uninterested students, Harvard made mathematics, Latin, Greek, and English optional after the freshman year. The impulse for this attack on the prescribed curriculum came from elitist, professionally self-conscious professors who shared Quincy's unwillingness to shift Harvard College from a classical to a utilitarian model. Benjamin Pierce's proposal for a two-year trial of an elective program in mathematics, adopted in 1838, was an admission that even Harvard must accommodate itself to a variety of demands—the utilitarian, the democratic, and the professional. Pierce's elective program offered Harvard students a choice among a one-year course in applied mathematics, a one-year theoretical course for potential schoolteachers, and a three-year course for prospective mathematicians.

This beginning of a serious sense of professional self-consciousness on the part of the professors was a development that owed something to the intellectual quality of Harvard Unitarianism, as well as to the absence of the overriding evangelical piety that characterized most American colleges. The offering of three electives in mathematics was a sign that Harvard was moving toward the preparation of specialists and that students were beginning to be left to organize their own course of study at the cost of the values that inhered in the traditional prescribed curriculum. By 1843 virtually all courses beyond the freshman year were offered on an elective basis, but the university builders had pushed their more reluctant colleagues too far. A reaction against the elective principle set in that year and was not reversed until the presidency of Charles William Eliot, who needed until 1883 to return Harvard to the largely elective curriculum of 1843.

In the meantime, individual members of the faculty were attempting to give the college a university style of teaching and learning. In 1842, Asa Gray accepted a professorship in botany with limited classroom obligations. His colleague in American history, Jared Sparks, had insisted as conditions of his accepting a professorship that he be free from teaching eight months a year and that he be allowed to do away with recitations altogether. Henry Wadsworth Longfellow, professor of modern languages, complained to his journal: "This having your mind constantly a playmate for boys—constantly adapting itself to them; instead of stretching out and grappling with men's minds" (Rudolph, 1977, p. 79). Harvard University was on its way!

Harvard succeeded in establishing the priority of intellectual achievement over other academic goals and purposes. It met the populist clamor for a practical education by upgrading the quality of its "impractical" curriculum. It recognized the winds of change emanating from German universities by encouraging professional self-consciousness among its professors. In moving the country's first institution of higher learning toward new expectations and new standards, Quincy used Harvard as an instrument for leading the United States away from a narrow provincialism and an unthinking equalitarianism.

Many at the time may not have noticed what was going on at Harvard, but quietly and effectively there were developing in Cambridge practices, priorities, and purposes that were giving promise of the transformation of a great old college into a great new university. Less dramatic than the reforms at Union, and for a time less enduring, Quincy's reforms not only ran counter to the mood and political realities of the time. They also pointed the way to intellectual sophistication and inquiry and attracted to Cambridge a faculty and a student body that would become accustomed to thinking of themselves as "the best." Certainly one way to be successful is to define the terms of success, live up to those terms, and wait for the rest of the world to adopt them.

A Second Period of Adversity: Between the Wars

Harvard, Johns Hopkins, and Clark universities, the great state universities, the instantaneous creation of fully developed institutions at Chicago and Stanford, the benefactions that placed Vassar and Smith and Wellesley into the academic firmament, and especially the bold adventure in Ithaca, New York, that spelled out the determination of Ezra Cornell and Andrew D. White to found an institution where anyone could study anything—these were the events that sent American higher education spinning in the late nineteenth century (Veysey, 1965). Some colleges never found out what happened to them, others simply went along with the current. But those last decades of the nineteenth century and first decades of the twentieth do not qualify as a time of adversity. Not only did the little colleges that were supposed to close their dormitories and become academies refuse to oblige, but their wealthy alumni provided them with facilities that allowed them to prosper into the twentieth century. Yale, Princeton, and Stanford wrestled with their identities and discovered that the United States was big enough and wealthy enough to encourage them to be lively and different. State legislatures in Michigan, Wisconsin, Minnesota, and California saw no reason why an English college and a German university could not be married to the American ideal of the university as an instrument of public service.

The next period of adversity for American higher education came after these dynamic years of university growth and collegiate accommodation. Between the two great wars the American college and university were no healthier than the economy that led to the Great Depression or the international order that led to the outbreak of the Second World War. All those great athletic stadiums—the Rose Bowl in Pasadena, the Yale Bowl, Franklin Field at Penn, and the great field at Michigan that could comfortably accommodate almost 90,000 people in 1927—were really not evidence of institutional health. Between the wars the universities and colleges were adept at fielding football teams; most of them, however, had given up control over their own identities and had surrendered themselves to alumni or student constituencies, all the while allowing their faculty members to flow in and out of classrooms, libraries, and laboratories like so many free spirits. Their sense of mission was muddled, their leaders were confused, and with it all only half of their football teams were victorious.

During this period higher education *looked* healthy; but, in part as a consequence of too rapid physical growth and the proliferation of degrees and programs, standards of admissions were low and the dropout rate was high. The best prepared students found their freshman year a repetition of secondary school, while the poorly prepared were bewildered. The professors were either frustrated by their students or had learned how to ignore them altogether (Pierson, 1955). And everywhere the fraternities and sororities, the athletic teams, the clubs and newspapers and literary journals were winning out over the curriculum for the time and devotion of students. Something significant had happened out there in the real world, where certain qualities of style and personality were rewarded by advancement in the new hierarchies of a corporate industrial society. And these were qualities nurtured more by campus facilities and style suggestive of a country club than by the intellectual life of the colleges. In fact, the success of these colleges hinged on their providing, both in facilities and style, the attributes of a country club. As the colleges and universities became more popular during the 1920s and 1930s—even during the Great Depression when they were something of a refuge—they also became more confused as to mission, less coherent in program, and more aimless in direction.

The great old colonial institutions that had set standards in the nineteenth century and had moved deliberately but thoughtfully toward university status were unable to function as beacons of enlightenment and symbols of strength between the wars. These were the years when Harvard and Yale were spending millions of dollars and exerting great energies to create physical environments capable of seducing their students into thinking of their universities as centers of intellectual life. The Yale colleges, Harvard houses, and Princeton eating clubs became instead new centers of loyalty and diversion that contributed to the idea of the university as a preparatory experience on the way to membership in an urban men's club and its suburban counterpart. Fraternities were performing a similar function elsewhere.

These same institutions, from the 1920s into the late 1940s, preserved themselves as bastions of a white Anglo-Saxon Protestant elite through the establishment of quotas for Jewish students (Synnott, 1979). While each university practiced discrimination against Jewish applicants in its own way, all succeeded in arriving at what was thought to be a comfortable policy of denying access to qualified Jews. Of course, where applicable, the policy also restricted entry by blacks, Catholics, women, homosexuals, and others considered unlikely candidates for the elite positions for which these universities prepared their graduates (Steinberg, 1974).

Harvard, Yale, Princeton, and the institutions that followed their lead were prompted to carry out their policy of discrimination in part because they were dependent on the financial support of a snobbish elite and in part because they had not yet altogether made up their minds to establish or maintain the priority of intellectual purpose over social considerations. All this was to change after the Second World War, but at a time when college and university students were celebrating the social values of college life, their elders were demonstrating how prejudice and social snobbery could also contaminate the atmosphere of academic life.

Of course, as in the decades before the Civil War, all over the country there were colleges and universities that quietly went about business as usual, doing the best they could with the material at hand. To some extent all of the rah-rah enthusiasm of college life in the 1920s and 1930s was a reaction to the success with which university ideals and practices had pervaded the academy. The 1923 lament of one student who had discovered that the curriculum consisted of a series of lecture courses may help to explain why he and others became caught up in the athletic and social possibilities of their campuses: "Instead of being a person, . . . I am now merely a suit of clothes pinned together by four or five seat numbers" (Rudolph, 1962, p. 449).

But at least three institutions made a significant mark

on the life of higher education during these years. Most of the older, bigger, and well-established colleges and universities did not so much thrive as tread water or mark time, as if somehow embarrassed at not being able to get their intellectual houses in order, bring undergraduate social enthusiasms under control, or move the curriculum out of the disarray that had followed the widespread intrusion of electives and vocationalism into academic practice. Between 1910 and 1930 these three institutions —one new, one old and on the verge of collapse, and one stable and secure but now led by an urbane reformer—turned themselves into laboratories of curricular innovation. Reed, Antioch, and Swarthmore in the first quarter of the twentieth century cast themselves in the tradition of Jefferson's Virginia, White's Cornell, Gilman's Johns Hopkins, and Harper's Chicago. They had to be paid attention to (Clark, 1970).

Reed College opened in Portland, Oregon, in 1911 as a protest against the trivialization of the academic experience by students with mainly extracurricular concerns. In the words of its first president, Reed proposed to free itself from "harassing traditions" and proceeded to do so by adopting simplified spelling, eliminating the extracurriculum, requiring a combination of thesis and oral examination of its seniors and a qualifying comprehensive examination of its juniors, importing a faculty of young enthusiasts from the East, and holding to high admission standards. This design, which would have been impossible to impose on an old institution, was workable in a new one because the bequest that supported it, the inclinations of the trustees, the encouragement of the general education board of the college, and the imagination of the president all favored an experimental model. In 1921, all of ten years old, Reed adopted a program that provided for two years of broad humanities courses with small discussion sections as a prelude to specialization in the junior and senior years. Reed's reform was not simply another version of concentration and distribution; it went beyond form to content and specified in the first two years a version of general education, that is, a synthesis of the knowledge and understanding it considered appropriate for a liberally educated person.

Antioch, an old college at Yellow Springs, Ohio, first presided over by Horace Mann, was so close to collapse in 1919 that when "the trustees tried to give it away to the YMCA, the YMCA returned it" (Rudolph, 1977, p. 241). Arthur E. Morgan, a trustee, took over and turned Antioch into a college that mixed traditional respect for the liberal arts with a progressive philosophy that emphasized work experience. Moreover, this mixture was itself combined with some of the social and group purposes of nineteenth-century America communal societies. Antioch proposed to do right by the humanities, careers, and the community. Antioch was a missionary movement that took as its challenge the development of the whole student, not simply his or her intellect.

Its five-year program, half spent on campus and half spent off campus in remunerative employment, centered on a work study plan that had originated at the engineering school of the University of Cincinnati in 1906; but the curriculum itself mixed culture, career, and community in equal parts. Antioch's style emphasized democratic campus relationships, a grounding in liberal learning, and self-directed study. The extramural phase of the Antioch experience, which had students working for 175 employers in twelve states in 1930, may have been vocational and financially rewarding in result; but Morgan thought of the off-campus experience as bringing students face to face with "practical realities in all their stubborn complexity" (Rudolph, 1977, p. 242) and as contributing to the education of the whole man and whole woman. It was already difficult for older colleges and universities to support liberal culture and general education in their courses of study, and now Antioch had presented them with a model that was completely beyond emulation: It offered a curricular alternative that, if adopted at all widely, would have required the dismantling of the entire structure of American higher education. In combination, Reed and Antioch proposed to repeal several hundred years of curricular history.

Swarthmore, in contrast, proposed a more modest and more easily adopted reform. Although the curricular transformation of Swarthmore was accompanied by the decline of the college's intercollegiate athletic program and an erosion of its social life, the honors program idea did not have to be taken as far as it was at Swarthmore in order to be an effective agency of order and focus in the course of study. Swarthmore used honors to cultivate a national constituency, to decrease its financial reliance on the Quakers of Philadelphia, and to define the college's uniqueness. Under the leadership of Frank Aydelotte, Swarthmore College pioneered in using an honors program to fulfill its obligation to liberal learning. Before the First World War a number of eastern institutions—Harvard, Yale, Princeton, and Columbia among them—explored the use of honors programs, of special opportunities and heightened expectations for especially able students, as a way of remedying a climate of undergraduate indifference to scholarship. Although these early programs were denied the necessary commitment and resources, they provided a clear challenge to the idea of the undergraduate college as a democracy of equals. As a former Rhodes scholar, Aydelotte had observed at Oxford the intellectually stimulating practice of separating honors students from pass students. Not until he took charge of Swarthmore was there an effective demonstration that the American undergraduate curriculum could embrace the values implicit in the honors idea. The demonstration cost the general education board $4 million, but it also created another remedy for curricular disarray and undergraduate apathy and introduced an element of diversity into the course of study, at a time when standardization may have been fostering a stultifying rigidity (Blanshard, 1970).

Aydelotte did not allow the Swarthmore honors program to depart from the spirit of liberal learning. "The central purpose of liberal education cannot be restricted to the study of any particular subject or combination of subjects," he wrote, as if to deny to concentration and distribution any exclusive or even necessary guardianship of the humane tradition. "Liberal knowledge is not a formula; it is a point of view," he continued. "The essence of liberal education is the development of mental power and moral responsibility in each individual. It is based upon the theory that each person is unique, that each deserves to have his own powers developed to the fullest possible extent" (Rudolph, 1977, pp. 230-231).

His notion of the Swarthmore honors program required that it be part of an educational experience that focused on the development of "intellect . . . character, and . . . sensitiveness to beauty—as over against merely learning some useful technique" (Rudolph, 1977, p. 231). On the one hand, Aydelotte did not intend to have the Swarthmore honors program confused with the purposes of graduate seminars in arts and sciences or contaminated by the narrow specialization appropriate to candidates for the degree of doctor of philosophy. On the other hand, the Swarthmore program, which was inaugurated in 1922, did set candidates for honors degrees apart from their classmates, allowed them to concentrate in a single field of study, exposed them to tutorial and seminar instruction, required them to write a thesis, and subjected them to a comprehensive written examination, as well as to an oral examination by outside examiners.

While other institutions were bedeviled by external and internal problems, held in the grip of a tenacious past, or thoroughly confused by the fallout of the explosive and dynamic university movement, these three colleges—Swarthmore, Reed, and Antioch—demonstrated that problems could be squarely faced and American higher education could be moved toward new definitions of soundness and responsibility. Swarthmore showed how the ingenious use of an honors program could promote both scholarship and specialization without impairing humanistic learning. Reed, unhampered by a past, recognized the advantage of a fresh beginning and proceeded to move intellectual purpose into the forefront of the college experience, neither piety nor social considerations being allowed to get in the way. And Antioch boldly chose to integrate the liberal and the vocational, the intellectual and the practical, on the sound grounds that education is a seamless web. At a time when most institutions were in the doldrums they led the way to higher ground.

Union and Harvard in the decades before the Civil War, Reed and Antioch and Swarthmore between the two world wars: successful institutions in periods of adversity. What did they have in common? How did they differ? In the first place, each of these institutions chose not to be defined by the prevailing practices of higher education nor by their more flamboyant critics. Union neither surrendered to the populist demand for utter utility nor held to the rigid purity of the traditionalists. Harvard actually swam against the tide, rejecting both the doctrinaire messages coming from New Haven and the populist hostility emanating from the Massachusetts General Court. Reed, Antioch, and Swarthmore all went their separate ways, resisting both the reactionary prescriptions of such critics as Irving Babbitt, Albert Jay Nock, and Robert Maynard Hutchins and the easygoing acquiescence with the times that allowed most American colleges and universities to confuse themselves with country clubs. In these examples of institutional success the laurels go to the brave.

Yet, of course, if they had failed, history would be recording their foolishness rather than their bravery. What made the difference? Each institution was headed by a determined, imaginative, and energetic leader, by a person who would not allow his colleagues and supporters to take the easy road—either to survival or to extinction. These men recognized in the educational environment implicit challenges to leaders of vision. For Nott and Quincy, doing something about the hostile climate was better than simply doing nothing, which was the path taken by most colleges, both those that disappeared and those that survived. That the "somethings" they did could be so different says a great deal about how open the United States was to the application of imagination and vision in the first half of the nineteenth century.

For the academic leaders who placed Reed, Antioch, and Swarthmore into the firmament of institutional success, the clear intention was to be different from the great majority of institutions either sunk in routine or coasting on tradition. They recognized that what was missing in most American colleges was an ethos of intellectual excitement and a commitment to practices and encouragements that would nurture it. Each of these institutions, in both periods, listened to its own heartbeat. No other institutions came near to duplicating the particular combination of factors that defined the uniqueness of these particular successes. The successful institutions paid attention to their own strengths and weaknesses, their own histories and opportunities, and went on from there.

Each institution entered upon a period of reform in a spirit of adventure, but the destinations they put before themselves were not so outlandish as to alienate a potential clientele. A Reed, Antioch, or Swarthmore would not have made much sense a century earlier, just as the programs of Nott and Quincy would have carried no special message a century later. It may be that it helps for an institution to have its back against some unmoving wall, to find itself in truly dire straits. Perhaps then a strong leader can relax the tenacious grip of tradition and unimaginative colleagues. But adversity is of no use to the uninspired and absolutely devastating to the timid.

References

Blanshard, F. *Frank Aydelotte of Swarthmore.* Middletown, Conn.: Wesleyan University Press, 1970.

Clark, B. R. *The Distinctive College: Antioch, Reed, and Swarthmore.* Hawthorne, N.Y.: Aldine, 1970.

Hislop, C. *Eliphalet Nott.* Middletown, Conn.: Wesleyan University Press, 1971.

McCaughey, R. A. *Josiah Quincy 1772-1864: The Last Federalist.* Cambridge, Mass.: Harvard University Press, 1974.

Pierson, G. W. *Yale: College and University, 1871-1937.* 2 vols. New Haven, Conn.: Yale University Press, 1952, 1955.

Rudolph, F. *The American College and University: A History.* New York: Knopf, 1962.

Rudolph, F. *Curriculum: A History of the American Undergraduate Course of Study Since 1636.* San Francisco: Jossey-Bass, 1977.

Rudolph, F. "Educational Excellence: The Secondary School-College Connection and Other Matters: An Historical Assessment." Unpublished paper, National Commission on Excellence in Education, 1982.

Rudolph, F. "The Power of Professors: The Impact of Specialization and Professionalization on the Curriculum." *Change,* 1984, *16,* 12-17, 41.

Steinberg, S. *The American Melting Pot: Catholics and Jews in American Higher Education.* New York: McGraw-Hill, 1974.

Synnott, M. G. *The Half-Opened Door: Discrimination and Admissions at Harvard, Yale, and Princeton, 1900–1970.* Westport, Conn.: Greenwood Press, 1979.

Veysey, L. R. *The Emergence of the American University.* Chicago: University of Chicago Press, 1965.

Wechsler, H. S. *The Qualified Student: A History of Selective College Admission in America.* New York: Wiley, 1977.

3

Mission:
A Statement of Identity
and Direction

Warren Bryan Martin

A riddle: What is deep yet lofty, broad yet complex, important yet ignored? Not metaphysics, though that's a good guess. Not politics in Argentina, though your persistence is admirable. Not a gingerbread house, though now you're getting close. The answer? College mission statements.

The mission statement is the foundation on which the House of Intellect stands. And lofty are the utterances that express the importance of our college's mission. Indeed, they float like puffy clouds over our solidly positioned edifice. Broad is the applicability assigned these statements; so broad that they are thought to cover every contingency. Yet, narrow is the gate to understanding them, and few there be that find it. No wonder, then, given the mission statement's depth and height, breadth and density, that it is so often ignored.

What I have just done, however, is what too many college administrators and faculty members often do. I have presented a caricature of the place of the mission statement in the life of the college or university. After a nod to its traditional authority and an acknowledgment of its lingering, albeit cumbersome, presence, I finally treated it like the House of Lords—all sound and fury, signifying nothing.

In presenting the mission statement this way, I am as wrong as are my colleagues. A good mission statement is as important to a college as is good management. Indeed, management is, or ought to be, guided by mission. And the same is true of the capital funds campaign and scores of other activities. Thus, if we express concern about the quality of student life on campus, and propose reforms, in all probability our definition of quality and our formulation of changes will be informed by the college's institutional mission. Or, to take another example, how can faculty development programs be effective without reference to institutional mission? Surely, they must be informed by the needs and goals of the college, not simply by outside professional criteria.

There is, of course, another way to look at all this. Perhaps a capital funds campaign should be designed, not with reference to institutional mission, but with an eye to the priorities of known sources of funding. He who pays the piper may still call the tune. Institutional mission be damned. Let the mission statement bend with the wind and follow rather than lead. As for student life, more than a few student deans, counselors, therapists, and other leaders concerned for the quality of student life have concluded that what is needed in many colleges is not pressure to bring student behavior into conformity with institutional standards but pressure to bring institutional objectives into agreement with broader, more inclusive societal norms. The individual student is not to defer to what is best for the institution; rather, the institution is to defer to the needs and interests of the individual. This nation, after all, places highest priority on the individual, not on the community. The institution's mission is to help the individual toward self-realization.

There are, I repeat, other ways of looking at these matters. Faculty development programs may, we know, have more to do with the values and goals of professional associations, that is, faculty guilds, than with institutional purposes. A college may emphasize teaching as compared to research in its statement of institutional mission; but for the young untenured faculty member, loyalty to the research orientation of the guild rather than to the college's commitment to teaching seems to be the way to success.

Well, if management is not brought into the service of institutional mission, the quality of student life is defined in the marketplace rather than in the quadrangle, and faculty loyalty focuses on the guild not the college, does this mean that the notion of institutional objectives stated in a mission statement has been discredited and can be discarded? Some say yes. Observers notice that mission statements are pretty much the same in all colleges, and so they conclude that the actual institutional mission is not to be found there. It is found rather in the curricular offerings, in the priorities of the capital funds campaign, in the features of student life. The processes of life in the college reveal the principles of the place.

Are we, then, at last free of old-fashioned and perhaps futile attempts to build changing structures on fixed foundations? Perhaps it is better to simply adapt old ideals to new realities, making the statement of mission conform to what the college or university is actually doing by giving that statement cosmetic surgery—a face-lift, a tummy tuck, a lancing of the old body politic's varicose veins. All the basic equipment can be left in place while the mission statement is given a more contemporary look. A related option is to deliberately leave the mission statement intact, striking down only offensive sectarian language. (As the college chapel may be left in place after the college goes secular, removing only the symbols that contradict pluralism.) Thereafter, college leaders can point to the historical traditions represented by the mission statement, thus preserving a claim to continuity while in fact marching to a different drummer and going in another direction.

But having said all this, can we go on to say that colleges have therefore freed themselves of the responsibility of specifying missions? Mission statements may be changed, may be ignored, or may be totally discarded, but have colleges thereby rid themselves, once and for all, of the traditional need for a statement of direction—for priorities, definitions, standards, and guidelines?

What Manner of Mission?

Can you name a college that literally has no sense of institutional mission, that is, no set of objectives? You may be able to cite a place with no stated institutional purposes, no formal mission statement. But, in fact, every college has a mission of some kind. The college president may acknowledge, even gloat, that "his" college has no elaborated mission, that it is not tied to a canonical statement of purpose. We understand, however, that what this president means is that the mission of his college is to remain flexible, to be responsive to changing times, to be improvisational and innovative. We are being told, in other words, not that the mission of this college is to have no mission but that the mission is to keep the college a moving target, always ready to jump over every dogma and run with every trend.

It is also possible, and fairly common, for a college to have a mission imposed on it, often by external forces—a constituency, a wealthy benefactor, a church, or a state legislature. Or a college may find its mission constrained, perhaps by financial exigency or by a sociopolitical agenda that carries government funding provisions irresistible to the college. So, if the president or faculty or board members say that they are committed in their college to process and to pragmatism, to that which is available and what works, they are telling us not that the institution has no mission but what the college's particular mission is. A mission imposed is, nonetheless, a mission in place.

The better way is to consciously go to work to clarify and specify the institution's basic purpose. Get straight about the mission. Sooner or later somebody will write those goals down—providing, yes, a mission statement. It is as certain as death and taxes.

The issue is not whether a college or university will have a mission or whether there will be a mission statement. Rather, the issue is, What sort of mission will it have? What will be the mission of this college as compared to that one?

Certain elements of almost any college or university mission statement will be the same. It will say something about the socialization of students—education for responsible citizenship, education that encourages self-realization and better interpersonal relationships, and so on. (The mating and marriage function is an unmentioned but unquestionably important part of college-level socialization. However parched the land appears, this underground river flows unvexed to the sea.) Almost all mission statements also affirm institutional commitment to the teaching of basic skills—reading, writing, computation, and verbal communication. They also speak of education in certain advanced skills—the methodology of a subject matter specialization and its essential content in the context of cognate disciplines. All this is presented by the college as providing education appropriate to later professional training or as providing education sufficient for entry-level positions in various careers.

Then, it is customary to profess, in the undergraduate mission statement, loyalty to general education—usually a Mulligan stew that includes such garden variety vegetables as history and literature, along with a dash of the arts. It will have a stock made of the social sciences—psychology or whatever else that pantry offers—and, finally, at least a little heavy stuff from the natural and physical sciences—meat and potatoes chemistry, biology, and so on. Around the edges of this stewpot, a college here and there will roll in a foreign language or some other speciality of the house. Finally, a pinch of math, and cook to taste.

The general education menu may be *prix fixe,* that is, a core curriculum with fixed ingredients and set fare. More likely, it will be a passel of distribution requirements, as with our Irish stew. Only occasionally will the student be encouraged to take the lead in concocting the recipe. Even less often will the corrolation between the institutional mission of the college and the general education program be so pointed and evident that an observer has no doubt about what drives the curriculum.

In this chapter we are not interested in arguing that an institution should write out a mission statement just for the sake of having one, nor do we think that one mission is as good as another. For us, the pivotal question, the question on which everything else turns, is this: If a college is to find opportunity amid adversity, what then could be characteristics in its mission that would set it apart from its competitors, help it find a special niche, give it a claim to "value added" by ensuring that it provides an added dimension in the education offered its students? There are, we believe, three useful categories of distinctiveness, three ways for colleges to position themselves so as to stand apart, not as eccentric institutions but as significant ones.

First, there are colleges with institutional missions that essentially feature one point of innovation. It is this distinction, this innovation, this characteristic, their leaders say, that makes them successful. We might call these institutions *unidimensional* colleges.

There are, in addition, those colleges that build an institutional mission that is conspicuously *two dimensional.* Life in these colleges has its warp and woof—woven deliberately so that certain innovations run through the length of undergraduate programs while certain other shared experiences reach across the width of the total endeavor. The fabric of the place has the dual strength of this weave built in and through it.

Another level of opportunity for colleges that would prosper in the presence of adversity calls for the distinctiveness of these institutions to appear to be *multidimensional.* They quite deliberately feature several innovations at once. Along the warp and woof they work in a distinctive design using both traditional and nontraditional patterns. The third dimension may be a depth dimension, perhaps a theological or philosophical commitment whose influence radiates from the center to the edges of the endeavor. In any event, the multidimensional character of the college extends from the mission statement through its every program and activity.

Standing Apart from the Crowd

Any taxonomy of colleges is somewhat contrived. To offer such a taxonomy may be useful in isolating distinguishing characteristics, as is the case here in classifying colleges as unidimensional and multidimensional. But of course no college has only one or two features; all colleges are in various ways multidimensional. They all have many characteristics—academic, social, financial, formal and informal. At the same time, however, in certain colleges something special identifies the place and sets it apart, gives it distinctiveness and maybe even character. Sometimes there is one point of distinction, one characteristic that stands out so much that it can be called the organizing principle.

Colorado College stands as a representative of this unidimensional approach to survival with distinction. The college's modular calendar, a one-course-at-a-time program of study, dominates the organization and ethos of the college. Colorado drew on the earlier Hiram College experiences with this calendar, tuned and refined it, marketed it skillfully, and, blessed by the sun and snow culture of Colorado Springs, marched out of obscurity into regional if not national recognition. Similarly, Cornell College was in trouble a few years ago, in part because it stood on a hill in Iowa surrounded by cornfields but more significantly because it was a good liberal arts college competing with several others equally good and located close by. How could Cornell stand out? And do so with integrity? One way was by adapting the Colorado calendar to its location and resources. Thus, Cornell has "an added dimension" that, to date, has brought lustre to the place and has, pardon the mercenary phrase, paid off handsomely.

What has been said for Colorado and Cornell colleges, could be said with Olympic-scale hosannas for Berea College in Kentucky. How often does a college with a reputation for educating Appalachian mountain students through a disciplined work study program not only succeed as an academic institution but accumulate an endowment of more than $90 million? Or, to make the point another way, how many colleges of Berea's size, yet with much better locations and more conventional programs, match Berea's reputation for excellence or its endowment? Let those with eyes to see, let those with ears to hear, learn the lesson of this focused, value-added concept of higher education.

In passing, it should be noted that certain colleges, given their location, affiliation, or other factors do not have the liberty to think of making themselves unidimensional in the way illustrated by Colorado, Cornell, or Berea. These colleges may be required through law or state mandate to be pluralistic communities offering a plethora of programs of study. Is there a way for them to stand out from the crowd institutionally, while honoring their obligation to serve a crowd of diverse individuals? Consider Brooklyn College, a unit of the City University of New York. This college offers an array of undergraduate programs appropriate for an urban institution, yet it has a point of distinction as difficult to achieve in that setting as Cornell's was in its location. As Robert Hess spells out in Chapter Fourteen, Brooklyn College offers a splendidly coherent and eminently sensible general education program expressed through a core curriculum. This curriculum offers, as William James would have it, a difference that makes a difference. Here, again, we see value-added education in a college able to carry through one-dimensional innovation—not holistic, but precise and to the point.

On the negative side of unidimensional distinctiveness, we note in passing those colleges that are just like every other college, except for being church related. When parents or pastors, students or high school counselors ask why a young person should go to one of them rather than elsewhere, the answer comes from that chorus of colleges singing the same anthem: One verse will be about a college small and friendly, offering plenty of time for the student to find himself or herself in a nonthreatening setting. Interpret that part of the answer to mean that the college practices mediocrity in an intimate setting. And the second verse will have to do with the college's historic affiliation with some church. Read that to mean, "We have been historically related to the church but that fact is now part of church history." It is painfully true, in too many cases, that the serious question—Why this college?—will be answered with a soft-shoe shuffle.

Extending and Enriching the Mission

The two-dimensional college, that institution that consciously weaves a warp and woof into its community life, has decisive advantages in the struggle to turn adversity into opportunity. For example, the vital church-related college that makes thoughtful and sustained efforts to ensure that all deliberations implement policy and are informed by the Judeo-Christian tradition brings a vertical as well as a horizontal, a transcendent as well as a humanistic, dimension to every aspect of the endeavor. That college joins faith and reason, worship and work in ways calculated to leave an indelible impression on all members of the community. To look into such a church-related college is to see a college that is unmistakedly different from its secular counterparts. It is a college committed to being not only church related but, to the extent possible, Christian.

There are, of course, other ways to conceptualize the mission of a college so as to make it two dimensional, indeed, to the extent that these points of distinction literally come to characterize the institution. At Princeton University, within the last five years, a multimillion dollar investment has been made to ensure that the quality of undergraduate life, especially for lower-division students, equals the already high level of the academic program. Princeton set out to gain recognition as a small university that works hard at quality and content not only in classrooms and labs but also in residence halls and social lounges. To this end, Princeton has reorganized its facilities to produce five undergraduate "colleges." In these colleges, freshmen and sophomores eat together in units of manageable size, enjoy common play and study areas, plan and carry out social events, have various counseling and guidance services, profit from the presence of selected upperclassmen, invite university professors to meals, and have a distinguished professor as master with quarters in the college. Here again is evidence of commitment to an added dimension; in this case, the excellence of the academic program is balanced by quality in the cocurricular elements of the undergraduate experience. This development is not, of course, the only thing that sets Princeton apart, but it is a development big enough and important enough to be an identifying feature of this university's mission.

Here is another institutional example: William Jewell College, Liberty, Missouri, has during the last decade or so moved to extend and enrich what we are calling the vertical dimension of life in the institution. The academic program has been qualitatively tightened up and quantitatively opened up. There are now options whereby the student can satisfy the general education requirement—one track offers a core, problem/theme approach, while the other provides a more familiar distributional arrangement. There is an Oxford University plan for selected students—a provision for a more individualized course of study on the Missouri campus and in Britain.

As for that other dimension, the so-called horizontal plane, William Jewell College has taken advantage of its physical proximity to Kansas City to develop a magnificent fine arts program. The presence of world-class artists at William Jewell has impressed the city's movers and shakers to the point that this college not only is becoming the area's cultural magnet but it is able to draw on widening sources of support for academic as well as cultural activities. William Jewell is moving up to a whole new level of significance by thinking in a lucid two-dimensional, even multidimensional way, emphasizing connections, programs, and relationships that strengthen and enrich the form and fabric of life in that institution. This college has a mission.

When the Whole Is More than the Parts

Could the more conventional college that is without distinguishing features, other than conventionality, move up to a new level of visibility and distinctiveness? We pull no punches. We are referring here to that college with a cautious and conventional faculty organized by departments and subject matter specializations. It is a college with only a few students who are sufficiently disciplined, motivated, and skilled to use the resources of the college to actually get an education, with or without the help of the faculty. It is a college where, in the end, perhaps only one-half of the students will grow and develop more than they would have out there in the real world exposed to the normal influences of family and friends, work and maturation. You see, this is indeed the conventional college we are talking about. Could such a college break out of the pack?

We hold the position that it can be done if this college will take William Blake's position that single vision is not good enough and that only multiple vision will do. The vertical spine for the college that would transcend conventionality should be a solid program in general education followed by disciplinary specialization. Variations are available on these familiar themes, and two will be stated later, but nothing is recommended that would require a faculty member's reach to extend beyond his grasp.

The horizontal plane in the life of this aspiring institution will make provision for another traditional function—the nurture of body, mind, and spirit, that is, the reconciliation of the academic curriculum with the cocurricular life of the students. Here is education for the whole person provided by faculty members who, it is hoped, will be role models of what it means to be a whole person.

The third dimension, the in-depth dimension, goes deep but it is not beyond normally available resources. It can be achieved when the college expands the notion of institutional mission to include the idea that a coherent "college culture" is both the goal and best expression of a vital institutional mission. The common college becomes uncommon, the average place becomes exceptional when a distinctive campus culture goes so deep and reaches so high that it comes to embody the institutional mission.

Consider, again, what could be done in the area of curriculum reform, so that the curriculum of this college would contribute to and not obstruct our ultimate goals. The vertical dimension might look familiar enough, featuring established approaches to career training. Here, faculty members would be expected to do, as stated earlier, mainly what they are trained to do—teach introductory and advanced classes in their disciplines. As a modest variation on this typical vertical dimension, however, the college might try a conservative form of a core curriculum for general education (see Boyer and Levine, 1981, for a viable conceptual plan). It makes sense to have a core curriculum at the heart of a college culture. Additionally, this college could make the upper-division majors blend better with career and professional interests. Most faculty members could, without too much trauma, accommodate these adjustments, thus improving prospects that students will get a more useful education.

More inclusive innovation, but still within reach of the college's human and fiscal resources, would call for the curriculum's vertical warp to feature, as it were, three threads—general or liberal education, vocational education, and integrative education—the trilinear curriculum (see Martin, 1982). By the use of such features, the college could provide an early introduction to career alternatives and carry general or liberal education into the upper-division years, where electives would give way to problem theme integrative seminars. Also, the college could respond to market demands and to its own traditions in responsible yet distinctive ways.

But how could the college's mission be made to cut, as we said, not only up and down but across and deep? Giroux (1984), along with many others, has pointed out that most current proposals for change in the institutional mission of both precollegiate education and higher education, in schools as well as in colleges, emphasize "economic rationality": "Within the boundaries of this discourse, schools become important only to the degree that they can provide the forms of knowledge, skills, and social practices necessary to produce the labor force for an increasingly complex, technological economy" (p. 188).

Under this version of educational philosophy, specific cognitive and technical outcomes are emphasized while the knowledge and skills necessary for a broader understanding—the principles, for example, of "cultural literacy" (Hirsh, 1983, p. 159) and "civic courage" (Giroux, 1984, p. 188)—are not acquired. A college must do more than increase individual student achievement as a way of serving industrial needs. Its challenge is to develop nothing less than a culture that expresses the institutional mission. This is, in fact, the crucial challenge for a college that would bestir itself and achieve distinction. But how to proceed?

As colleges struggled to make ends meet, it came to be assumed that management-oriented corporations had a lot to say to colleges. Corporate executives taught college administrators lessons in management systems and corporate strategies— portfolio theories, cost curves, computer utilizations, econometric models. "Run your college like a business," "Remember that management is a science," thus spake confident corporate officers to quaking college leaders. And in this way the institutional missions of many colleges came to be shaped by management strategies.

Now, however, a different emphasis is emerging in business and industry as corporate consultants, office managers, and chief executive officers look for ways to ensure success in their own operations by putting emphasis on something called the *corporate culture,* that is, the traditions and assumptions, values and purposes, ceremonies and rituals, programs and "carrying mechanisms" that, taken together, differentiate an institution from its competitors. One impressive sign of this emphasis is that a book featuring attention to "cultures"—Peters and Waterman's *In Search of Excellence* (1982)—sold over 1.3 million hardcover copies.

What is noteworthy for educators is that the corporate model at its best involves a culture that has amazing similarities to a college culture at its best. Corporations, therefore, have as much to learn from colleges as colleges do from corporations. College officials should, in fact, become a resource for company officers, given the current emphasis on corporate culture. After all, most colleges still have some shared beliefs and values, rituals and ceremonies, informal communication networks, and a residual sense of community—all of which are also elements of a corporate culture. The college has something to teach the corporation when the culture of that college is an accurate expression of the institution's mission.

However, because of the problems caused by flaccid enrollments and sagging budgets, administrators, board members, and some faculty have tended to ignore or even to deliberately play down the distinctive features of their own cultures in their institutional mission statements and, instead, have tried to imitate corporations on the level of management systems and marketing strategies. Also, college leaders have seemed willing to strike a deal with corporate leaders: If the corporations would show the colleges how to survive by instruction in management efficiencies and program economies, the colleges in turn would emphasize preparation of students for careers in business and industry and release faculty for contract research in corporations.

What is plain is that corporations and colleges aspire equally to excellence but both fall equally short of it. Neither side dare preach to the other. Neither partner can be a missionary to the other. Sensing this condition, corporate as well as college leaders are now advocating a return to fundamentals in mission, as shown by one partner's attention to the characteristics of successful corporate cultures and by the other partner's interest in reviving and improving college cultures.

Two recent books, the one by Peters and Waterman already mentioned and a second by Deal and Kennedy entitled *Corporate Cultures* (1982), offer guidance to corporate consultants and chief executives who are searching for the essential elements in strong corporate cultures. For example, these authors point out that almost all corporations have key words and phrases in their advertising to signal corporate priorities. Most managers and chief executives have understandably doubted that slogans such as "IBM means service" were anything more than promotional "gong" words. Now comes research, reported in the aforementioned books, drawn from a sample of eighty corporations, demonstrating that eighteen companies with clearly stated beliefs or values were uniformly high performers in the marketplace. There was a correlation between what the British call "word chimes" and institutional performance, between success in the marketplace and what these researchers call the corporate culture—when that culture was painstakingly developed and faithfully cultivated throughout the organization and when it not only represented the best elements of the institution's mission but was in fact the mission at work day-by-day.

There are certain characteristics of a cohesive culture, sometimes intangible but very influential, that will always be elements of that institution's mission. One of these characteristics is a set of commonly held values or standards. They guide "product" development, quality control, human relationships, competition, and planning for the future. These values—justice, civility, fairness, decency—are based on beliefs and attitudes about human nature and social organizations whether the organization is Proctor and Gamble or Washington and Lee. Basic ideas about values will not be the same for every institution, but every strong corporation and every strong college will have beliefs that stand as foundations on which the culture and mission statements are built.

What else? Investigations into corporate cultures by Peters and Waterman, as well as by Deal and Kennedy confirm what observers of vital college cultures already knew: Rites and rituals, heroes and exemplars, ceremonies and convocations are important. In these ways the underlying purposes of the organization are made visible, initiates are drawn into the fellowship that sustains old-timers, the community is given not only models of appropriate daily behavior but examples of the kind of risk takers and visionaries needed to revitalize the enterprise.

Storytellers, priests, cabals, even eccentrics will also be present in a culture with a mission. These people may appear to spend most of their time punching holes in the fabric of a corporate or college culture. In fact, they are specialists in an essential service. They not only circulate commentaries throughout the community but also serve as posts to hold up the very tent they seem to want to tear down. Standards cannot survive without these informal communication networks that, in the process of exposing weaknesses in the standards, end up helping to repair or reform them.

Again, what else? Successful corporations, like successful colleges, stay close to their customers, emphasizing service to the point of making it an obsession. They are also "tight-loose," meaning that these benchmark corporations are "tight" about certain basic objectives and values—they emphasize a few features that are nonnegotiable. But, paradoxically, these same corporations are "loose" in the sense that they encourage individual initiative, innovation, and creativity even to the point of errors. If we're not making errors, said one chief executive, we're not making progress. As for the role of the chief executive officer, Peters and Waterman are persuaded that this person's main assignment is to manage the values of the organization, taking the comprehensive or synoptic view and stressing the connectedness of things.

It would be a mistake to conclude that, because corporate cultures share certain characteristics with each other or share those characteristics with college cultures, there is a single dominant culture. Corporate consultants Deal and Kennedy (1982, pp. 107–108) have identified four distinct or generic cultures:

> *Tough-guy/macho culture*—the domain of spunky individuals accustomed to high risks, as in most advertising agencies; persons accustomed to quick feedback on successes and failures.
>
> *Hard work/play hard culture*—where action is everything—movement, activities, and persistence. To persist is to prevail. This is the culture of computer companies and door-to-door operations—Tandy and Mary Kay Cosmetics. Helping to keep morale up, and the energy level high, there are quick and conspicuous rewards.
>
> *High-stakes/slow feedback*—Boeing Aircraft, Mobil, and Exxon are positioned here. It is the world where one decision can determine the health of the corporation for a decade. Consequently, moves are deliberate, and when the commitments are made the sense of relief is quickly replaced by anxiety as the long wait for the big payoff begins.
>
> *Low-risk/slow feedback culture*—process and precision are the key words for most insurance companies, regulated industries, and various bureaus of government. Rewards and sanctions are both slow in coming. Technical skills are prized. Order is the framework for progress.

In any large corporation, all four of these generic cultures will be found. Strong companies may actually build their corporate cultures so as to blend the elements of this taxonomy.

This interest in strong corporate cultures and the finding

that "organizations have, in fact, gained great strength from shared values—with emphasis on the 'shared' " (Deal and Kennedy, 1982, p. 22) have their counterpart, please remember, in liberal arts colleges and other undergraduate colleges of arts and sciences that now, like so many corporations, realize the need to build or rebuild working cultures in their organizations.

A strong college, research and observation show, has a distinctive mission. Certain features of that college will be variations on themes stated in strong corporate cultures, not because the college is imitating the corporation but because any community or culture of distinction will have certain characteristic features. However, the culture of a college, when that college and its mission are strong, transcends a corporate culture. The college will, therefore, have something special to say to the corporation—and to society at large.

The college culture will show beliefs and values, as does the corporate culture, but it is more likely to go deeper into basic issues than will the corporation. Notice the superficial level at which Deal and Kennedy (1982) position the corporate culture when discussing values: "We think that society today suffers from pervasive uncertainty about values, a relativism that undermines leadership and commitment alike. After all, in this fast-paced world, who really does know what's right? On the philosophical level, we find ourselves without convincing responses. But, the everyday business environment is quite different. Even if ultimate values are chimerical, particular values clearly make sense for specific organizations operating in specific economic circumstances. Perhaps because ultimate values seem so elusive, people respond positively to practical ones. Choices must be made, and values are an indispensable guide in making them" (p. 22).

It was the dominance of "immediate" values of the tough-guy/macho culture of salesmen, and similar values among the high-risk/slow feedback culture of executives, that caused American airframe manufacturers—Lockheed and McDonnell Douglas, for example—to tolerate bribes and other illegal incentives to promote the sale of the L-1011 and the DC-10. "Practical" values, especially in the specific economic circumstances in which those "values" were employed, had quite specific outcomes not all of them foreseen or desirable. Perhaps corporations should now and then institute a search for values beyond monetary success. At any rate, a strong college culture will not allow specific economic circumstances to determine the scope of inquiry. Success will not be determined by the popularity of "practical" values, anymore than failure will be signaled by a paucity of easy responses to the question of "who knows what's right?"

The college of distinction may be able to stay longer at the task of tracking the effects of its culture than will the corporation. The college can be informed by persons who left the college culture ten and twenty years ago, that is, by graduates who come back to report on the positive and negative effects of the college experience in their lives. This evidence contributes to a more comprehensive assessment of the college than is likely to be possible for the corporation. While the purposeful college has an educational philosophy that goes deeper and farther than the beliefs and values basic to a meaningful corporate culture, the college may also reach higher than the corporation; it can reach up to consider questions of religion and ethics, thereby assuring the college of another added dimension, one that enables the values of the college to transcend both philosophy and education.

Good colleges, like good corporations, tend to locate themselves in generic categories: the research university, that is, the university as pathfinder and disseminator of new knowledge; the community college, or the college as a center of educational services; and the comprehensive liberal arts college, or the college as contributor to vital connections, including those of body, mind, and spirit. The educational institution most likely to have something of importance to say to emerging corporate cultures is that third one, the college that is able to point to faculty and administrators who, while professionally competent, are more loyal to their college than to their guilds; to colleagues who, while generous and responsive toward researchers working on the growing edge of knowledge, prefer to be teacher-scholars best known for another contribution of equal importance—success in the synoptic function, success in synthesizing old and new knowledge. The culture or mission of a college of character features attention to the connectedness of things.

The college culture in the institution with a strong mission statement will encounter certain problems endemic to strong corporate cultures—the risk of obsolescence, resistance to change, and the likelihood of inconsistency. The breakup of AT&T and its subsequent reorganization provided a classic study in the problems of effecting change in a corporate culture. Yet certain colleges with a distinctive way of life should have something of importance to say to certain corporations. Bethel College (Kansas), a Mennonite college with a definite ethnic orientation, has leaders who can speak about how it is possible to effect change in a strong culture when the changes effected constitute innovation within a tradition. Career education in a liberal arts college is an appropriate development as long as the career programs are consistent with the values and location of that college—in this example, agricultural management at a college located in North Newton, Kansas. Also, a college may be better able than a corporation to keep changes external to the institution in perspective, if we remember that societal changes in America occur often and stay in place briefly, while changes in a college's culture take effect slowly and endure about as long as it took for them to come into being.

For a decade or two, college and university administrators have imitated executives and managers of business and industry. If executives favored consolidations and conglomerates, administrators hurried to design higher education's equivalent to the corporate example in comprehensive schools, state systems, and coordinating councils. If the style among corporate managers featured decentralization, the campus response was community colleges, cluster colleges, and a proliferation of institutes and centers at universities. Or, if the word among corporate leaders was "strategy," imitative college leaders force-fed campus data into computers and tried to make computer literacy the hallmark of the new literati.

Now, the vogue for business and industry is corporate

cultures. This, however, constitutes not only a change but a transformation, a move from the periphery to the center, from less important to more important considerations. Now, more than ever before, there is reason for colleges to be informed by the corporate example as they attempt to create or revive strong college cultures. To do so will not only help the colleges but, for a change, give the colleges an opportunity to teach the corporations something in return. In education, as in choral music, there are times to join the chorus and times to take the lead.

Advice to a Mission Maker

The approach to determining the institutional mission or the college culture must be conscious and deliberate. Otherwise, it will be improvised or imposed. Furthermore, if the college is to find opportunities for significance in a period of adversity, this mission or culture must give that institution an added dimension, a certain distinctiveness and character. This level of accomplishment is available to colleges that would otherwise be in the "undifferentiated middle," to colleges of limited financial resources, and to colleges not blessed with prime locations. It will happen when the basic mission of the institution becomes that of shaping a coherent, vital college culture.

The place to begin when your committee is assigned to write an institutional mission statement is *not* with the existing one. To begin with such a statement may put you in bondage to that from which you need to be free. There will be plenty of time later, when you are feeling stronger, to refer back to that from which you can never fully escape but to which you can never fully return. Begin writing the new institutional mission statement, then, by thinking about the college in three dimensions: the academic program(s), the cocurricular life of students, and the general ethos of the place. This exercise will give you a reading on the institution's height, breadth, and depth.

Try next to fit those elements together. See if you can develop a composite, three-dimensional picture of the college. Then ask: Are these institutional features in focus, balanced, and connected with each other? Is each component living in the present, is it informed by the past, and will it be relevant to the future? More simply, do these institutional features serve worthy purposes?

Are there also leaders on campus who have a sense of shared mission and who will work cooperatively with colleagues even as they use management technology? Do they show that the protection of core values is that for which they would ultimately give their all? Remember that, according to Peters and Waterman (1982), the management of institutional values is the main task of leadership. At about this point in the process you will have a purchase on what we have been calling the college culture—that amalgam of multidimensional qualities and characteristics drawn from that which has gone before, combined with what is, and pointed toward goals and objectives appropriate for the next era in the life of the institution.

From this institutional pattern or mosaic, next consider the salutary distinctions: that which gives accent to the composition, that which provides the design in the warp and woof of the fabric, that which distinguishes this college from its competitors and gives it a competitive edge. If you are unable to call up such features, then weigh institutional resources and canvass the aspirations of the people most committed to the college. In this way, you will discover if you have ingredients that can be molded into a one-dimensional, two-dimensional, or three-dimensional educational program.

It would also be helpful to look for relevant models in other colleges and universities. If your college is small, look to Guilford College (North Carolina) or to Messiah College (Pennsylvania). If you are in a university or a large college, probe developments over the last decade at the University of Wisconsin, Green Bay, or at Evergreen State College in Washington. The point here is to identify elements that might have transfer value.

Why spend time on the statement of an idea, as in a mission statement, when we can predict that practice will fall short of it? Because actual practice, procedures, arrangements, settings, and appearances must always be measured against an ideal. A statement of institutional mission, at its best, formally represents assumptions and purposes that will guide the planning, as well as the activities, of a college or university. Despite its flights of rhetoric and sweeping generalizations, a good mission statement informs behavior and helps members of the community decide when to say no and when to say yes. It is a statement of intention that affects practice. It is informed by tradition and experience and yet transcends both. It relates to reality but is basically an ideal. And we need ideas and ideals even more than techniques and dollars (Martin, 1982).

The end to which all of this is the means is to see that now, or for the future, certain points of uniqueness, the culture and its character will stand out. Write, then, about that culture and its distinction. Make this the main theme of the statement of institutional mission. You will be telling the truth, and the truth will make you and the college sing.

References

Boyer, E. L., and Levine, A. E. *Quest for Common Learning.* Washington, D.C.: Carnegie Foundation for the Advancement of Teaching, 1981.

Deal, T., and Kennedy, A. *Corporate Cultures.* Reading, Mass.: Addison-Wesley, 1982.

Giroux, H. "Public Philosophy and the Crisis in Education." *Harvard Educational Review,* 1984, *54,* 188.

Hirsh, E. O. "Cultural Literacy." *American Scholar,* 1983, *52,* 159–169.

Martin, W. B. *College of Character: Renewing the Purpose and Content of College Education.* San Francisco: Jossey-Bass, 1982.

Peters, T. J., and Waterman, R. H., Jr. *In Search of Excellence.* New York: Harper & Row, 1982.

4

Leaders:
Presidents Who Make
a Difference

David Riesman
Sharon Elliott Fuller

Whenever college and university presidents gather in coteries small enough for candor, they tell each other "war stories" about their difficulties in making effective use of the authority they are nominally granted by the board of trustees and by the formal constitution of the academic enterprise they head.[1] In addition to the constraints imposed by legal and administrative regulations and the increasingly frequent intervention or threatened intervention of the judicial process, they remark on the participatory power of faculty and to some degree of students, often won as concessions in the ardent destabilizing efforts of the late 1960s and early 1970s. Well before those events, what Jencks and Riesman (1968) termed the "academic revolution" gave power to mobile faculty and the disciplines to which they owe allegiance, as against the institutional loyalties that, though muted, persist not only in some church-related colleges but in certain major and selective institutions as well. Today, presidents must take account of the waning legitimacy of authority as such and also confront a situation of lessened faculty mobility. At present, institutions not in the demographically prospering areas of the country and not rapidly expanding present a picture of entrenched faculty who cannot readily leave, but who can dig in (less effectively against student customers than against presidential leverage).[2]

One captures the flavor of an earlier era in Clark's *Distinctive College* (1970), which offers the reader historically grounded accounts of the creation of Reed College through the academic vision and entrepreneurial energies of William T. Foster in 1911, and of the re-creation of Swarthmore by Frank Aydelotte in the 1920s, and of Antioch College by Arthur Morgan during the same period. These colleges are said to have a *saga* or, as one might also say, an ethos or moral penumbra that helps shape the outlook of their graduates, quite apart from the academic or other skills accumulated during the course of their education. These three dynamic presidents had the authority to engender such a saga, one that is recognizable in Reed's case over two generations later.

Most college presidents do not now have the authority of these three inventive academic entrepreneurs. But there remain nevertheless a large number of academic executives who have found room to maneuver and have made a visible difference to their institutions. In this essay we shall briefly discuss two colleges, Mary Baldwin and Carleton, and their presidents, Virginia Lester and Robert Edwards, with an eye to determining the degree to which a president can today influence the development of a small liberal arts college by building on its saga.

The biases of this essay include a belief that leaders make a difference, that they are a very scarce human resource, and that for the sake of higher education and what it portends for the country and the world, we need to find ways to select and support them effectively.[3] Clark Kerr (1984) has reported on behalf of the Commission on Strengthening Presidential Leadership that only a small minority of presidents have or seize the opportunity to pay serious attention to the undergraduate curriculum and to faculty selection and retention; the great majority, estimated at four-fifths, leave these crucial matters entirely to their principal academic subordinates. Through subordinates, presidents can influence curricula even in large research universities. But our focus here is on institutions so small (Mary Baldwin with 800 and Carleton with 1,850 students) that the president can know all members of the staff and faculty; these are institutions of manageable scale.

In general, the better the institution in terms of faculty distinction and prestige, the more powerful the faculty is likely to be vis-à-vis the president, and the more likely to possess a few relentless guerrilla warriors against authority. The irony is that the authority of the president is almost always less than it may seem to student and faculty antagonists and is therefore more likely to excite counterattack because of its very vulnerability. These limits on the presidency are aggravated by the fact that there has been a decrease in recent years in the terms of office that presidents commonly serve. The average duration is now seven years. Moreover, as one president quoted by Kerr (1984) described the way a faculty accumulates grievances, "Eventually one manages to make at least one decision against the convictions of virtually every member of the faculty" (p. 54).

In the liberal arts colleges we have examined, we have sought to understand the characteristic attachments faculty members have to an institution and their respective definitions of its saga, as against the pull of their academic discipline. Faculty members who see themselves almost purely as institutional loyalists, disconnected from their disciplines, may view presidents and deans with jaundiced eyes when they propose changes incongruent with the faculty members' sense of tradition. Other faculty members will regard movements into adult and continuing education or new vocational programs as desecrations of their disciplinary commitment and sense of personal craftsmanship. Some faculty members will harbor both impulses. Still others may seek presidential support for their own entrepreneurial energies, while others will resent presidential support for more favored colleagues.

Presidents who seek to make a difference must of course

take account of the various ways in which faculty can be persuaded, on occasion even inspired, to redefine institutional, departmental, and disciplinary loyalties in pursuit of, at one level,
institutional survival and, at another level, institution-wide improvement. As we write, Mary Baldwin College is searching for a
new president to take office after the conclusion of Virginia
Lester's ninth year. Her accomplishment is in part reflected in
the fact that, of eight finalist candidates, six are presidents now;
this must mean that they must regard Mary Baldwin College as
an opportunity as well as a challenge.[4]

In helping bring about the changes necessary for Mary
Baldwin College's survival and for incremental improvements at
Carleton College, both presidents have had the full support of
their boards.[5] Presidents, however, often require more than passive consent; they may be able to use nonintrusive advice, but
they also need personal support as individuals facing complicated dilemmas. Such support is essential in coping with resistance as well as with attacks from faculty. This is particularly
true if, at the outset of a presidency, the board has mandated a
change from previous policies.[6]

The research enterprise of which this essay is a necessarily
compressed installment led us to a preliminary examination of
several dozen liberal arts colleges. After brief visits to most of
these institutions, we narrowed our focus to a handful of private liberal arts colleges, more in search of challenges for leadership than in search of adversity, for the latter is indeed both
widespread currently and, so to speak, overdue demographically.[7] The academic landscape presents a number of endangered
species. When it is not under the patronage of an eminent evan-
gelist, the small church-related liberal arts college, committed to
the formation of intellect as well as of character, is in many
cases endangered. The historically black private institutions are
also in a condition of jeopardy, as public and private colleges
and universities bid for black faculty members, administrators,
and students.

Even the most eminent of the women's colleges are
threatened in their selectivity. When numerous men's colleges—
Ivy League, Catholic, Protestant, and public—became coeduca-

tional with a rush in the sixties and seventies, a number of women's colleges followed suit. But whereas women were eager to "integrate" Yale, Williams, Holy Cross, and the University of Virginia, the reverse has not been the case. America is not, and it is not likely to become, an androgynous country. Correspondingly, we believe that single-sex education will continue to serve some women far better than do coeducational institutions. However, the women's movements helped in the 1960s to define single-sex institutions as somehow odd, even "unnatural." This is not the place to argue the case for single-sex education, particularly for women, but simply to note that the cultural pressures toward homogenization of education are so powerful that it is unlikely that a particular variety such as women's colleges, once extinguished or reduced to ecological rarity, could ever be reestablished. For this essay we have chosen to discuss Virginia Lester's decade-long work at Mary Baldwin College because it faced even more serious dangers to survival than other women's colleges in the South—dangers that, despite growing success in recruiting students and financial support, remain for the future; it provides the clearest case in our purview of a "turnaround" situation.

In addition to having to confront the widespread belief that single-sex education is aberrant, segregated in the pejorative sense, as well as out of tune with the times, Mary Baldwin possesses a handicap common to many of the best of the country's liberal arts colleges, namely, their location in rural areas and in small towns. Today's students are more sophisticated than their predecessors. They have left their families' protection earlier; and they not only prefer urban locations, provided that these are not too depressing and crime ridden, but also like the opportunity for part-time work that larger communities offer. Mary Baldwin College traces its origin back to a female seminary in Staunton, Virginia, in 1842; today Staunton has a population of 28,000.

Carleton College is located in Northfield, Minnesota (population 13,000), along with St. Olaf College, forty miles south of the Twin Cities. In the Northeast and Middle Atlantic states, where private higher education retains strong hegemony, a rural or small-town location is only a marginal inhibitor of recruitment. Amherst, Williams, Wellesley, Bowdoin, Swarthmore, Franklin and Marshall, and others are all in varying degree heavily overapplied. In Carleton's case it is the combination of small-town locale with midwestern location that acts as a brake on the potential traffic from the seacoasts of the East, West, and South.[8]

The two accounts that follow have been prepared with the cooperation of the institutions, including generous facilitation from their presidents. Although our model is ethnographic (see Riesman, 1978), we have done neither the extended fieldwork nor the archival research requisite for more than a preliminary report. Although particular passages may sound definitive, we insist on our tentativeness. We begin our saga of each institution with the coming of a new president.

Mary Baldwin College

Mary Baldwin dates its history back to the mid nineteenth century, although it did not become a four-year institution until 1923. It prospered after the Second World War, notably under the leadership of Samuel R. Spencer, Jr. (1957–1968). Like somewhat better-known Sweet Briar and Hollins, Mary Baldwin was then attracting a number of northern students to mix with its southern ladies. The focus was on the liberal arts, with the accoutrement appropriate to jobs before and after marriage as well as for the married state, including preparation for the education of one's children, along with suitable volunteer work; of course, for many, these would not turn out to be the sole realities.[9] At the very time of President Spencer's departure, cultural attitudes were turning against the single-sex colleges. For much of the country outside the Northeast and South, and for the overwhelming bulk of public higher education, these had been anomalous for decades. The latent egalitarianism of the 1960s that found a voice in the counterculture opposed boundaries of any sort, and certainly those based on gender, as exclusive and nefarious; what seemed merely traditional and archaic interested only a small minority of young women.[10]

After the departure of President Spencer, who was esteemed although regarded as autocratic, a year elapsed before a successor was found in William W. Kelly. He is reputed to have charmed the search committee, the college community, and the trustees. Everyone speaks of him as an immensely likable person, and if he had a fault, it was the need to be liked—common in most of us, but a negative quality in a president. He faced extraordinarily difficult decisions, consulted widely, and then postponed. His decisions came belatedly, and consultation did not save him from criticism for incompetent stewardship. He lost the respect of the faculty and the board. Indeed, the faculty's increased role in governance created a difficult situation for Kelly's successor, for the faculty had gotten into the habit of dealing directly with the board. Such habitual "end runs" are inevitably extremely threatening to a new president who believes the faculty were instrumental in the release of the former president. Matters were made more difficult because in the sixties the faculty had been enlarged beyond what increasing enrollments required; moreover, money was borrowed to expand the physical plant, and its maintenance costs were a factor in the deficits that began in the first year of Kelly's incumbency. Several years later, enrollment started to decline on a moderate slope, but in 1976 it dropped precipitously by 100 to a total of 645. The previous year the trustees had installed a controller; they also asked the president to appoint an executive assistant, since the president was on the road so much, seeking endowment support.

The New President. Concerned for him and for the college, the trustees retired President Kelly and looked around for a successor who could rescue a college whose closing had been rumored, one obvious reason for the drop in enrollment. The trustees discovered the array of difficulties confronting the college only when a number of prospects they had sought as candidates to succeed Kelly turned them down. In fact, the trustees had not only been lulled into unawareness of how large a deficit the college was running by the assurances of the now departing administration but also were so out of touch with academic realities that they failed to realize that the presidency of the college had become an unattractive prospect.[11]

In selecting Virginia Lester in 1976, the trustees broke with the sequence of Southern gentlemen. Moreover, Virginia Lester did not bring with her a typical academic and administrative background. After receiving an undergraduate degree from Pennsylvania State and a master's degree in education from Temple, she taught school, married, bore two children, then entered higher education as a part-time administrator and teacher in the Department of Education at Skidmore College. Divorced and for many years a single mother, Virginia Lester earned a doctorate "at a distance" through the Union of Experimenting Colleges and Universities, a Cincinnati offshoot of Antioch College. At the same time, she held the position of dean at Empire State College, the State University of New York's experiment in distance learning. Her writings have been almost entirely in the field of higher education, occasional essays rather than research works. But her work at Empire State College had been combined with some visibility as a consultant to other academic institutions, and she had become a part of what might be termed the "old girls' network" of women helping other women advance in academic administration. Lacking formal disciplinary training, she has also lacked the frequent prejudices of academics against corporate and financial leaders, and she has moved easily in their worlds as well as in those of state and national government and of the foundations.

Lester realized that many things must be accomplished immediately in order to save Mary Baldwin; she addressed herself first to the obvious adversities. She saw herself as a competent expert with a mandate to defend the institution and the people in it and prepared to act decisively when requisite. Moving quickly, she consulted faculty, but she was not prepared to be as consultative as her predecessor had been. Nor was she prepared to acquiesce in the commonly protracted debates characteristic of frightened faculty members deeply involved in critical decisions. When, after consultation, she took actions contrary to the wishes of some of the faculty, those faculty who might appreciate the necessity for the decision would often nevertheless conclude that their views had not received serious consideration. She asked the board of trustees to reject the deficit budget they had been given in order to allow her the time to draw up an alternative one. Without enjoying what in happier circumstances might have been her honeymoon period, she set about to trim faculty and staff perquisites (she also sold the elegant presidential mansion) and asked the board to institute a tenure ceiling. The expert who brings bad news, and who competently takes responsive action, is rarely popular on campus; Lester tended to be deprecated as brusque as well as admired for her effectiveness. Indeed, most faculty members agreed then and still agree today that she deserves full credit for turning around the college and for eventually securing substantial increases in faculty salaries (American Association of University Professors, 1984). Faculty members also recognized that Lester shared with them all the stress-inducing institutional data from which her predecessors had shielded them. Lester recalls an early faculty meeting where a faculty committee and a marketing consultant made such an extensive report that a senior faculty member declared, "I don't know what the president wants to do, but I want her to do it." As is commonly the case, as conditions grew less desperate for the faculty, support for the president also diminished.

In Staunton itself, her institution of competitive bidding severed the college's traditional ties with local merchants, and the resulting antagonisms are a reminder of the hazards facing administrators in lean times in small communities, where almost everyone is related to or friendly with almost everyone else.[12]

One of the first steps Lester took showed her willingness to accept risks. Staunton Military Academy had folded, and the college was threatened with the possibility of having unsightly or noisome real estate developments as neighbors. To avoid this, the trustees and Lester decided to buy the property, permitting expansion of the college and some real estate development by or on behalf of the college (the headmaster's home on the academy campus became Lester's presidential house). The ability to carry off the purchase of the land, along with profitable resale of portions of it, signaled that the college was here to stay.

Turning her attention to the curriculum, Lester led the

college toward re-imagining what college age women require for occupational and personal viability in the contemporary world. This required considering both the short-run aims that might help recruitment of students and the long-run aims that might be engendered among undergraduates. Such a double perspective, and the promotional and educational programs needed to support these aims can never be final, and at Mary Baldwin they of course remain incomplete. The college already had a program in education, as many liberal arts colleges do; it also had one in medical technology. Lester added business management and communications. To have shifted too sharply away from the traditional liberal arts and sciences toward such vocational programs would have damaged the morale of many faculty, antagonized alumnae, and even failed as a recruiting tactic in competition with established state and private schools long oriented toward undergraduate professional programs. Some faculty members have in fact concluded that the college has abandoned its traditional devotion to the liberal arts and are not satisfied by the redefined program, with its requirement that half of the undergraduate work must be in courses qualifying for general education credit. Faculty dissatisfaction has been increased by Mary Baldwin's tight budget, which has not been adequate to pay equal salaries or give equally fast promotions to professors in such fields as English, foreign languages, or art history, as to those in money and banking, communications, and computer science. Since Lester was clearly in charge of academic policy, the college's shift in pedagogical focus, although in line with national shifts, did not earn her any warmth from faculty who saw their fields and hence themselves as in effect demoted. Furthermore, Lester drew on the corporate chief executive officers she had recruited as members of the board of trustees and of the advisory board of visitors, as well as others, both to provide externships for undergraduates in their own enterprises and to speak at the college concerning potential careers in industry, finance, and other areas.

Tradition and Modernity. By noting that she balanced the college's budget in the very first year, we can perhaps visualize Virginia Lester as the not unfamiliar leader who seeks to modernize in a traditional environment, retaining the advantages provided by the tradition while meeting and bettering the competition. Lester mobilized alumnae in a way that had not been done previously, seeking to generate excitement through the prospect of re-creating a women's college in an era of radically changed relations between the sexes. (The focus on women was highlighted in the fall of 1984 by the invitation extended to Ann Firor Scott, a professor of history at Duke University, to lecture on the history of higher education for women, with one lecture devoted specifically to Mary Baldwin College's own trajectory.) Judging by the distribution of student majors and by the new catalogue that highlights general education more dramatically than earlier ones had done, Mary Baldwin College has not tilted so heavily toward direct vocational tracks as many other private colleges have. Although 18.8 percent of its students major in business and management, 14.5 percent major in fine and applied arts, including some who have studied arts management. Indeed, within the traditional departments, externships supplemented by career workshops and counseling tempt students to learn now and earn later.

One of Lester's most controversial changes was made in her very first year, when she instituted an adult degree program for mature women. Coming at the same time as the college's stronger emphasis on careers, this made senior faculty in the liberal arts uneasy. To such faculty, or to new faculty socialized in their mode, those who teach adults are not quite respectable, not true colleagues. But opposition was muted because the adults are not residential and secure their degrees through individualized programs similar to those with which Lester had worked at New York's Empire State College.[13] Regular faculty often seek to do this tutorial work, for which they receive extra compensation. More recently Lester has instituted a new Program for the Exceptionally Gifted, that is, precollegiate girls. None of the regular faculty are asked to teach in this program. Still, there are those who are discomfitted by any departure from the college's tacit compact with the liberal arts tradition and who do not view it as something that might independently be worth accomplishing.

None of the changes brought about at the college would have been conceivable without Lester's energetic fund raising from alumnae, corporations, and foundations. The hostility of some faculty toward undergraduate preparation for business was to a modest extent softened by her ability to secure an endowed chair of business management. However, Lester faced the problem common to higher education generally: the relatively few members of the faculty who are in high demand in the current market are not always those who are prepared to carry the heaviest burdens of teaching, advising, and committee work. The shift in students' capacities and interests naturally shifts the work load of faculty, much as would occur in any faculty competition for student "customers." For example, the faculty in business management carry an extremely heavy student load, along with their full share of committee work, while as elsewhere, faculty in some of the traditional liberal arts seek to sustain a major in the face of a paucity of students. Lester has managed to raise faculty salaries across the board as partial compensation for those bearing unevenly heavy burdens, but there is no ready way in view of the college's limited resources and still uncertain prospects to provide faculty with salaries they would consider comfortable, let alone to provide them with long-run security. Also, many faculty members who have been at the college for a long time complain that current students do not know how to write and are too vocational—the same complaints heard elsewhere, even in the most selective colleges. However, *Miscellany,* the literary and arts magazine of the college, contained in the three issues we examined a number of fine examples of contemporary poetry—occasionally using vocabulary and exploring themes that must be anathema to many alumnae and some faculty.

Style and Substance. Corporate and governmental leaders in and out of Virginia admired Lester's intelligence and spunk, but she was shy of friends in Staunton itself. Decidedly a Yankee, she is also a convinced Quaker with the Friends' belief in consultation and consensus, goals more easily attained when she was dean at New York's Empire State College. The situation at Mary Baldwin College called for decisiveness, and the very difficulties of the consultative processes she sought and helped institute clashed with both board and fiscal imperatives. Moreover, her often impatient manner, readily accepted as it might be at Skidmore College or in the State University of New York system, appeared to Virginians to be lacking in the small touches of courtliness and generosity that they expected.[14] From the outset Lester understood that the future prospects of a somewhat isolated liberal arts college with a primarily regional clientele are precarious. One might say that the situation Lester faced at Mary Baldwin College ignited her impatience as well as her ingenuity. Moreover, while many presidents discover in the course of their incumbency that even when they have come from the faculty they are no longer regarded as colleagues but rather as "mere" managers, Lester's relative absence of a conventional academic background may have made it difficult for her to identify with the specific disciplinary commitments of many faculty members.

Where there was turnover of administrators, particularly in the development office, Lester respected her subordinates, defending them when necessary until it seemed imperative to replace them. But she lacked the time and perhaps the skill to develop their individual qualities and capacities. Even a few changes in such a small enclave forced Lester to spend time and energy searching for and selecting replacements and placed a certain strain on these deputies in their relation to one another. Leadership in the liberal arts college is more difficult than in corporate settings, not only because the tests for accomplishment are even more amorphous in academia than in the business world, but because those who select themselves and then are socialized into the academic professions are generally less given to teamwork and more inclined to solipsism than the gamesmen and institutional loyalists of the business world. In both milieux, leaders must achieve the ability to mobilize others where consultation and sharing of problems may itself create anxieties. It is only seemingly paradoxical that when Lester exhibited ordinary human frailty rather than her more typical sangfroid and decisiveness, her associates were likely to become anxious rather than nurturant—no doubt because they depended so much on her continuing energy, presence of mind, and alert entrepreneurship. Lester sought out advice from outside, not only from the Association of Governing Boards, whose Board-Mentor Program was used to help give faculty a sense of how board committees and boards as a whole generally operate (Lester, 1983), but also from consultants in the area of group dynamics, in the hope of engendering a more commodious and generous climate for her staff and herself. Nevertheless, she found no way to break through the image of herself as a driving, efficient person, more able to share tasks than warmth and ideas.

Another observer—Ellen Earle Chaffee—who examined Mary Baldwin College during Lester's presidency has also concluded that she was effective in rescuing the college from rapid or slow desuetude.[15] Not only was she consulted by leaders of other institutions facing somewhat comparable problems, but she was also regarded as someone who helped sustain the women's colleges at a time when these make up a very small proportion of academic enterprises, particularly outside of the still single-sex, once-Catholic colleges founded by religious orders. Under her leadership, Mary Baldwin College became one of the women's colleges that promise to put the kind of spin on their graduates that will take them as far as their talents allow, relatively unhampered by the traditional reluctance of American women to become overtly competitive and assertive. Had Mary Baldwin College failed, the mistaken conclusion might have been drawn that there was little support for a *women's* college rather than that geographically isolated, nonaffluent liberal arts colleges had become marginal enterprises.

And Virginia Lester herself? When one discusses leadership in the terms of this volume, the physical and psychological toll on the leaders themselves (and the sometimes even greater toll on their families) is not a major part of the reckoning. We have but one life, and all of us spend it in one way or another. Virginia Lester has been able, through the presidency of Mary Baldwin College, to conclude that she has made a difference. But for a cosmopolitan person who needs and wants friends there has been a cost in spending ten years in a town of 28,000 people where the college is just about the only game in town.

Of course, her position of leadership enabled her to come to know people in major metropolitan centers, and these connections were both useful to the college and consoling to her.

In November 1984 Lester announced her resignation as of the end of the academic year and her decision to attend law school. She was admitted to Stanford, Harvard, and other major law schools and plans to attend Stanford. In the last months she refused to become a candidate for other colleges, even those in more cosmopolitan settings; apparently she has had enough of that sort of academic combat duty.

Carleton College

Carleton College opened in 1866 as a coeducational institution with sponsorship from, but not control by, Congregational churches. Its saga of midwestern style plain living and high thinking was reshaped by Donald J. Cowling, who served as president from 1909 until 1945 and made Carleton an almost-national college. Laurence Gould, who had been professor of geology, famous for his explorations in the Antarctic and elsewhere, succeeded Cowling and stayed on as president until 1962, adding greatly to Carleton's programs as well as its national visibility. John Nason, who had been president of Swarthmore College, took over from Gould in the era of student and faculty protests and was in turn succeeded by Howard Swearer, now president of Brown; Edwards came in 1977. (For more on Carleton's history, see Headley and Jarcow, 1966; Edwards, 1984.) Carleton resembles Clark's "distinctive college" in its strong traditions of faculty self-governance and idealism; like Antioch, Reed, and Swarthmore, it combines strong academic emphases with intense intellectuality. It shares with Oberlin an international focus toward the Far East as well as toward Europe. It possesses a legacy of Minnesota liberalism and midwestern breeziness and lack of hauteur.

In the middle 1970s, however, Carleton's relative eminence was imperiled. This was due to factors already mentioned at the outset of this chapter, notably its small-town location (it is just barely within commuting distance of the Twin Cities). Furthermore, the daily television maps of national weather point to frigid temperatures in that part of the country; unlike Dartmouth, Carleton offers only rolling country for cross-country skiing, not the resort slopes of Vermont.[16] One has to have visited the college or to trust what others say about it to appreciate the charms of its buildings and its surrounding arboretum, playing fields, and countryside.

Prospects for admissions were among the greatest long-run hazards facing the college. In the past, Carleton has drawn nearly three-fifths of its student body from the Middle West. However, even in Minnesota, it has no constituency on which it can count, since it competes with the great research University of Minnesota, with its negligible tuition, its location in the Twin Cities, and its own history of capable leadership. In the same small town of Northfield, Carleton has a regional rival for some students in St. Olaf College, the most distinguished of the colleges related to the American Lutheran Church and also the flagship college for Americans of Norwegian or Danish descent. Northwestern and Wisconsin are also regional competitors, as are some nearby liberal arts colleges, notably Macalester. Most of all, Carleton competes with the Ivy League schools, with Stanford, Berkeley, and Duke, and with those state universities —Virginia, Chapel Hill, and Vermont—that at public expense offer much of the atmosphere of a private institution. It also competes, notably in the East but also everywhere else, with the national small liberal arts colleges, with Amherst, Williams, Wellesley, Swarthmore, Pomona, Haverford, and Bryn Mawr. Some of these colleges, and also Smith, Mount Holyoke, Middlebury, and Bowdoin, are in the Northeast, in rural areas or small towns that are not handicapped by their rural or small-town locale. But to some extent, all such colleges compete with those colleges and universities where metropolitan locations make for numerous internships—though Carleton has in recent years organized an excellent alumni network to help provide these—as well as readier access to part-time jobs.[17]

Up to the present, Carleton has maintained its commitment to admitting students on a "need-blind" basis, that is, ad-

mitting students without reference to their capacity to pay.
However, once admitted, if a student is in need, the college has
a financial aid package of scholarship, loan, and work-study aid
geared to the financial situation of the student's family in line
with the criteria set by the College Scholarship Service. The
immensely overapplied and wealthy institutions that compete
with Carleton—Harvard, Stanford, Amherst, Swarthmore—attract many capable students from wealthy families who do not
require aid and have been able to make up appropriate aid pack-
ages for all the rest. Moreover, many of Carleton's private competitors, and also some state universities, have courted topflight
students by offering so-called merit scholarships, that is, discounting tuition irrespective of the student's need, much in the
way that many universities and some colleges recruit athletes.
In this altered competitive climate, Carleton's policy has become both less effective and more costly than it formerly was.
Correspondingly, the report by a student-faculty-administration
financial aid task force has recommended that the proportion of
students receiving financial aid not greatly exceed the current
55 percent. After extensive debate by the College Council, the
report was accepted, with its painful conclusion that there may
be a few students at the college (estimated at no more than 6
percent) who were chosen ahead of those ranked higher because
the former can pay their own way. The aid that is offered will
continue to be merit-blind; that is, Carleton will not enter the
increasingly mercenary competition for able scholars. The new
admissions policy aims to maintain, within anticipated fiscal
constraints, the ability to provide adequate aid to a student
body of the widest possible diversity in terms of accomplishments and of economic, geographic, ethnic, and racial backgrounds.

The New President. When Robert Edwards came to Carleton in 1977, he succeeded a successful and reasonably well-liked
president in Howard Swearer. Since Swearer had been persuaded by Brown University to leave Carleton at midyear, Harriet Sheridan, formerly the dean, was appointed interim president. Hence Edwards arrived after a certain interregnum. He
was the unanimous choice of the trustees but not of the faculty,

a number of whom preferred the effervescent former president of Haverford College, John Coleman.[18]

In announcing Edwards's appointment in March 1977, Thomas M. Crosby, chairman of the board, noted that the search committee had found Edwards to be "extraordinarily able," declaring: "His lack of professional experience in academia is felt to be no disadvantage, for Carleton's issues and opportunities can be viewed in a fresh perspective." This statement put in the best possible light the choice of someone who had not met any of the usual academic criteria. A magna cum laude English major from Princeton, Edwards read law for two years at Cambridge and graduated from Harvard Law School. After working in Africa and in the State Department, he joined the Ford Foundation, eventually heading its program for the Middle East and Africa. Understandably, Edwards moved cautiously as he learned more about the college and vice versa.

Grounding the Future. Edwards saw right away that the first step toward planning Carleton's future had to be a strong push to enlarge the admissions pool and then to move toward establishing a healthier endowment. Faculty salaries and campus facilities were in need of improvement, and outside funds would provide a necessary margin of safety and an essential resource for the development of the curriculum and of the scholarly capacities of the faculty. Edwards hoped to move toward all these goals in rapid succession without provoking anxiety among faculty and staff.

To accomplish these goals, Edwards works with Frank I. Wright, vice-president and treasurer, who is now, after three decades, serving under his fourth president, or fifth if one includes the acting presidency of Harriet Sheridan. Wright has been the dedicated "goalie" of Carleton, exceptionally competent and trusted, yet recurrently facing attack from faculty and students, and indeed other administrators, for a frugality that has at times allowed Edwards and the trustees to take some risks that would otherwise have appeared foolhardy. It is never easy or comfortable to protect the future of such a highly egalitarian college as Carleton against its current inhabitants. Yet Wright seems to have done just that.

Edwards persuaded Richard Steele, a Harvard College alumnus with a Ph.D. degree in English from the University of Wisconsin, who had done admissions work at Vassar and Bates and was director of admissions at the University of Vermont, to come to Carleton College, presenting Steele to the search committee after first himself eliciting his interest. Steele reports directly to Edwards and works closely with him. Edwards also recruited Daniel Sullivan from the sociology department, first as dean for academic development and planning and then as vice-president. Sullivan is a sociologist of science who has studied but not managed organizations, and he possesses professional knowledge of national demographic and cultural landscapes.[19] Working with an admissions staff of six professionals in addition to alumni and faculty who attend professional meetings in communities where there may be Carleton prospects, Steele has greatly enlarged Carleton's effort to recruit a national and diversified student body, including students from the Far East and elsewhere outside the United States. When Edwards arrived, Carleton was accepting four-fifths of its applicants, of whom less than half enrolled; by 1984, it was accepting only 48 percent of applicants, of whom 42 percent enrolled.[20] One factor that maintained and increased the college's visibility and attractiveness for applicants has been the mobilization of its alumni into the same sort of network of alumni admissions representatives that other schools have also found useful.

Edwards has brought imagination and energy to the tasks of development, as well as to the whole administrative team that he has largely built and encouraged. In regular fund raising and in the capital campaign, Edwards and Sullivan frequently form a duo; they meet with potential donors singly or in groups, and the lively Sullivan provides a counterpoise to the gravity that Edwards's wit does not undercut. The board of trustees that Edwards inherited included some exceptionally competent, effective, and dedicated corporate leaders, particularly from the Twin Cities, the usual quota of lawyers, several academicians, and a number of public figures. For many years, Carleton benefited from the inheritors of the lumber fortunes, such as that of the Weyerhaeuser family.[21] However, there are now few such heirs on the Carleton board. Edwards has known all along that the endowment needed to be dramatically increased if Carleton was to maintain its present standards in the face of demographic decline and increased competition and certainly if Carleton was to improve within the boundaries its saga would encourage and permit. After much discussion and exploration, Edwards and the board decided to plan a capital campaign. The plan and the campaign have required an enormous amount of Edwards's time. At this writing, however, it appears likely that the campaign will meet its goals.

In his career at the Ford Foundation, Edwards had developed good judgment of people and projects abroad and at home. Thus he could make bets on people such as Sullivan and Steele, whom he courted to join his administration. Working with his colleagues, Edwards turned his attention to faculty development and curricular planning. In these areas, Edwards has had to contend with his lack of academic credentials—only in a formal sense, however, since his intellectual range is formidable. Even so, his relation to faculty members was not easy at the outset, for Carleton faculty think of themselves, as faculty almost everywhere do, as superior to mere administrators. It helps that he is physically tall and personally impressive and that he speaks and writes with elegance. He is patient, but clearly determined. In time faculty members began to relax in their suspicions of Edwards, except for a few who are inclined to oppose all established authority. However, Edwards has been able to solidify his support from the board of trustees. He has devoted great energies to working with a committee of the board, less likely to be inheritors of wealth, but capable of soliciting from corporations and from some of the new self-made multimillionaires, not only of the immediate area, but of the country at large.

Clarifying the Future. With admissions and finances on sounder footing, Edwards was able to pursue the possibility of leading a faculty that had a justifiably high opinion of itself and Carleton College toward an even more distinguished position of leadership in academia. He could not lead the faculty directly; he needed a dean. After her acting presidency, Harriet Sheridan

had returned to the deanship. A redoubtable person, highly intelligent, with a talent for wit and a degree of acerbity, she was
in the position of virtually all acting presidents who stay on in
a subordinate position, where a comfortable match with the
new incumbent is a statistically unlikely prospect. After two
years, she followed Howard Swearer to Brown to occupy the
position of dean there and indeed to achieve an eminence wholly unclouded by the awkwardness of having had to return to the
second-in-command position at Carleton.

Edwards appointed a faculty search committee and
worked closely with it to recruit a new dean. Edwards hoped
that the committee would find someone who had the background of a research university but who would regard undergraduate education at such a university neither as a model to
imitate nor as a "negative identity" to reject. Relying on his
own ability to enlarge the span of control of his associates, Edwards recruited Peter Stanley, who has both his baccalaureate
and his doctorate from Harvard and who was then teaching history there, but who had had virtually no prior administrative
experience.[22] (That Stanley's specialty is American-Philippine
relations was an additional asset for a college with strong interests in the Far East.) From his own experience, Stanley appreciated the advantages for undergraduates of being at a research
university. But he could also articulate with the authority of
that background an appreciation of the compensating advantages for students at Carleton and other academically demanding liberal arts colleges of confronting faculty members who
manage to combine intense but not always specialized teaching
with their own often extremely specialized research.

Working together, Edwards and Stanley sought to maintain a delicate balance to avoid the temptation of moving
Carleton further in the direction of such protograduate university colleges as Swarthmore, Amherst, and Wellesley. Maintaining the balance has meant persuading faculty that "state of the
art" scholarship could be reflected in their teaching even in
small departments that have to cover a relatively large segment
of the academic waterfront. Edwards and Stanley wanted faculty members to regard themselves as members of their aca-

demic guilds and as supportive mentors for their students. Successfully to combine these tasks, given the heavy teaching loads, might imply—so Edwards and Stanley suggested—that faculty members needed to find some private space, even an occasional degree of aloofness, in contrast to Carleton's tradition of easy accessibility.

Indeed, given Edwards's own Ivy League background and his intellectual breadth, a number of Carleton faculty feared that he would try to move the College in just such a direction. Although Carleton has many faculty members with undergraduate and graduate degrees from Ivy League and other notable research universities, there has been a touch of a sometimes adopted midwestern chauvinism in the Carleton ethos.[23] Especially in the sixties and early seventies, some faculty members wanted to present themselves as "just folks," as of course in many elite schools radical faculty identified with "the kids."[24] In contrast, Edwards was seen as "eastern," which is synonymous with the Establishment, and of course there are the Princeton and Harvard connections. Ellen Edwards is an interior designer, Wellesley educated.[25] The Edwardses have style, but style is something just slightly deprecated by many Carletonians. Edwards reads widely and enjoys intellectual discourse; yet we know very few institutions where faculty members feel sufficiently comfortable with the president (see Fisher, 1984), even when they truly like him and have no fear for their own futures, to discuss ideas or intellectual matters. Many presidents discover that students enjoy seeing the president at campus events, athletic and otherwise; Edwards has generally found his relationships with undergraduates (several of whom have reported their astonishment at how much he seems to know about students) relaxed and agreeable, in contrast with the heaviness that can hang over his encounters with faculty. Understanding the limitations on his freedom of maneuver, Edwards set about to make himself familiar with Carleton's saga as a teaching college, with its intimate and informal faculty-student relationships that reflected not only the smallness of the college's enrollment but the faculty preference for small classes. Although many of Carleton's faculty and students are aware of the somewhat greater eminence of its eastern competitors, Carleton ranks with Oberlin as the best liberal arts college between the Alleghenies and the Rocky Mountains.[26] The fear of Carleton faculty and students of being pulled toward a saga other than their own has its admirable side, even though it also seems possible that, as Sisk (1984) has reflectively contended, Americans are too fearful of imitation, ending up imitating each other's searches for eccentricity and exorbitant individualism. Concerned not to lose Carleton's special character, Edwards and Stanley worked together on many projects for incremental improvement of the quality of teaching and learning.[27] Currently, for example, there is a committee in place concerned with "quality of student life." (Let it be noted here that the *Carletonian,* the admirably written student weekly, was an invaluable resource for us.) Stanley has continued Carleton's method of evaluating teaching by having recent graduates, as well as current students, submit reports on particular faculty members. This procedure can elicit more detached judgment from graduates, while minimizing the power of individual faculty members to campaign for themselves through showmanship, ideology, easy grading, and so on (see Riesman, 1975).[28]

For detailed discussion of Edwards's strategy, however, we select two major initiatives. The more visible one was the decision greatly to expand the library, long regarded as inadequate in collections and equipment. The other was a program of faculty development primarily geared to encouraging individual faculty members to maintain and strengthen their disciplinary connections through leaves of absence for research and in other ways as well.

The Library. As student tour guides reported to the admissions office, prospective students and their parents visiting Carleton responded favorably to the observatory but remarked on the unimpressiveness of the library, which was small and, because built on a hillside, looks smaller than it actually is. More important, faculty members and students complained about crowding in the library, whose holdings are adequate, particularly as they are supplemented through exchange programs with St. Olaf College and the Universities of Minnesota and Wisconsin.

One of Edwards's major efforts was to keep things moving toward a plan for expansion of the library in the face of indecision and resistance on the part of faculty committees. Some had hoped for an entirely new library; others wanted to delay any changes until brighter economic times. There was not only a fear, shared by some important trustees, about the estimated capital cost of $8 million but also a concern about the carrying costs in facilities that the revamped library would pose. In Edwards's initial years, some faculty were not reassured about the college's long-term future and could readily envisage competition in a time of declining resources between sustaining salaries and sustaining the library. It was not a happy trade-off to envisage. After much initial planning, the relatively conservative decision was reached to renovate and greatly extend the current library.

There was a more subtle undercurrent of barely voiced opposition to the library reflecting the fear that the Edwards administration was Avis imitating Hertz, wanting a library as posh as that at Trinity, as stunning as that at Wellesley. Moreover, some thought that emphasis on the library of the planned size implied a library larger than needed for undergraduate education and for faculty who were teacher-scholars but in general not publishing- or discipline-oriented. And of course the notion of using the library as a marketing tactic would be anathema to faculty, as would be any sign of unnecessary display. Edwards was all the more inclined to move warily in this situation because, as we shall see in a moment, the theme of faculty development posed some analogous threats to those faculty members who had thrown themselves with admirable dedication into teaching and nothing but teaching, of course with a good deal of committee service and departmental curricular planning as part of that enterprise.

Nevertheless, Edwards and those of his persuasion were greatly tempted to make a start on the library when it appeared that the capital campaign was going well and that the goal of $8 million could readily be reached if some exigency did not befall.[29] It was frustrating to watch building costs rise, and still no library begun. It was in fact one of the trustees who came to the conclusion that it would be an undue risk to proceed with the library until all the funds were actually in hand, a view that soothed some faculty anxieties.

Finally, however, Edwards's patience and pertinacity were rewarded. In anticipation of the funds to be raised in the capital campaign, members of the board made contingent pledges of capital. If capital funds were secured, the pledges would be released. It was these pledges by the trustees that served as a loan guarantee and allowed library construction to proceed. And this bet, as Edwards termed it, helped the campaign itself gather momentum; trustees contributed more than a third of the total goal of $51.5 million (Edwards, 1984, p. 5). Although some faculty may still be critical of Edwards for not accepting the pace and mode of the established committees, for most the outcome is a happy one. The redesigned and expanded library is handsome; it is light and spacious, with ample cubicles for students and exhibit space for collections of photography and painting. Many faculty members who prize their independence have since been inclined to trust Edwards's intentions for the college.

Faculty Development. As in any other long-established college, there are quite different academic generations represented at Carleton. In the decades of expansion, from 1958 to 1977, nearly half of Carleton's present faculty members were recruited. During the Edwards presidency, from 1978 to the present, there has been some growth of nontenured faculty with nearly a third of the faculty at the assistant professor or instructor level. One route toward improving faculty quality that Edwards has eschewed has been the recruitment of tenured faculty who have made their reputations elsewhere. To bring in new permanent faculty would undermine Carleton's saga and, even if judiciously pursued, such a policy would destroy the fragile truce already attained between what are perceived to be Edwards's elitist ambitions for Carleton and the college's own assertively egalitarian ambience. What Edwards has done, which is in the Carleton tradition, is to encourage and enable departments or interdepartmental concentrations to bring in visiting professors, a few of them on a regular schedule such as one term every second year, to fill vacancies created by leaves of absence.

But there is a problem here: The salary ceiling generally placed on these replacement appointments handicaps recruitment of someone whose preferential status might threaten the equilibrium of a department, even if such a person were willing to leave his or her home base for a nontenured position.[30]

This policy of recruitment of tenured faculty only from within the college means that the rejuvenation of a particular department is a matter that requires extraordinary patience and tact. There are no permanent department heads at Carleton; rather, the college employs the rotation system common in the more eminent private institutions where the task is seen as a chore to be shared and shed rather than as an honor or reward for institutional (or personal) loyalty. Carleton recently instituted regular meetings of department chairs as a way of helping the more amateur ones get a sense of their responsibilities and to share common problems with more experienced hands. Incremental improvement of departments from within is periodically facilitated by the requisite five-year review in which an ad hoc committee of outsiders from the field and insiders from neighboring fields sometimes quite strenuously participate.

Nonetheless, it does not take a virtuoso student of higher education to recognize the dangers of intellectual anemia for faculties composed of some older professors jealous of more recent recruits with more up-to-date disciplinary skills and also of a large number of professors who are probably not mobile and for the majority of whom retirement is many years away.

Three foundations in particular, the Mellon Foundation under John Sawyer, the Hewlett Foundation under Roger Heyns, and the Bush Foundation under Humphrey Doermann, were prepared to respond to proposals from Carleton that might lead to some degree of renewal from within. Mellon and Hewlett said they would match on a one-to-three basis funds the college itself raised, and Edwards was able to persuade the trustees and alumni to meet this rather high threshold. The outcome was an endowed discretionary fund of $1 million to be awarded to faculty members who proposed some sort of activity that would renew their ties to their field of specialization, preferably away from campus. This could include money for travel, small re-

search stipends, and of course the travel to professional meetings that Carleton has regularly proffered. Faculty members are
invited to submit proposals for a grant from this fund; these
proposals are then reviewed outside the college, and small
awards are made—commonly of $10,000 to $12,000, approxi-
mating a term's salary—supplementing the paid leave that the
college would already be providing and perhaps permitting the
extension of sabbatical leave to a full year. What makes this
program different from many others is the insistence that the
awards go to those faculty members who are likely to use the
results of their extramural study and research in their teaching.
The aim has been, not to substitute an audience of peers for the
Carleton student audience, but to encourage the faculty member to find a way to perform simultaneously or in short consecutive intervals for the two overlapping audiences, abroad in
the subdiscipline or craft and at home for students and for faculty colloquia.

The announcement of the faculty development program
led to a challenge by those faculty members always vigilant
against any exercises of presidential or decanal authority, particularly any that inferentially suggested that total commitment
of one's scholarly energies to teaching was not enough. But one
cannot hope to offer students state-of-the-art teaching as a fairly regular matter if faculty members are not exposed to the
stimulus and threat of peer judgment (see Trow, 1977; Kramer,
1981).

These grants have helped maintain and strengthen the
visibility of certain Carleton faculty within their disciplines.
Such an enhancement and the larger opportunities for research
make it less difficult for the departments, prodded and encouraged by the dean with the president's support, to recruit junior
faculty in such fields of high demand (from companies as well
as from research universities) as economics, computer science
and its mathematical bases, and biology.[31] Moreover, the initial
faculty development grants, and the evident lack of favoritism
in awarding these, have appeared to create a virtuous circle:
Faculty members who get grants are put in a position where
their work and interests will bring them further grants and wider

orbits of connection beyond Northfield. Simultaneously, the capital campaign is under way to improve laboratory facilities and faculty offices.[32] These developments are of crucial importance for improving the vitality of teaching and collegiality among Carleton's tenured faculty now in their thirties and forties. These faculty members are chairing departments, serving on standing and ad hoc committees, and taking their share of representing Carleton not only to their disciplines but also to prospective students who visit the college or whom they plan to see when they attend professional meetings in cities where they may also speak to Carleton alumni.

Even so, Edwards has an almost preternatural awareness of the risks of this sort of success. Some faculty members, truly excited by their research and the responses it has evoked from peers, may grow ever more resentful of the fact that a small college can hardly ever provide them with true peers in their subspecialty. For that they need a research university, an institute or center, or a metropolis. In Northfield, some of their colleagues may even regard their work as too arcane for faculty colloquia, let alone for undergraduates. Moreover, in small departments, virtually all faculty members must take a hand in the introductory courses, which is equitable in the sense that Carleton does not have a two-tier faculty. To be sure, teaching neophytes can be reasonably refreshing for the specialist (with the possible exception of introductory language courses). In this arena as in others, Edwards and Stanley proceeded through Carleton's participatory channels, emphasizing their commitment to the Carleton saga.

It is a truism to say, though few curricula recognize the fact, that the methods of introducing students to substantive areas of study are important. Already, Carleton students in their regular courses do a great deal of writing, far more than at many undergraduate colleges of research universities. But because classes are small and faculty prefer seminarlike discussions to lecturing, students are not always exposed to models of elegant oral expression. As one prescient Carleton alumnus remarked to us, Carleton College students do occasionally get Rhodes scholarships but might get more if they had more exposure to eloquent faculty and more opportunity to imitate them.[33] (His is an attitude most unlikely to be shared by more than a handful of Carleton undergraduates, and a number of faculty would observe that some departments, such as history, do approve a more formal style of class presentation.) Edwards himself, as we have already indicated, has presence; at convocations and commencements and at other less ceremonial occasions, faculty and students have an opportunity to hear him employ an elevated vocabulary and to speak with distinction. Many of the faculty who are attracted to Carleton and who have made a choice to stay there, like many faculty and professionals elsewhere, prefer potluck suppers to formal dinners, and informal discussion to finished addresses. Edwards, and Stanley with him, have helped create occasions of a different style.

Edwards's own experience at the Ford Foundation makes it natural for him to want to intensify Carleton's traditional concern that its students have an international perspective. At a time when America has become "domesticated," and there is little interest in foreign cultures and less in foreign languages, Carleton has maintained a serious language requirement and an active program of current study in Japan, Western Europe, Latin America, and the Middle East.

There is also a great concern at Carleton that students be exposed to internal American diversities. There is a continuous emphasis on American race relations, as well as an effort to ensure that white Carleton undergraduates are exposed to materials on Afro-American culture and history. More recently, the somewhat separate cultures of the two sexes have received attention, and there have been faculty seminars aimed at the inauguration of courses that would carry a feminist perspective into the disciplines where such a perspective is now manageable, as in the humanities and the more social of the social sciences.

It should be evident from our account that the changes at Carleton during Edwards's presidency have not been easily achieved. He has proceeded cautiously from being primarily the extramural spokesman for the college to becoming also one of the intramural sources of reexamination of previously taken-for-granted levels of performance. The Carleton College faculty and student body can perhaps be led to the margin; they cannot be pushed.

Outside of Carleton, Edwards has not sought to use the "bully pulpit" of the presidency of a leading college to register his views on national affairs. But these are evident within the college, for he has taken controversial positions, sometimes at odds with strong student and faculty idealism, on such issues as the Solomon Amendment, South African investment, ethical purchasing, and CIA recruitment.[34] Outside of Carleton, he has been actively if quietly concerned, along with the Associated Colleges of the Midwest and similar organized groups, with the financial aid policies of states and the nation and, as an active supporter of the Consortium on Financing Higher Education, with developing agreements concerning admissions and aid policies among the country's leading private liberal arts colleges. Although he is a modest man who does not like to make off-the-cuff pronouncements, he has in recent years become a leader among Minnesota spokesmen for higher education, and nationally in the area of undergraduate education in the natural sciences and mathematics.[35] He tries not to neglect his family, a none too easy task for a college president. Given the regard in which he is held by his fellow presidents, and by many trustees and others with whom he has come into contact over the years, Edwards must already be deluged with invitations to become a candidate for major university presidencies. The prospect has not distracted him from what Veblen would have called an "eye single" to Carleton College.

Searching for the "Perfect" College President

We draw our heading from a chapter in Bennis's *The Leaning Ivory Tower* (1973). We do not believe that there is such a person as an all-purpose leader or a "perfect college president." Leadership is inevitably contingent. To be sure, there are qualities that commonly help leaders. It helps to be tall, to be articulate, and to have personal magnetism—unless these assets, despite the leader's conscious efforts, make others too fearful

and apt to fight back as a defense against feeling small. It helps
to have energy—but if that energy makes one impatient in the
face of unavoidable delays and detours, then it becomes a negative asset. In his book *The Leader,* Maccoby (1981) presents
profiles of six leaders who range from a U.S. Congressman to
Volvo's chief executive officer. Maccoby emphasizes the opportunities some of his leaders have had for clarifying the purposes
of an organization, being trustworthy (but not too trusting),
and working cooperatively toward the development of subordinates' talents. But the leader's chance to exercise moral and intellectual alertness occurs only in particular constellations and
at particular moments in history.

Indeed the chanciness, the contingencies of fate strike us
whenever we look at college and university presidents in their
settings. A fumble in a football game or an accident to an oppo-
nent's star player can make or break a public university's chief
executive at the outset of an incumbency. Let us take the not
necessarily hypothetical case of a president of a reasonably well-
endowed liberal arts college who comes in with a mandate from
the board of trustees to upgrade the institution academically
and to make it more selective. And let us posit further that, in
his first year, there happens to be a vigorous student campaign
to achieve tenure for an extremely popular but highly controversial assistant professor who has been denied promotion by
his or her department. The president will somehow have to decide whether he can afford to simply let this crisis run its natural course, while he concentrates on longer-range issues, or
whether he will permanently cripple his authority if he fails to
intervene.

In our judgment, presidential originality is demonstrated
by selective adaptation of the various available models to the
idiosyncratic human and ecological landscape of a particular institution. Many established institutions, unless prodded, will remain on a plateau, slightly inclined downward in some cases of
incremental mediocrity, slightly inclined upward if there are
enough ambitious faculty and staff seeking to bring about improvement. In such a setting, a really bad president might temporarily damage the institution in terms of its morale, might

divide and even sour alumni, and might begin to tarnish its attraction for students. But any system with built-in redundancy can withstand a great deal of damage before actual ruin arrives.

Notes

1. For support of the research on which this chapter is based, we are indebted to the Carnegie Foundation for the Advancement of Teaching; this essay is drawn from work in progress to be published by that foundation. We also acknowledge the support of the Exxon Education Foundation and the Association of Governing Boards of Universities and Colleges. We have had the benefit of helpful conversations and comments from Marian Gade, Zelda Gamson, Michael Maccoby, and Martin Trow.

2. Where the threat of a censure resolution has not deterred an administration, unionization and litigation have been other devices to inhibit selective rather than wholesale retrenchment.

3. In one of the most important and influential books on the presidency, Cohen and March conclude that there cannot be significant leadership in what they term an "organized anarchy"; the people in positions of leadership are fungible, and are believed by themselves and others to be important but resemble —our metaphor—the generals in *War and Peace,* around whom the battle flowed while they imagined that they were in command (see Cohen and March, 1974). This view is a useful counter to simple-minded exaggeration of the role of leaders who may be only nominal. But in the social sciences, where the belief is quite general that social "forces" are what matter, and individual wills kid themselves both that they exist and that they can influence outcomes, the tilt is generally in the direction of what John Gardner once termed "the antileadership vaccine." Our view is consonant with the one forcefully expressed in the report of the Commission directed by Clark Kerr on Strengthening Presidential Leadership (1984).

4. Riesman was himself inclined to underestimate what academic leadership could accomplish. In "The Collision Course

of Higher Education" (Riesman, 1969), he predicted colleges would be bankrupt. They would suffer, as would most of higher education, from demographic decline. They would suffer from the fact that the labor-intensive costs of higher education were rising faster than inflation, sometimes with a doubling time of seven years or so. They would suffer as a result of the student-faculty protests of that epoch, from lowered public esteem and lowered public willingness to subsidize higher education. It is obvious today that the generalization was premature, if not mistaken: Many of the colleges Riesman thought would be defunct by 1980 are still floating above the Plimsoll line. Indeed, some new ones have been started in both the public and the private sector. In retrospect Riesman believes his predictions missed the mark because he underestimated the power of institutional leadership drastically to cut costs and to recruit more of the desperately sought-after adult clients to their particular colleges. Likewise, he underestimated the flexibility of faculty in adjusting to new student interests and markets.

5. Such support is not something one can take for granted in the liberal arts college. Some board members are only intermittently attentive; some undermine presidents by having direct dealings with vice-presidents or faculty—ties all the more likely if they are themselves alumni and the president comes in from outside (Wood, 1984; Kauffman, 1983).

6. However, it is quite common for individual board members to begin to undercut a president who has been attacked by faculty for decisions agreed on and even insisted on by the board as a whole. And there are few examples where a board will continue to support a president against virtually unanimous faculty opposition; fewer presidents still will want to continue in such a setting if they can find another way to make a livelihood.

7. Admissions officers in the most selective private and public undergraduate institutions have been astonished by the fact that applicant pools have shrunk for them marginally, if at all. It is in the less selective institutions that the gap is already seriously felt. It would appear that the uncertain economy and the competitive future for the able young people of college age

has led to a choice of colleges that combine prestige and post-baccalaureate visibility with higher costs of attendance.

8. Carleton does its best to alert prospective students to its attractive campus, the scenic charms of the surrounding woods, the lake, and the ample playing fields, and to the opportunities for cross-country and, at some distance, downhill skiing. In the Midwest, it is a bit more selective than Oberlin.

9. A not uncommon practice for southern women was to spend two years at a selective women's college and then transfer to the flagship campus of their home state for the purposes both of vocational training and a wider pool of eligible and perhaps preferably older males, such as law or business school students; of course some also were claimed by matrimony before graduation. Today Mary Baldwin College experiences attrition of 30 percent, far below average for the country; only the most highly selective liberal arts colleges, and only at most three or four women's colleges, maintain a cohort of 90 percent or more until graduation.

10. Some wings of the women's movements are today inclined to defend the women's colleges, recognizing that for women to be able to compete effectively with men, some fare better if they have the benefit of preparation in institutions explicitly attuned to their needs, and where they are not in diurnal competition with one another for male company. But all through the Sixties and Seventies, the women's movements, for the most part, insisted on equal but not separate treatment for women and, on the model of the civil rights movement, sought equality through integration.

11. In the search now under way for a successor to Virginia Lester, the board of trustees has in Richard J. Ernst, president of the Northern Virginia Community College System, a member who is sophisticated in understanding the complexities of a search, someone who can help guide the search committee (trustees, faculty, students, and alumnae) in their procedures.

12. Several presidents have reported to us the local traumas occasioned by their cancellation of food service contracts in order to sign up with a national or professional food service. Alumni may also be involved in such "conflict of inter-

est" at a level not usually thought of as significant for the presidential career. There is no log on the presidential path so small that it cannot be stumbled over!

13. Undergraduates in selective private colleges frequently complain that there is not enough diversity in the student body, by which they indicate that, for example, there are too many of those tiresome preppies, or not enough black or Hispanic students, or enough students who come quite obviously from working-class backgrounds. But it is rare, almost unheard of, for students to complain about the true homogeneity of the residential liberal arts college, which is one of age. Yet in those cases where adult degree program students take daytime classes along with undergraduates, they are not generally welcome; they work too hard and are sometimes seen as setting the curve or, in a perhaps antiquated phrase, as DAR's, Damned Average Raisers. When former President Alberta Arthurs at Chatham College instituted an adult degree program, called the Gateway Program, some of whose adult women students came to live on campus, many students complained not only about their classroom but also about their residential presence. For some of the problems faced by former President Alberta Arthurs at Chatham (one of the colleges in our own original orbit of inquiry), see cases prepared by Chatham Trustee and Harvard Business School Professor Louis Byington Barnes and by Frederic Jacobs.

14. Lester is quoted on herself in a newspaper story recounting her contribution and her decision to resign the presidency: "What I'm not is tough and aggressive, but I'm different. What I am is hard-driving, intense, energetic. And I am willing to make hard decisions. But that gets labeled differently down here." (See Nardi, 1985, p. F-1.)

15. See Chaffee (1984, "Enterprise College," pp. 93–106). Chaffee's account, shared with us by Lester, has been of great help to our own work, and we have drawn freely from it.

16. Carleton's market research discovered that in the Washington/Baltimore "market" from which a number of students are attracted to Carleton, highly educated parents were more favorable toward Carleton and less favorable to California

schools than were their children, who knew less about Carleton and more about California (Litten, Sullivan, and Brodigan, 1983).

17. Under Edwards's presidency, Carleton has intensified earlier efforts to increase its recruitment of black students and some supportive faculty and staff who are black. This latter task is particularly difficult in a small town without a black middle class.

18. During his visit to the campus as a finalist, Coleman met robust faculty questioning from faculty members not actually opposed to his candidacy, but rather demonstrating the Carleton ethos of faculty self-governance and skeptical curiosity concerning anyone who would presume to lead them. The interchange spurred Coleman's already large misgivings about accepting another presidency; despite urging from the very faculty who had perhaps somewhat abrasively questioned him, he declined to remain a candidate, choosing instead to head a major foundation oriented to the health sciences.

19. Sullivan is coauthor of a College Board publication (Litten, Sullivan, and Brodigan, 1983) that describes efforts toward the inevitably inexact rapprochement between what Carleton claims to offer, the students it enrolls, and what the latter might pick up in terms of "value added" during their college years. The volume emphasizes the necessity for marketing to be scrupulous in seeing to it that the curriculum and faculty provide the advantages proffered in promotional literature, referring, of course, not only to Carleton itself, but to other colleges where admissions policies are controlled by the administration and faculty and not exclusively by the market or by coaches. The work is the combined work of Larry Litten, former director of Institutional Research at Carleton, Sullivan, and David L. Brodigan, current coordinator of institutional research, registrar, and assistant professor of psychology at Carleton.

20. In both periods, Carleton has attracted about a fifth of the 1,700 students with combined scores of over 1,400 on the College Boards. It now (1984-85) enrolls 240 National Merit Scholars.

21. In an issue of the alumni magazine devoted to trustees, Edwards has written: "At the beginning of the century our own graduate, Thorstein Veblen, in *The Higher Learning in America,* observed sourly about boards of trustees that 'poor men and men without large experience in business affairs are felt to have no place in these bodies.' One wonders what he would make of the fact that, of his alma mater's trustees today, a quarter come from education, religion, and journalism; another quarter from the professions; and half from business and banking" (Edwards, 1984, p. 8).

22. A sequence of earlier deans had come from faculty positions in the humanities: Bruce Morgan from religion and American studies at Amherst, Bardwell Smith from religion at Carleton, and Harriet Sheridan from English at Carleton. That Stanley also came out of the humanities added to Edwards's academic legitimacy in a way that would have been less salient had he and the search committee with which he worked found someone from the social sciences or even the natural sciences; many of the latter are more likely than people in the humanities to have been involved with external consulting. In part as a beleaguered minority group, academics in the humanities have often made themselves the gatekeepers of academic purity.

23. Three-quarters of Carleton's faculty of 211 have their bachelor's degrees from good small liberal arts colleges, from the Ivy League, or from eminent non–Ivy League research universities; of 94 tenured faculty, all but 12 have their graduate degrees from eminent institutions.

24. It is important not to exaggerate this element in Carleton's saga. Howard Swearer had also come to Carleton from the Ford Foundation and had attended Princeton as an undergraduate; however, he came originally from Kansas and had taught at the University of California at Los Angeles. But John Nason, Swearer's predecessor, an alumnus, had been a Rhodes Scholar and president of Swarthmore College, and, prior to Carleton, president of the Foreign Policy Association in New York. Twin City elites value their international and cosmopolitan connections, reflected in Carleton's board of trustees.

25. The look of the campus has been greatly enhanced

since the Edwardses' arrival. Ellen Edwards, who comes from a family of architects, has had an unobtrusive interest in improving maintenance. Apart from his own concern as an individual, Robert Edwards as president has seen the importance for faculty and students of living in attractive surroundings (including Nutting House, the president's house, to which students come in the course of the year in large numbers) and recognizes that it also makes a difference in recruiting prospects who visit Carleton—faculty as well as students.

26. Paradoxically, according to some of Carleton's market research, Carleton is derogated by some families in the East because its tuition is lower than those of the "Little Ivies" and of some others in the East, and therefore naturally cannot be as good, although for the Middle West Carleton is seen as relatively expensive.

27. This work and the close cohesion of the administrative trio of Edwards, Sullivan, and Stanley was interrupted at the end of the 1983–84 academic year by Stanley's resignation to accept the directorship of the Ford Foundation for higher education and the arts. Roy Elveton, a respected professor of philosophy, has acceded to the request of the president and of his colleagues that he become dean for a four-year stint, while all involved consider when and whether to look for a successor.

28. A careful story in the *Carletonian* compared grading over a three-year period in the different departments, both in terms of introductory-level courses and of required courses, noting the generally slightly higher grades in humanities than in mathematics and science courses. Peter Stanley commented that overgenerous grading "has the destructive effect of giving the student an unrealistic sense of how easy it is to do well in the world," whereas "exceptionally hard grading results in an undesirable increase in stress among students." Stanley's practice, if he feels that a department or instructor has been too lax or harsh, is to discuss the problem with department chairs; he declared, "There is a question of academic freedom in grading standards, however, the college must be more than just individuals" (see Brennwald, 1984).

29. There was also some marginal discussion of whether,

in addition to raising salaries and assuring their continuation, there were not other needs the college had to consider other than the need for a library. One of these was the pressure for improved physical facilities for which some money was already available. The pressure came from students, particularly reflecting the search for new intercollegiate competitors in women's as well as men's sports, and the increased desire of faculty and staff who, like sedentary adults elsewhere, have become physical fitness buffs. There were occasions when an outsider, knowing Carleton's reputation for academic seriousness and lack of excitement for spectator—in contrast to participative—sports, would have been puzzled by faculty members who apparently preferred a year-round track to a larger library!

30. These issues have recently been dramatized in the case of a new recruit of unquestioned abilities as a scholar and teacher who gave up tenure at a distinguished university to come to Carleton to a named chair, but with eventual tenure by no means guaranteed. The issue of fairness arose when his promotion to tenure was proposed after two rather than three years' service—an issue aired in the *Carletonian*—with some faculty members contending that such a person should wait his or her turn along with everyone else recruited as an assistant professor with no speeding of the calendar, while others thought some expedition was justified under these particular circumstances.

31. The kinds of conflicts that can tear apart a small college community arose in the 1983–84 academic year over the request of a woman faculty member who was planning to have a child for permission to return after a maternity leave to half-time teaching, so as to permit care for the prospective infant. The already overworked department responded that all the fields covered by the assistant professor seeking such a status were essential for their majors (including many students whom Carleton has traditionally sent on to Ph.D. programs), and they could not hire a part-time person to fill the expected gap; hence, they denied the request. The women's movements are powerful at Carleton, as one might suppose; the women's caucus and many male faculty members and students supported

the request for the humaneness that no one denied, indeed a modulated new feminism more philoprogenitive than otherwise. The dean and president supported the department in the face of increasingly bitter attacks—amply and, on the whole, fairly covered in the *Carletonian*. The memory has lingered, but the harshness of thought and rhetoric have become attenuated.

32. Some of these have been in basements, by no means claustrophobic, but still at times depressing. One of the minor crises that erupted in the second year of Edwards's administration was the discovery that a recently erected building had been so poorly designed and constructed that it threatened to collapse. It had to be rebuilt virtually from the ground up. Eventually the college received a $2.4 million settlement from the architect and contractor.

33. Recently, the Career Center offered Carleton applicants for Rhodes, Watson, and other fellowships a chance for a simulated trial run at presenting themselves to a screening committee, and a number took advantage of the opportunity. Some faculty members who view Carleton, not incorrectly, as having a less competitive atmosphere than, for example, Reed or Swarthmore, were surprised at the readiness of these students to learn how to compete in a wider forum. Yet, as Cass and Birnbaum pointed out (1983, p. 75): "Despite very strong emphasis on the liberal arts, Carleton, nevertheless, ranks among the top 100 most productive institutions in developing business executives."

34. In the fourth year of his presidency, Edwards and the college were confronted by a strike by the housekeeping, food service, and maintenance staff, who had been rapidly organized. Some faculty members actively cooperated with the strike's organizers and at the outset a number of faculty members and students sympathized with the strikers. There was a demonstration in front of the president's house that created some anxiety among Edwards's three young children. The strike had strong support on television in a generally pro-labor milieu. But after a time, the *Carletonian* cooled on the strikers and their tactics, and in the end the strike failed to achieve its aims. The *Carletonian* reports that union members are now on the

whole reconciled with the college and generally supportive and, by the same token, resentful of the union's leadership. The strike might have been a dreadful blow to Edwards's presidency had it occurred as his incumbency began. As it was, the board had full confidence in him and showed this by not interfering: There was no backseat driving at all, except for the characteristic extravagant caution of Carleton's lawyers warning against any genuine act by the president that might be interpreted as an unfair labor practice. The wounds the strike caused within the faculty appear completely healed. The same is true of the conflict that occurred under Howard Swearer's presidency when one of the social science departments denied tenure to a radical, extremely popular activist, who has made the whole state his arena. Dean Harriet Sheridan and the president concurred in the department's decision to deny tenure. But then there was such a storm of protest that the president asked the appropriate disciplinary association to recommend two outside reviewers; these recommended tenure, which was of course granted. Such actions inevitably undercut a department's leadership, but here too reconciliation seems to have occurred.

35. Along with the presidents of Oberlin, Reed, Williams, Swarthmore, Mount Holyoke, and Franklin and Marshall, Edwards has sponsored a report by David Davis, Van Atta, Sam S. Carrier, and Frank Frankfort, "Educating America's Scientists: The Role of the Research Colleges," issued by Oberlin College, 1985. Edwards has also joined the board of trustees of the Carnegie Foundation for the Advancement of Teaching and has been active in the Association of American Colleges.

References

American Association of University Professors. "The Annual Report on the Economic Status of the Profession 1983-84." *Academe*, 1984, *70* (2), special issue.

Bennis, W. *The Leaning Ivory Tower.* San Francisco: Jossey-Bass, 1973.

Brennwald, P. "Departmental GPAs Compared: Some Disparities Shown Between Humanities, Sciences." *Carletonian*, 1984, *103* (20), 1, 21.

Cass, J., and Birnbaum, M. *Comparative Guide to American Colleges.* (11th ed.) New York: Harper & Row, 1983.

Chaffee, E. E. *After Decline, What? Survival Strategies at Eight Private Colleges.* Boulder, Colo.: National Center for Higher Education Management Systems, 1984.

Clark, B. R. *The Distinctive College: Antioch, Reed, and Swarthmore.* Hawthorne, N.Y.: Aldine, 1970.

Cohen, M. D., and March, J. G. *Leadership and Ambiguity: The American College President.* New York: McGraw-Hill, 1974.

Edwards, R. H. "Trustees Today: A Presidential Report." *Carleton Voice,* 1984, *50* (1), 2-8.

Fisher, J. L. *Power of the Presidency.* New York: American Council on Education/Macmillan, 1984.

Headley, L. A., and Jarcow, M. E. *Carleton—The First Century.* Northfield, Minn.: Carleton College, 1966.

Jencks, C., and Riesman, D. *The Academic Revolution.* Chicago: University of Chicago Press, 1968.

Kauffman, J. *At the Pleasure of the Board.* Washington, D.C.: American Council on Education, 1983.

Kerr, C. *Presidents Make a Difference: Strengthening Leadership in Colleges and Universities.* Washington, D.C.: Association of Governing Boards of Universities and Colleges, 1984.

Kramer, M. "In Defense of Distribution: A Critique of the Carnegie Essay on General Education." *Change,* 1981, *13,* 26-31.

Lester, V. L. "Ask Mary Baldwin . . . AGB Board-Mentor Approach Really Works." *AGB Reports,* Sept./Oct. 1983, pp. 30-34.

Litten, L., Sullivan, D., and Brodigan, D. *Marketing in College Admissions.* (Foreword by D. Riesman.) Princeton, N.J.: The College Board, 1983.

Maccoby, M. *The Leader: A New Face for American Management.* New York: Simon & Schuster, 1981.

Nardi, G. " 'Nobody's Going to Know Who I Am,' Says Mary Baldwin College President." *Richmond Times-Dispatch,* Apr. 7, 1985, p. F-1.

Riesman, D. "The Collision Course of Higher Education." *Journal of College Student Personnel,* 1969, *10,* 363-369.

Riesman, D. "Can We Maintain Quality Graduate Education in a

Period of Retrenchment?" 2nd David Henry Lecture, University of Illinois at Chicago, Apr. 28, 1975.

Riesman, D. "Ethical and Practical Dilemmas of Fieldwork in Academic Settings: A Memoir." In R. K. Merton, J. Coleman, and P. Rossi (eds.), *Qualitative and Quantitative Social Research: Papers in Honor of Paul F. Lazarsfeld.* New York: Free Press, 1978.

Sisk, J. "The Fear of Imitation." *Georgia Review,* 1984, *43* (1), 9–20.

Trow, M. "Departments as Contexts for Teaching and Learning." In D. E. McHenry and Associates, *Academic Departments: Problems, Variations, and Alternatives.* San Francisco: Jossey-Bass, 1977.

Wood, M. *Trusteeship in the Private College.* Baltimore, Md.: Johns Hopkins University Press, 1984.

5

Leadership:
Golden Rules
of Practice

Leon Botstein

Since the era of student rebellion in the 1960s, which was followed almost immediately by a period of contraction and economic reversals for colleges and universities, the position of college president has come to be viewed as a singularly unenviable—even a beleaguered and impossible—one. An exaggerated premium is now placed on a president's management and mediation skills, and the standard of success for college presidents is defined too frequently as the maintenance of equilibrium rather than the building of progressive institutions.

The college president is rarely seen as a *primus inter pares,* an intellectual figure who can be looked to for the setting and implementing of policies directed at the heart of the university or college enterprise—the functions of teaching and scholarship. Rather, the president has emerged as a consummate broker of competing interests, at best an arbitrator who is asked to represent institutional unity and coherence to external constituents for purposes of fund raising (from legislatures or private sources), despite the obvious and persistent lack of unity and coherence on American campuses. In the 1980s, the president is expected to resist pressures from divergent factions on the campus, but that same president usually lacks the resources and authority to exercise decisive judgment and choice. Few presidents, when they are appointed, seek or receive an initial mandate to concentrate on the intellectual and curricular character of an institution, even though sound institutional management and sufficient resources most readily emerge when a coherent and distinct academic philosophy has been articulated.

While the appearance of presidential authority and prestige is officially maintained, both by presidents and their constituents, the authentic capacity to exercise this leadership has been eroded. This paradoxical situation accounts for three salient characteristics of contemporary college presidents: the shortness of their tenure, the ineffectiveness of their actual leadership and impact, and the shrinking pool of talented new individuals who find themselves drawn to the career. Few who possess even a modicum of intellectual courage and achievement, of eloquence and character, can be lured into applying for or accepting a college presidency. Unlike political executives in the public realm, such as governors and mayors, college presidents rarely maintain an active public constituency outside their institutions that can serve to outflank and contain competing factions within a campus. Bereft of an internal or external mandate or an autonomous base of authority, the college president has not only become quite marginal in intellectual terms but possesses little real power.

The mundane duties of daily management, administration, and public relations, along with the task of polite begging —euphemistically called development—have become the central obligations of the president. The psychic exchange extracted by incumbent presidents for these services, in a context which militates against serious academic and intellectual leadership, is the quiet toleration by all within and outside the campus of the public appearance of power. All that remains of a once-prestigious position is the image of authority, but that image continues to be deeply cherished by incumbent presidents. They want to act as if they still had the power to influence the essential academic character of their institutions.

The need to sustain this illusion is shared by faculty, trustees, and alumni. The illusion of presidential power and authority, in the face of the persistent and evident ineffectiveness of the presidency (for which these constituents are, in part, responsible), offers a shield that protects from criticism the intellectual inertia of these same constituents with respect to the future of an institution. The "bad" president becomes an easy scapegoat—the necessary, ritualized object of derision. His or her failures provide a plausible excuse for the lack of vision and progress within a campus. It is therefore not surprising that among serious scholars and teachers the expressed ambition to become a college president is itself plausible grounds for doubt and suspicion. In most circumstances, the willing candidate, by the mere fact of his or her expressed eagerness to be chosen, ought to be disqualified. Most search committees choose candidates whom they know little about and trust that the presidential tenure will last long enough for the incumbent and the institution to understand one another and for the president to effect serious change.

Needed: A Strong Presidency

The historical irony is, of course, that forceful, decisive, and memorable leadership, exercised for longer than a decade, was the key ingredient in the development of distinguished colleges and universities before 1960. Eliot, Meiklejohn, Hutchins, Conant, Butler, and Sachar are just a few names that now evoke periodic nostalgia from precisely those constituents in the university that today, as members of a search committee, would reject comparable individuals as too outspoken, too strong headed, and too opinionated. These men might now be deemed too sharp and powerful to "get along" with all the vested interests that fear any loss of status or leverage under a strong president. Yet history indicates that, without a strong presidency, significant progress and intellectual ferment in a college or university are highly unlikely.

The final irony of history is that it has been the strong presidency that has successfully brought forth, despite the vested interests that resist it, the most productive moments for faculty, students, alumni, and trustees. Faculty will be better teachers and engage more actively in scholarship and research when internal politics are under control, when management is sound and short-term crises are rare, and when a strong guiding hand motivated by curricular and scholarly goals governs a campus. In such circumstances, campus life and politics provide faculty few ready excuses not to do that for which they are uniquely qualified: to teach and conduct research. A president who is not jockeying for support from within a board of trustees and is not frightened of them need not constantly curry favor. He or she can be a much more compelling raiser of funds. Trustee confidence in the president becomes expensive for the trustees—in terms of philanthropy. The same holds true for alumni who may well use the superficial dimensions of a particular president to justify stinginess. A well-run institution with a strong, respected president who focuses on the intellectual and academic purposes of the college is more likely to generate an atmosphere that encourages students to strive for high standards of achievement. On the undergraduate level, such an environment can inspire students to pursue the initially less tangible and pragmatic ideals of liberal learning.

Despite this bleak and somewhat cynical characterization of the college presidency, it remains a function that, even in poor hands, influences the future of an institution. It remains implicitly vested with a serious intellectual agenda, even if that agenda lies dormant. The *effective* college presidency is also a delightful and possible task. In the decades ahead there may even be a gradual shift back to the conviction that once dominated the history of higher education: that the hiring and support of a strong, long-tenured president are directly in the self-interest of every campus constituency.

Evidence for this proposition can be found in those institutions that, during the past decade, have demonstrated the truth of an axiom dear to the classical historians of Greece and Rome: Necessity is frequently the effective cause of virtue and courage. Institutions that found themselves in difficult predicaments in terms of finance, academic quality, and enrollment during the 1970s discovered that the conventional manager, the glad-handing president, was not able to solve serious institutional problems. Furthermore, the best of these conventional presidents—and some were certainly ambitious and clever—were deterred from accepting presidencies loaded with serious risks of failure. Much like the Spartans at Thermopylae under Leonidas (at those institutions that fell despite valiant leadership) and the Athenians under Themistocles at Salamis (at those institutions in crisis that triumphed under sound leadership), institutions faced with serious danger in the 1970s created the context, often inadvertently, for the recruitment and support of strong college presidents.

Conversely, those institutions whose financial status and self-image did not inspire a sense of fear and danger continued to hire bland and unexceptional presidents and continued (perhaps wisely) to limit their substantive influence. For these colleges, the stakes were never survival. All dimensions of campus life continued to proceed as in the past. All there might have been to lament were missed opportunities. The complacency allowed by accumulated wealth and prestige—including secure public funding—is understandably hard to overcome. Well-endowed and prestigious public institutions may be the last to consciously reach once again for dynamic, powerful scholars and teachers as presidents. Memorable leadership in such institutions will more likely emerge unexpectedly, as it has in the past, from an appointment that promised to be unexceptional—from "dark horse" candidates chosen hastily, after other offers fell through.

A career of fifteen years as a college president is neither easy to summarize nor necessarily sufficiently interesting to warrant writing about. Many presidential experiences are *sui generis*. The sense of competition and feudal pride among institutions in the United States is strong enough to disqualify claims that experiences at one institution apply to another or that the insights of one college president can be useful beyond the confines of a single college. Yet there are common aspects, as well as shared predicaments and challenges, to be found within all college presidencies. My own experience since 1970 has included the presidency of a prestigious but relatively unendowed liberal arts undergraduate institution (Bard College from 1975 to the present); the presidency of an experimental, unaccredited college that I found in Chapter 11 bankruptcy and that later closed in 1978 (Franconia College, 1970–1975); and the presidency of a vital, unique institution, America's only early college (Simon's Rock) that Bard took over in 1979 and that is now flourishing as part of Bard. All three institutions are or were private, undergraduate liberal arts colleges located on beautiful rural sites in the Northeast. Bard has a few small graduate programs. Both Bard and Simon's Rock maintain distinctive curricular commitments and exacting intellectual standards, and they can point to productive and ambitious faculty, elite, outspoken students, few alumni, and generous trustees. Franconia offered the challenge of rescuing, albeit temporarily, an impoverished, debt-ridden, cooperatively governed alternative institution without a serious physical plant in a politically hostile environment. Franconia College was a child of the intellectual and social currents of the 1960s (when it was founded) and the 1970s (when it closed).

Lessons from Experience

The following ten maxims are distilled from these fifteen years of being a college president. The intent is to offer guidance as to what a college president ought to do to influence the success of the institution that he or she has been chosen to lead. At a minimum, these "golden rules" are intended to provoke, if not infuriate, the reader. A word of caution. The author enjoys being a college president and expects to continue to do so for years to come, even though he falls consistently short of living up to the rules that he has composed for himself and others.

The following advice is cast in the spirit of Richard Strauss's "Ten Golden Rules" for young orchestral conductors that he wrote at the end of his life in 1949. Strauss's first two rules were: "(1) Remember that you are making music not to amuse yourself but to delight your audience; and (2) you should not perspire when conducting: only the audience should get warm." Since both these maxims apply in spirit to the college president, I will begin with them and add, with the appropriate glosses, eight supplementary rules to make a full complement of ten.

1. *Strauss's first bit of advice underscores the need to remember that the overriding obligation of a college president is to have a lasting impact on others.* The president must inspire and bring the best out of all the constituent elements within a college. The position is not designed for self-celebration. It is not a forum for one's own ambitions, a platform for social or political activities that have no direct bearing on the purposes of the college or university. Rather, this rule demands that a president be sustained by a driving sense of what ought to be done in and for the college and by a guiding vision of the academic community and the intellectual enterprise. And, while that vision must be realized in practice and produce concrete results, it cannot be managerial in content. Efficiency, economy, and smooth administration in a university or college derive from the distinction, coherence, and adequacy of its academic ideals and strategies, not the other way around. Academic administration is not an autonomous science with its own normative goals. It is contingent on the teaching and research mission of a college, its educative and scholarly functions.

Even though colleges have different histories, personnel, and student markets, no institutional strategy will work if it is not informed by a substantive image of how best to conduct scholarly inquiry, train professionals and preprofessionals, educate undergraduates in critical understanding, and spur research within the confines and constraints of an individual institution. The formation of that vision is the first task of the president. A decisive curricular and intellectual goal demands both a firm, well-reasoned philosophical principle and a sensitivity to particular circumstances. But its intent must be to extend existing institutional limits and resources. Inherited definitions of evident practicality never provide a sufficient argument against the radical ambition of ideals. In fact, presidential conduct based on such intellectual ideals can be incorporated into any existing institution effectively, either by introducing new goals or by reviving dormant traditions. Authentic, intelligent leadership can inspire others and, in the end, will accrue much more to the benefit of the president than even the cleverest of short-term management schemes, if these are predicated on the assumption that dramatic, long-term changes are not possible. "Management by objectives" is a perfectly useful notion, as long as the objectives are grand and intellectually substantive.

If the constituencies of a college see that the president is motivated by convictions that transcend existing resources, personalities, and mere personal ambition on his or her part, they will be more inclined to listen and help. The possession of a clear point of view about the academic character of a college, in fact, demonstrates the deepest loyalty on the part of a president to an institution. No matter how difficult the internal circumstances at an institution, its various constituencies will accept his leadership if he or she has succeeded in gaining their intellectual respect. Enlightened leadership, moreover, increases the chances that virtue and self-interest will not come in conflict and may prevent a president's inevitable opponents from charging that his strategies are designed to benefit himself, not the college.

2. *Presidential leadership demands the display of confidence, even in its absence.* Tentative behavior and the display of anxiety reduce the willingness of others to take risks on behalf of a new program. Given the many pressures and the persistence of seemingly insoluble problems, nervousness legitimately plagues all college presidents. But finding a way to control it is essential. Failure to communicate that one is in command of the situation (which often involves the willingness to compromise and admit error) invites doubt.

A president's unwillingness to take firm stands despite his or her authentic commitment to particular courses of action is often motivated by overeagerness to mollify everyone, to exit quickly from minor crises, and to be liked by all concerned, consistently, always. The need to be popular triumphs over the will to be right. Obsessive concern with how one is perceived and regarded by others leads to actions calculated merely to please. Keeping everyone happy requires a sequence of short-term, pragmatic strategies, not the implementation of a long-range vision.

Strauss's maxim, therefore, calls for the president to set the agenda and the terms of the exchange between him or her and all constituents, from trustees to students, with a maximum of self-control. This in turn requires a long-range commitment on the part of the president, so that his or her colleagues on the faculty, on the board, and among the alumni cannot assume that they will outlast the president and therefore can resist presidential initiatives with impunity. The idealism, determination, hard work, and focused plans of the president should make others "perspire," about the magnitude, danger, and rewards of the new tasks ahead. A campus should be stirred and motivated—even made to feel anxious—by the leadership that the president seeks to offer, as well as by the nature of his ideals and the actual strategy he employs.

Last but not least, behavior by presidents predicated essentially on a calculation of immediate political responses leads inevitably to feelings of contempt on the part of the president's constituents. Academic colleagues are exceptionally articulate and gifted. They have the uncanny capacity to penetrate maneuvering, flattery, short-term balancing of vested concerns, and actions intended merely to appease. While they may resist leadership initially, they deeply despise mediocrity, lack of self-confidence, and failure to take risks. Without dramatic leadership and the will to seize the initiative, the president will find himself in trouble, since his or her function will lose its initial claim to legitimacy. Trust will be hard to develop. Constituencies within the academy, with all their eloquence and cleverness, have shown themselves to be ruthless with weakness and hesitancy, with the effort to manage merely by consensus and not by conviction.

3. *Never form a committee unless you know exactly what you want it to do; never issue statements or memoranda that cannot or will not be followed by visible action.*

The time of faculty and trustees is valuable and should not be wasted. In matters of curriculum, for example, unless a committee realizes the precise intent of a presidential initiative, the conclusions it reaches may be rejected or tabled. This only invites anger. No committee whose purpose is to offer input and consultation can generate a solution without a clear indication of the substantive objective, well beyond general cliches and rhetoric. In turn, consultative mechanisms should not be created unless the president is willing to take their advice seriously. Faculty prefer to respond to direct presidential action without any claim of consensus or consultation than to waste their time in a complex process propelled by a hidden agenda to which they are not privy.

Trustees in particular want their volunteer time well spent. And presidents need to direct that time toward the task for which trustees are uniquely suited: augmenting institutional resources. Trustees would rather sacrifice the appearance of conventional participation than do something a president could do just as well without them. The price one pays for the judicious use of committees is fewer but more dedicated committees and the greater risk that presidential actions will be blocked, countermanded, or accepted with some initial resentment. A president should use informal consultation and personal communication to pave the way for unilateral actions. He or she should be willing to justify such actions after the fact. However, the president should exercise unilateral authority only for the most significant long-range purposes, and not solely in moments of crisis.

Finally, no committees should be set up to change governance or procedures. The notion that some new structure will render serious change easier to come by is a classic presidential illusion. There is practically no existing system of college or university governance that cannot be adapted to the objectives of a strong, decisive president. Fussing with processes, like forming superfluous committees, is a symptom of lack of ideas. Presidents can and usually should stay within the bounds of an institution's traditional protocols.

4. *When you feel impelled to sing a song of praise about how well the institution is doing or how outstanding the college is, talk about something else altogether.*

Most college presidents misunderstand their public relations function. To alumni, donors, foundations, and corporations, as well as to the larger community, the internal activities of a campus are often less interesting than one might imagine.

Instead, these groups want to be informed about broader issues of culture and society. The best demonstration of an institution's achievement is often oblique. Supporters want to feel that they are making contributions toward goals in education, public policy, or scientific research that transcend the confines of any single institution.

For the most hard core alumni who appear entirely under the spell of a reflexive nostalgia, the president should try to alter their perspective and not pander to it. This holds for interested friends of the college, and parents. What people want to know is why the activities of a particular college are important to the future of culture, the nation, politics, science, or education. The president must be an individual whom the public wants to listen to and talk with. Standing for issues and points of view larger than the presidency itself can make a president that kind of person.

The office of the presidency offers an opportunity for the incumbent to emerge as an individual of substantive insight and eloquence on matters well beyond the realm of college administration. Students and faculty in particular must be able to witness how a president seizes this opportunity. In doing so, however, the college president must never lose sight of how to illustrate a larger issue through an example of something that is being done on the campus—something that has been accomplished by faculty or students. The president must place the institution into the larger context and argue its significance. If he does so successfully, he will augment the sense of pride among trustees, faculty, and students in their college.

Never seek refuge in inherited tradition, the past reputation of the college, or the assumption of past loyalty. Anticipation of a brighter future for the college, one that will be more memorable within a larger social and cultural context, is the most powerful motivator of public support and philanthropy. This is particularly so if those to whom the president is speaking as representative of the college sense that they can share in the accomplishment of noble goals and programs. When speaking to the faculty, the president should try to convince them that the larger cultural and social issues that affect academic policy are more critical than in-house political concerns. But a president must never engage himself in larger realms (foreign policy and business or domestic affairs) in a manner that cannot be demonstrably shown to benefit the campus.

Finally, a president should seek to involve trustees in discussions of serious policy matters and ideas, even if trustees seem unwilling to do so. Presidents need to keep trustees away from the details and trivialities of day-to-day management. In the same vein, the president should share aspects of financial strategy and other trustee matters with faculty and students. Above all, a president should seek opportunities to discuss serious subjects with students, faculty, and trustees that have nothing whatsoever to do with institutional issues. The president must be more than a professional college president and use that fact on behalf of the college.

5. *When you think you are being candid, try to be even more open and honest.*

Political considerations sometimes require the use of discretion. But never try to pass off partial disclosure as an act of true candor. If secrets are to be kept, remain silent. When you feel the need to underscore the fact that you are being candid, you are probably being defensive about the extent of your candor. Either remain quiet or be brutally honest. Your constituents must trust you, not only to be straightforward (no matter how harsh the truth) but also to be sufficiently intelligent to avoid speaking when that is the best course. You can declare openly that there are matters that cannot and should not be revealed. Therefore, do not use your unique access to information as a back-room political tool.

It is when conditions are bad, when enrollment is off, when grants and money are scarce that you should especially remember this maxim. In this regard, there are three common errors committed in bad times. First, too many presidents become defensive about institutional crises that are rooted in the historical condition of an institution. Ironically, adversity (as this book attempts to show) gives a president room to exercise leadership and initiative. Security and complacency in institutions militate against new efforts at change. Therefore, resist the temptation to be defensive about difficulties that cannot be avoided or solved quickly. A clear sense of the essential problems facing an institution, if shared by faculty and trustees, strengthens the hand of the president who has a strategy designed to counter problems and overcome them. Even if the first try fails, a pattern of calculated effort will be admired.

Second, presidents often cannot tolerate danger or risk—the anxiety of responsibility. But open disclosure of imminent disaster in the absence of a strategy for dealing with it and purely for the sake of candor is only evidence of a failure of nerve. If a president cannot solve a major problem, then he should either resign or be willing to risk failure despite his best efforts. Talking about the problem publicly and indiscreetly serves no purpose except to make the president feel better. It may even increase the likelihood that a threatening danger will become an actual disaster.

The president should reveal her concerns fully and without euphemisms to those who might be in a position to help. This judicious mix of silence and honesty will help in two ways. The president will seek out genuine help more aggressively and will try to solve the problem more energetically if she senses the depth of her own responsibility and accepts the inappropriateness of hiding behind "I warned you" or similar public declarations. A president must be prepared to accept a defeat engineered by others without necessarily exposing those who are actually at fault. Otherwise, first-class professional administrators will not work with her. A college president must be willing to accept the consequences of the work, good and bad, of others.

Faculty and students, particularly in matters of finance, will only become paralyzed by dangers about which they are informed but over which they have no influence. The press, which often hears about bad news before the fact, revels in catastrophe and rumors, and press reputations linger on. If a president cannot muster a believable optimism, perhaps he should step down. Honesty and candor, therefore, demand both rigorous silence and full disclosure, each chosen appropriately within a strategy for success.

Third and last, presidents sometimes talk about serious

matters in vague generalities or in platitudes. But this is a mistake. Presidents should either hide their fears or overcome them. They should not share them obliquely or gratuitously. If a president chooses to talk about problems, he should be precise, since the imagination of faculty can often infer a worse result than the president himself suspects or foresees.

6. *Never become too friendly with a small, exclusive circle of faculty or trustees; never find yourself in a position where you must cut the budget against your better judgment.*

Always remember that your social life on a college campus is a function of your position. Do not try to divide and conquer through the cocktail circuit. Cherish the structural loneliness and distance of the job. Do not delude yourself that you are being courted or flattered because of your personality apart from your job. This, in turn, does not mean that affection for you is not genuine. Rather, it means that the affection you receive derives not from your personality but primarily from your performance as president. Friendliness, affection, and warmth on a campus are indispensable, but they can be developed only on the basis of your role and your leadership.

Do not hold grudges or become enmeshed in internal or historical emnities on a campus. Instead, take advantage of the fact that your role as president may allow you to alter the historic relationships among faculty and students for the better. Reach out to professed opponents out of decency but never out of a desire to retaliate. Seek out the redeeming features of everyone you deal with. Concentrate on those features. There are always grounds on which to respect someone and to develop a modicum of affection and regard for him or her.

In turn, do not camouflage anger or annoyance. Honesty of response bespeaks a serious regard for those with whom you are dealing. Be cautious about those who openly seek to align themselves with you for purely strategic reasons. But signal clearly your gratitude to those who openly support you because they actually agree with you. Always use reason and discussion and do not rely on social compatibility to achieve political support. Try to understand why you are being either opposed or supported. Then accept and acknowledge the grounds for both.

Do not expect consistent support from your allies; in fact, such consistency may damage the usefulness of their support at critical moments.

Minimize the pain of political losses for others. Do not gloat over victories. Never say anything in confidence that you are not prepared to defend in public, and try to anticipate, as you speak, the inaccuracies that will emerge in the retelling of presumed confidences. Know that your position inevitably encourages duplicity in others' dealings with you, but do not feel morally superior as a result. Concentrate on what people say to you directly and not what they say behind your back. Read Machiavelli's *The Prince* but do not forget to read *The Discourses* as well.

Since an environment of cooperation ought to be generated by a president on the grounds of a common intellectual and curricular enterprise, a president must never hide behind the authority of the trustees. If a president feels that he cannot get something done through the board—get a new expenditure approved, for example—he should not try to. A president must not emerge as the "good guy" with students or faculty in a situation in which the trustees refuse to do what the president believes in and others know should be done. He should take the blame for that which cannot be done. A president must operate from strength by presenting serious proposals that trustees are likely to accept. This prevents a president from being circumvented and the authority of his office from being undermined. Presidents should never fear the trustees. If possible, they should work without contracts and should be prepared to be dismissed at the pleasure of their boards. But presidents should know and respect the role of trustees and never come in open conflict with them. Shield them and they will shield you. If trustees will not approve something a president really believes must be done, he or she must either convince them or be prepared to resign.

Study finance. Concentrate on the income side, not the expense side. Resist conventional wisdom in matters of finance. Some individuals think unendowed institutions can be run like Harvard. Trustees of small colleges frequently want to act as if they were trustees at Yale. Discourage these temptations and instead get trustees to allow you to act as an entrepreneur. They too should become entrepreneurs, but without putting the entire enterprise at risk.

Remember that one can sink on an even keel. As an entrepreneurial president, remember that the consequence of failure is stark, but that the rewards of success are far greater than those that come from serving as caretaker of inadequate or declining resources. For some institutions, survival without distinction or the provision of much-needed services—survival merely for the sake of tradition and the past—is not enough justification for the work of a president. However, survival alone may be a virtue if only because it permits someone else to try to succeed where you have failed. Recognize when your plan is not working, even though you deeply believe in it. By the same token, never do something that you do not believe in for the sake of keeping your job.

7. *Just when your work load and schedule seem intolerable and overwhelming, agree to teach a course or do some research and scholarship in addition to your current duties.*

Presidencies invite obligations that are neither necessary nor useful. Set your own schedule and reevaluate the way you are spending your time. Keep only those traditions from your predecessors that you discover are essential. Start your own traditions and consistently use the element of surprise. Do not act because you think "this is what a president is supposed to do." Do not travel unnecessarily or involve yourself in superfluous commissions, higher education organizations, and the like unless you can see some benefit in them to your college. Delegate as many administrative duties as you can. Keep your intellect active on a regular basis. Do not be consumed by others' demands and realize that inaccessibility will make the occasions when you enter the picture or meet with someone that much more significant.

Always remember that you are in a college. Risk success and failure as teacher and scholar. Do not permit yourself to become only a bureaucrat or public relations officer. If you have no time for substantive research work, writing, and thinking, you are managing your time poorly. If you have lost your taste for teaching or research, do not continue to administer a college or university. Get a job in business or government. As a college president, you must also be prepared to work harder than others and to set the pace for your colleagues, both in the administration and on the faculty. Despite the demands of the job, much of what presidents do is inefficient and vague in intent, and could be done better in less time. This is especially true of fund raising and public relations. Find your own ways of accomplishing these things so that your work as teacher and scholar can continue.

8. *When you think you have raised as much money from an individual or an institution as you can, begin to ask for more; when you feel that everything would be fine if you just had more money, undertake a significant new program that adds to the amount of money you must find.*

There is always more money to be raised, even for public institutions. One never reaches the limit, for the overall limit is incrementally flexible. No one is offended by being asked for too much money. The worst that people can say is no. Concentrate on large gifts and develop lead gifts of significant magnitude that can raise the level of the lowest gifts. Giving reflects commitment. No trustee, alumnus, or alumna with whom you deal directly should remain a nongiver, even if the gift is small. Demand that all give to the highest level of which they are capable. Individuals who give well relative to their means inspire others and often make the best fund raisers. Wealthy individuals who give little stand as deterrents to generosity. Take no pride in being a good fund raiser. Give the credit to others, and remember to raise money from yourself.

Don't complain about not having enough money. Simply raise more and remember that people will not give money just because a college needs it. Philanthropy derives from the satisfaction of personal needs on the part of donors. Discover that need and develop a way to offer a means to respond to it. Gifts promised in wills by individuals who do not give while they are alive cannot be relied upon. Such promises are usually strategies to avoid annual gifts. Press donors hard, for doing so reveals the strength of your own conviction. The more a donor gives, the happier he or she will be. Remember the wisdom of the Talmud: "Philanthropy robs the rich man of his poverty."

9. *When recruiting students becomes more difficult and retaining them becomes increasingly hard, don't fire the admissions staff or look for more personnel. Make the academic program more rigorous and mobilize all the other staff and faculty of the college while leaving the admissions office and student services staff alone.*

Few admissions officers or counselors can dramatically change the appeal of a college. Its reputation among potential students derives from the work of the faculty and the administration at large. You are the chief admissions officer yourself. Your public posture and visibility are essential, second only to that of the college itself. Find new ways of recruiting, but never use ways that concentrate on the hotel, resort, and restaurant dimensions of residential campuses. Do not pander to students as if they were buying a car or joining a record club. Do not demean the intellectual purposes of a college by using an inappropriate mode of recruitment. Marketing wisdom and experience must be adapted to your college. You must sell serious programs to students who can benefit from them. Recognize those institutions with which you are in competition and outline clearly the differences and shared qualities. Recognize that most of the rhetoric in college publications is interchangeable. Mere assertions of distinction are as ineffective as pretty photographs. Fraudulent admissions work leads to extensive attrition. Make the admissions process the first encounter a student has with your institution's curricular philosophy.

Be careful not to misrepresent the degree of your college's selectivity. If your college is not selective, students will soon find that out. If your college is selective, you should not make an issue of the difficulties of getting in. Point to what might be involved in *getting out* of college in four years. Participate in the training of your admissions staff and mobilize the institution on their behalf. If institutional distinction is what you seek, create it; do not merely claim it. Involve faculty in the admissions process, not by using them as recruiters, but by asking them to develop those academic programs you feel are necessary to improve the admissions picture. Disabuse faculty of the illusion that a better admissions office will alter a pattern of decline in either the quality or quantity of applicants. If you remember that students should come to college to rectify their ignorance, you will find yourself concentrating on extending and improving your academic program and curriculum. These are the only aspects of a college that, in the long run, can ensure a healthy enrollment. Do not follow student tastes in curriculum. Offer a program based on principles that challenge student assumptions and intellectual habits.

Remember that success in admissions and success in fund raising go hand in hand. Both depend on the internal quality of the institution, as well as on the external recognition of its character, standards, and program. This also holds true for student services, except for the fact that inadequate housing and social conditions can interfere with the successful provision of an academic program. A poor social atmosphere among students is usually a symptom of an inadequate curriculum—of the paucity and triviality of the academic ideals that inform a campus. Changing all that is your job, not someone else's.

10. *Delegate responsibility but never resist accepting it; don't search for new ideas, find them. In moments of failure, accept the blame and laugh at yourself. In success, thank others and assume immediately that your triumphs are ephemeral.*

Remember what Herodotus taught in his mythic presentation of a conversation between the Athenian lawgiver Solon and the Lydian King Croesus. Success and happiness are ephemeral. Disaster strikes the immodest, and success breeds blindness and arrogance, which in turn invite catastrophe. A healthy campus depends on all its constituents; and it depends not simply on their loyalty to your administration but on their devotion to the ideals of the enterprise that you represent and help sustain. Recognize your weaknesses and failings but not with false modesty. Take pride in what you do, but use humor to reveal a recognition of your many limitations. Laugh at yourself and not at others. When others whom you appoint fail, either reprimand them or fire them, but take the blame yourself.

Search for new ideas everywhere, all the time. Copy and adapt. Do not overrate originality in the enterprise of education. It is, ultimately, a deeply conservative endeavor, properly tied to tradition.

Commitment to the Future

A final word. A president should love what he or she does, for in the America of the late twentieth century, the college presidency is a critical public position. Few roles have such potential for disinterested leadership in the public interest. Few positions are so well cast for making a contribution to the public debate on the future of our culture and the preservation of democracy. Few institutions will be as critical to the national future as will colleges and universities. In the private sector, the healthy survival of a diverse group of smaller institutions is critical to the tradition of the liberal arts. But it is precisely these smaller private colleges that now find themselves in the greatest danger. They require the strongest possible intellectual and academic direction from presidents who must, at the same time, be consummate risk takers. The reform of education at all levels in America is needed desperately, but it will require participation by colleges throughout the nation, particularly those dedicated to liberal learning. The investment of decades and, in some cases, centuries on behalf of individual institutions must not only be preserved, therefore, but it must be extended.

In the final analysis, both professionals within the academy and the public at large want and expect presidents to lead. Leadership from a college president, however, must involve more than rectifying past oversights or reforming the practices of previous incumbents. Curricular and institutional renewal requires of the president that he or she come to a principled understanding of past and present. The work undertaken by presidents must respond to the intellectual needs of the future. The serious adaptation of tradition—one that reflects more than a faith in change itself or a dubious, if not arrogant, claim about what the future will actually bring—constitutes the challenge facing today's college president. The presidency of a college, because it influences the shape of study and scholarship—the way in which we conduct the learned professions, education, and research—must be driven by a commitment to what the future *ought* to bring; by some faith that the actualities of tomorrow will, even in a minor way, mirror the concerted efforts of the present.

If these "golden rules" provide no insight, try to write your own, whether you are a president, a would-be president, a faculty member, a trustee, or a concerned citizen sufficiently engaged in higher education to have picked up this book.

6

Program:
A Focus on Purpose
and Performance

Arthur Levine

Focusing on curriculum is one of the best ways for colleges and universities to thrive in hard times; and, to come right to the point, the best solutions to the present demographic, financial, and political problems of such institutions are educational ones. But few colleges are proceeding in this fashion. Since the Second World War the curriculum at most colleges has grown by accretion. New programs have been continually added to the old ones, and the old have been retained. Today's curriculum is thus a hodgepodge of five decades of change.

The curriculum reforms of the 1940s, for example, are still with us. After the war, the rallying cry of the American college was education for democracy. The curricular response was institution of a rash of new and varied general education pro-

Note: The data in this chapter are based on a study of a random sample of 309 four-year college catalogues stratified by Carnegie typology; the study was carried out for the Carnegie Foundation for the Advancement of Teaching.

126

grams, and a study of recent college catalogues shows another general education revival today. In contrast to the situation a decade ago, colleges now have programs with more structure and more requirements in science, social science, English, humanities, fine arts, and religion. General education is definitely back.

The innovations of the 1950s linger as well. After the launching of Sputnik in 1957, academic excellence became the rallying cry of higher education. The college curriculum accented science and foreign languages, honors programs, and accelerated study. Courses for the gifted mushroomed. We see the same trends now. Excellence is once more a watchword. Honors programs are booming. For the first time in two decades, a majority of colleges have such programs. Intensified or time-shortened programs are on the rise. More than eight out of ten colleges nationally accept Advanced Placement and College-Level Examination Program credits. In the past decade, the number of colleges enrolling superior high school juniors has doubled.

The reforms of the 1960s have persisted as well. Education for life, or "relevance," became the theme. New subject matters entered the curriculum—ethnic, urban, and environmental studies, arts and crafts, and so on. Reduced requirements, independent study, student-created majors, and pass-fail grading were much in evidence. All these options still exist at a majority of schools. Only the "relevant" subject matters have declined in number, and even these remain quite widespread.

The curriculum trends of the 1970s are also collegiate staples today. They emphasized the need for social justice and reflected a commitment to universal higher education. The curricular focus was on the nontraditional—new students, variable scheduling, alternatives to courses, off-campus study, credit for life experience, and compensatory education. The data show that all these curricular options spread like wildfire. Today a majority of colleges offer credit for off-campus study, remedial instruction, and prior learning. In fact, one out of every five colleges now has an external degree program. More recently, an emphasis on education for work has come to occupy center stage. Increased specialization, vocational majors, career counseling, internships, and credit for work are all part of the contemporary scene. In fact, a majority of institutions engage in each practice.

In short, the curriculum at most colleges and universities has grown by accretion in a haphazard fashion for some fifty years. Today it is blurred and confused, misshapen and bloated. It has taken on the appearance of a junkyard, littered with the reforms of five decades and the assorted legacies of 350 years of collegiate history. Colleges are more confident today about the length of an undergraduate education than they are about its content. In fact, most colleges ask little more from their students than that they scrounge around the yard for four years, picking and choosing from among the rubble in accordance with the minimal house rules.

Some would celebrate this situation. They would speak of the importance of diversity or of the value of letting a thousand flowers bloom. But in doing so they would mislead us. Diversity certainly should be cherished. Institutional differences are essential. To the extent that colleges have expanded their enrollments, broadened their curricula, and responded to variations in the students they enroll, they have made important strides. This is not the difficulty. The shortcomings of the current curriculum are merely symptoms. The real problem is that, at many schools, the curriculum simply lacks a purpose.

Of course, this is not a new problem. It has existed in varying degree for at least 200 years. But in the post–Second World War era, it has grown worse. Enjoying bounteous resources and feeling enormous pressure to expand, colleges did not contemplate the whys and wherefores of growth in the past. It was too heady a time. And these questions are not being considered today either even though resources have shrunk and the pressures to contract are constantly increasing. The implications are simply too frightening.

In this sense, the junkyard curriculum hurts. It is a liability to colleges in hard times. It is not only expensive but it lacks educational merit. A junkyard curriculum costs more to maintain than a leaner, more carefully thought-out alternative. A junkyard curriculum also has a leveling effect on quality. It encourages mediocrity. Both good and bad programs are maintained, and institutional resources are stretched to support them. Good programs arc thus denied the support needed to make them excellent, and poor programs are supported to a larger extent than they deserve.

Finally, the junkyard curriculum does not seem to increase enrollments, but rather to diminish them, particularly in small schools. Apparently, when a college offers a tad of this, that, and the other thing, students see the glass as half empty rather than as half full. The school is viewed as deficient rather than comprehensive. In every area other colleges with more sharply defined missions have more complete programs.

Thus, colleges that hope to once again become thriving institutions must clean up their junkyards. They ought to do this, not out of nostalgia for the past, but out of pure pragmatism. What they have now isn't working, and it will only pull them down if they try to retain it.

Blind Alleys

In their search for better curricula, many institutions run up against serious obstacles. Some of these obstacles come in the form of myths—misconceptions that most of us share about what is fundamental, perhaps even intrinsic, to curriculum success.

Five myths stand out. The first is that money is success: The more money a college spends on its curriculum, the more likely it is to excel. In his book *Investment in Learning,* Bowen (1977) shows that such thinking has serious limits. He reports "a rather indistinct but positive relationship between institutional expenditures for education and outcomes in the form of value added" (p. 288). So money does make a difference. But Bowen also finds that "affluent institutions could perform as well, or nearly as well, with less money and that many institutions could achieve greater results with the same money. . . . Increases in affluence do not automatically result in improvements in performance as is often claimed" (pp. 166-167). In short, although money helps, it does not guarantee institutional success, and lesser resources do not spell failure.

A second myth is that sky-high admission standards are

the key to curricular excellence. But this belief confuses selectivity with quality and institutional achievement. Extremely selective schools occasionally offer students poor programs, and some open admissions institutions provide first-rate curricula. As a historic rule, poor programs ultimately cost a college its students. A survival mentality and a more or less rapid erosion of selectivity are common phenomena in many schools with weak programs. Hence the conclusion that selectivity has little bearing on institutional success.

Another common myth is that success is the province of a particular kind of institution—public rather than private, urban rather than rural, comprehensive rather than single program, and so on. But the simple reality is that there are curricular success stories in every category of institution, even if on the whole some sectors are doing better than others. Berea College in Kentucky seems to be in all the wrong categories—it is a rural, private, liberal arts college—but it is nonetheless thriving.

A fourth myth is that a particular course of study is the answer for institutional success. Traditionally, the liberal arts were considered the cream of academic studies, and occupational courses carried the least prestige. Today, that balance has shifted. Vocational subjects are now regarded by some as the only sensible curriculum, while the liberal arts have decreased in popularity and enrollment due to a tight job market. But the point is this: Neither curriculum has a lock on success. It is true that vocational programs are doing far better in enrollment than are the liberal arts. Business programs, for example, have doubled in size in the past decade and a half while the liberal arts have declined by a third. But the fact is that in the past several years quite a few vocational programs at institutions as varied as the General College at the University of Minnesota and Flathead Valley Community College in Kalispell, Montana, have been discontinued for financial and educational reasons. And, as Part Three illustrates, an impressive number of liberal arts colleges without unusual resources have been among the nation's greatest success stories—Birmingham-Southern, Hood, Bradford, and others. In short, in terms of subject matter, there are many paths to success.

A related misconception is that one form of instruction surpasses all others. Many educators believe that small classes are superior to large ones and look with disdain on courses that are "taught" by computers. In truth, considerable research demonstrates that while small classes and teacher-taught courses are better suited to some students, computer-taught and larger classes are just right for others. In actuality, students have different learning styles, and the college that responds best to the needs of its particular students is likely to do better in some very pragmatic ways—admissions, retention, and development.

A last myth is that curricular quality can be measured in classroom hours. A week consists of 168 hours. Of that time students spend only an average of 15 hours in class. Yet we tend to concentrate almost exclusively on class time when we think about curriculum. Few colleges make use of the other 153 hours. The irony is that extracurricular or cocurricular activities have at least as much impact as does the curriculum itself. We have known this since the Bennington studies of a half century ago, and scholars like Newcomb, Chickering, and Astin have made the point time and time again.

The point is this. There are colleges that have seen carefully crafted classroom programs both undermined and strengthened by out-of-classroom activities. One such institution enthusiastically adopted an all-new interdisciplinary environmental focus for its curriculum. But the unplanned cocurricular program put a premium on activities and values that were quite at odds with the curriculum. When students were surveyed about their curriculum two years after its implementation, their opinions for the most part echoed the sentiments of the young man who said, "It doesn't get in my way. I can study what I want in spite of the environmental program."

In contrast, there are institutions such as Spelman College in Atlanta and Bowdoin College in Maine that have joined living and learning, classroom and residential life. We can also point to the University of South Carolina, which created an orientation course to introduce students to the world of college; to Empire State in Saratoga, New York, and Metropolitan State in Minneapolis, which focus on the outcomes of learning rather than on the place in which learning occurs; and to Berea College, which built extracurricular activities into the curriculum. The attention of these schools to out-of-class learning has brought them excellent rewards in terms of the quality of campus community and student learning, not to mention such pragmatic benefits as increased enrollment and retention of students. In short, colleges that consider curriculum in its broadest sense—classes as well as cocurriculum—have the best chance of offering their students a quality education.

Finding the Right Curriculum

This brings us to the $64,000 question: What curriculum should a college adopt to ensure success? Variations on that question include: What is the best advising system to improve retention of students? Which grading system will help students most with employers and professional schools? What kind of general education program will most likely attract foundation support? Not long ago I received a phone call from a college dean who asked me what kind of general education program his school might adopt to bring about an enrollment upturn. When I said that no such program existed, he replied, "I thought you were supposed to be knowledgeable about curriculum." We talked awhile longer; but after our conversation had ended, the dean was clearly disappointed, as much in me as in his failure to find a new program to present to his colleagues.

My point is this: There are no curricular panaceas. In fact, successful programs taken over lock, stock, and barrel by one college from another frequently fail in the new environment. A good example is the national response to the Harvard general education reform of the 1970s. A number of colleges, believing the Harvard program to be the product of careful planning by the best minds in the country, produced carbon copies of it. Three years later, at least two of those colleges are already actively looking for another answer, having failed with the first.

The best program an institution can adopt is the one that best conforms to its situation. It is this curriculum alone that has the potential to help an institution succeed in hard times, to answer the "bodies and bucks" problem that plagues us all. A curriculum, any curriculum, is probably best described as a road. It is a means and not an end. It has neither its own agenda nor an independent life. A curriculum is simply the path a college uses to move what it already has—a certain student body, a particular faculty, specific resources, and a unique history—to what it hopes to achieve—a set of goals or a vision of what its graduates should become.

Every college should have a vision, that is, a clear sense of what its graduates should attain to receive a degree. We call this a mission. A curriculum should reflect that mission and serve as a mechanism for achieving it. To accomplish this, a curriculum must correspond to the abilities and needs of the students attending the college. Thus, if two colleges desire precisely the same achievements of their graduates but have enrolled different student populations, they might require very different programs. Say, for instance, that one school enrolled a fairly homogenous, high-ability student body and the other consisted of a heterogeneous mix of students—some poor in basic skills, others extremely able. These two student groups would require very different courses of study. The students at the first school might need little compensatory education, those at the second much more. The first school could offer a group of common studies to all freshmen; the second, owing to the heterogeneity of its students, would be more successful offering a variety of alternatives. And so on. Instruction, support services, and even evaluation might vary sharply; yet, despite these differences, the programs could both be high in quality and be exactly right for the two institutions.

It is also essential, if a curriculum is to bring success, that it be consistent with the training and interests of the faculty who will teach the program. About fifteen years ago, a major university adopted a new, progressive, student-centered curriculum. It required, for example, that faculty members spend much more time advising undergraduates, that they provide students with written evaluations as an alternative to grades, and that they spend more time teaching outside their specialties. The curriculum failed quickly. It was inconsistent with the faculty's strong disciplinary training and its primary interest in and commitment to research and graduate teaching. With time and effort, a faculty can be changed. But in the final analysis, the curriculum must be adapted to the faculty, not the faculty to the curriculum. Loss of quality and institutional decline are the price paid for mismatching.

Another requirement is that the curriculum be consistent with the resources available to the institution. Several examples of inconsistencies come to mind. In one instance, a liberal arts college decided that all its students should take one course together. The class was designed and ready for enrollment when it was discovered that the college did not have a room large enough to accommodate the whole student body. In another instance, a rural institution created a three-credit internship program only to find that its rural location made the program impossible to implement. In yet a third case, an educational policy committee designed a new freshman seminar program. The committee spent more than a year developing the proposal, creating courses, and so on when it suddenly came to light that the college could not afford the new program, which turned out to be much more expensive than the curriculum it replaced. In short, programs implemented without adequate resources do not work.

One more requirement is that the curriculum be compatible with the history and traditions of the college. In the late 1960s, a university president and a nationally renowned scholar agreed to establish an experimental college at a very traditional university. The idea earned acclaim in the higher education community and even in the press. But seven years later, the experiment had failed, and the university had said good riddance to it. Cause of death: terminal incompatibility. The goals of the college, the nature of its faculty, and the character of its students clashed with the mission and traditions of the university. The experimental college did not seek to achieve goals comparable to those of the university, and it could not be considered a high-quality operation. Hence, it failed.

Despite these cautionary tales, it is important to recognize that any college or university in America has the potential to be a curricular success story. And the payoff can be enormous, much larger than most presidents, deans, or faculties would imagine. Frederick Rudolph makes this clear in his account of the early history of Union College in Chapter Two. In many respects, in fact, the 1840s and 1850s are reminiscent of the present. That era, like ours, was characterized by shifting demographics, a turbulent economy, changing national priorities, a lack of political support for higher education, a labor market and social institutions in transition, and a technological revolution. It is worth noting that the institutions that most successfully overcame the demographic, economic, and social problems of the earlier time were those that responded best to the educational needs of the day. They were for the most part lesser known institutions such as Vermont, Brown, Michigan, and Union whose reputations grew out of their accomplishments during this period. Such colleges attracted students, even though the number of students was diminishing, and they obtained financial support despite a troubled economy. These institutions became leaders in the face of more pressing national priorities.

The same appears to be true today. Recently the Ford Foundation brought together a number of small liberal arts colleges that were experiencing success. The colleges were asked why they were doing so well. Each cited a focus on the curriculum as the main ingredient of their success. This focus resulted in distinctive programs that in turn had created unique niches in the marketplace for these institutions. It brought them increased enrollments and better faculties. It built morale on campus. It created a sense of excitement among alumni that translated into increased giving. It got them numerous grants from major foundations, and it brought them media coverage that increased applications and contributions. For these small liberal arts colleges an emphasis on curriculum resulted not only in educational vitality but in healthy bottom lines. Resources followed programming, not the other way around. For the most part these colleges concluded that they could not succeed simply through a focus on enrollments and resources, marketing and management. They believed that the challenges facing col-

leges and universities today are at their base educational, not
demographic, economic, or social.

It is true that one challenge for colleges today is to offer
an education that will serve a population that is growing older,
changing in composition, increasing in numbers of minorities,
and moving constantly. Colleges today must also offer students
an education that will prepare them for a world in which jobs,
the labor market, and technologies are constantly changing. Finally, colleges must offer an education that is responsive to the
problems caused by the decline in civic participation, social institutions in transition, a shrinking globe, and confusion about
values and beliefs. But if there is a lesson that grows out of the
experience of the liberal arts colleges mentioned earlier, it is
that curricular vision is perhaps the only effective remedy for
the problems that ail higher education today. We can be certain
that new social issues and new demographic patterns will continue to emerge, as the twentieth century gives way to the
twenty-first, and that these developments will present fresh
challenges to higher education. But are our colleges to be nothing
more than mere weathervanes, acted upon rather than acting?
Or will they now set out to establish their own curricular identities and, in the process, learn how to give shape to the very
forces that would shape them? The choice is ours.

7

Faculty:
Ongoing Development
and Renewal

Jerry G. Gaff

The employment outlook issued by the U.S. Department of Labor (1984) lists college faculty among the occupational groups
facing the greatest percentage decline in numbers by 1995. As if
to add insult to injury, professors rank just below oilworkers,
ranch hands, and other unskilled or transient laborers in anticipated decline in numbers. Recently, faculty members on a budget
committee of a college noted in a discussion that some of their
students had secured jobs upon graduation at salaries higher than
those of their teachers. Pride and satisfaction at the success of
the students were mixed with resentment over investing the time
and expense to gain a doctorate, spending several years to hone
professional skills, and still earning less than students who have
only baccalaureate degrees.

Midlife crises can strike faculty members with special
force. Even successful professionals looking ahead to ten,
twenty, or thirty more years of the same work in a grim climate
occasionally ask themselves, "Is this all there is to it? Would a
different career add another dimension to my life? Am I too old

to go back and take that path rejected earlier?" These examples can be multiplied, and they all add up to the mood of gloom and doom that hangs over the professoriate these days. Like Rodney Dangerfield, many faculty members feel, with some justification, that they get no respect. Given the fact that most current faculty members have never lived through rough times in their professions and institutions, the historical success stories described by Frederick Rudolph in Chapter Two, the less visible contemporary success stories discussed in other chapters, and even the stories of what some of their older colleagues experienced during the 1930s and 1940s—the last recession in higher education—lack salience. Faculty members, simply stated, have not had to develop the survival skills to cope, let alone thrive, in a difficult era. What to do?

Faculty Development Essential

The starting point is to acknowledge that the faculty are the heart blood of a college or university. The faculty are responsible for defining the overall instructional program, for providing instruction to students in individual courses, for giving advice to students about their studies and careers, and for serving as role models for students. It takes years for a college to assemble an outstanding faculty, an enormous amount of effort and experience for faculty members to develop their various talents, and expenditures of large sums of money to support their ongoing professional development. The college that is fortunate enough to have high-quality faculty members will devote a great deal of time, energy, and resources to their continual growth and development. Always a concern, the development of faculty is absolutely essential during the hard times that now beset the profession. This is precisely the time to turn to faculty development for solutions to some of the most vexing problems confronting individuals and institutions.

What do faculty need for their development? There are as many different answers to that question as there are faculty members; each person is unique and possesses his or her own blend of dreams, strengths, weaknesses, anxieties, and so on.

But two general kinds of answers have emerged at different eras, and a third answer is now emerging.

The first desideratum can be put quite simply: Faculty need to be experts in their disciplines. Throughout much of academic history there has been debate over what kinds of qualifications teachers should possess, but during recent decades professional standards have predominated over such criteria as religious affiliation or faith, character, or other personal qualities. Today this typically means completion of an advanced degree in one's specialty at a recognized institution of higher learning. Most faculty members in colleges and universities in this country meet this standard, but this is not the case everywhere in the world. Discussions of faculty development with academics from Brazil, India, or Indonesia, for example, often focus on the problem of securing faculty with sound training or of securing more adequate training for the ones they have. Many college students around the world are still instructed in science by the local physician and in literature by the publisher of the local newspaper. Securing adequate training is a first-order need for faculty; and although this problem is less apparent in this country than in others, one hears the concern voiced that many of today's best graduate students are spurning the academic life. Keeping the academic pipeline filled with talented individuals, some of whom will move into the professoriate, is a necessary step to ensure an adequate supply of intellectually exciting college teachers for the future.

Paralleling the emphasis on hiring faculty who possess professional qualifications is a distinctive set of practices by which colleges and universities seek to promote the continual development of faculty. These practices, which assist faculty in upgrading or updating their knowledge, include support for completing dissertations, research assistance, sabbatical leaves, and travel allowances. Such devices have become standard operating practices at all but the backwater institutions of higher learning, and they are crucial to any faculty development program. Unfortunately, when budgets get tight, the tendency is to reduce the funds devoted to these activities. Although such funding can be reduced for a short time without serious consequences, if continued for a long period of time it is a prescription for disaster.

Knowing one's subject, however, does not automatically make one an effective teacher. This point was driven home during the late 1960s when students protested irrelevant courses and uninspired teaching, especially at the very places with the greatest concentration of leading scholars—Berkeley, Columbia, Harvard, Chicago, Wisconsin. At about the same time, a great deal of research was being undertaken on the process of learning, student development in college, faculty impact on students' learning and development, the components of effective teaching, and evaluation of teaching. This research found learning and teaching to be complex activities that involve a knowledgeable instructor as only one of a series of factors in sound education. The publication *Faculty Development in a Time of Retrenchment* by the Group for Human Development in Higher Education (1974) made the case for greater attention to the teaching role in the development of faculty and argued for campus programs to assist development in this area. These concepts fell on fertile soil, and during the 1970s such programs sprouted like mushrooms after a spring rain.

These new programs were of different types, and they served differing purposes (Gaff, 1975; Clark and Lewis, 1985). Some focused on faculty members themselves and sought to help individuals learn more about their profession, their students, or their institutions; acquire new instructional skills; gain feedback about their own teaching behavior; explore their attitudes, values, and feelings about teaching; or apply some principles of learning in their courses. Other programs focused on instruction itself and worked with faculty members to set specific objectives and to measure their achievement; to produce instructional materials using a variety of media, to design courses with the aid of experts in learning and technology, and to develop learning systems such as mastery learning or the Personalized System of Instruction. Still others emphasized the fact that teaching should occur within a supportive environment and helped faculty members to create such a climate by setting group goals and objectives, improving relationships among colleagues in departments, training leaders such as department chairpersons and administrators, and establishing clear policies about the importance of teaching in the reward system. However the programs were conceptualized—and most, in fact, combined several features—the majority were administered by means of an office or center separated from the formal authority structure. Development of faculty is most effective if it relies on the carrot rather than the stick. Lasting change can best be brought about if it is the result of the intrinsic motivation of the faculty members; others can best help by enticing, stimulating, supporting, and reinforcing the positive efforts of individuals. This means they should not be in an authority relationship with the individual.

There is evidence that these newer campus programs can be effective in assisting faculty members to improve in their instructional roles. After interviewing over 500 faculty members who had participated in faculty development activities in twenty private liberal arts colleges, Nelsen and Siegel (1980) concluded that "effective faculty renewal is possible" (Preface). In their report of a project involving sixteen colleges and universities, Gaff and Justice (1978) state, "At this point faculty development can be considered not a high-risk experiment but a set of tools that can be used as one component of total institutional renewal" (p. 97).

None of these findings are new. Several writers have discussed them in greater depth. What *is* new is that yet a third general answer to what faculty members need for their development is emerging. The various concepts and model programs that have been fashioned to foster intellectual and instructional development continue to play important roles, but a new agenda is taking shape that changes once again the character of faculty development. This new agenda relies on the generic qualities of the development activities to date but applies them to particular needs of the institution. If the earlier forms of faculty development required the institution to help faculty members become knowledgeable and effective teachers, the new phase turns the tables and asks the faculty to assist the institution in achieving specific needs—needs that are very much in the self-interest of individual faculty members as well. Faculty members increasingly are able to renew themselves by participating in activities aimed at renewing their institutions. Evidence can be found in four different areas: reforming the curriculum, striking a new balance between professional and liberal education, recruiting and serving new student clienteles, and developing the faculty as a collective. Each of these will be discussed separately.

Reforming the Curriculum

There is a veritable curriculum revival taking place on the nation's college campuses. Literally hundreds of colleges and universities of all types are bent on correcting the problems that led the Carnegie Foundation for the Advancement of Teaching (1977) to declare general education a "disaster area." The problems with the general education portion of the curriculum are usually laid at the feet of students—their interest in vocational preparation has turned them away from the liberal arts, and the loose distribution requirements found at many institutions were a response to student demands for greater choice. At times, however, blame is placed on the institution for countenancing fragmented or disjointed offerings and for offering a curriculum that is the result of expedient political compromises rather than the expression of a conviction about the best education for its students. But the problem at base derives from the faculty. It is the faculty that devise, approve, teach, monitor, and alter the curriculum. If the curriculum neglects general education in favor of their specialties, if it lacks a basic educational rationale, if it fails to balance professional and liberal education, that is the result of faculty decisions.

But the good news is that if faculty are in large part the problem, they are also the key to the solution. Curriculum committees or specially designated task forces have taken the lead on campus after campus in reviewing the curriculum, fashioning broad agreements about educational principles among competing factions, bringing greater integrity and coherence to the curriculum, and overseeing the implementation and evaluation of new, usually trimmer, programs.

Curriculum revisions, always difficult to accomplish, are particularly vexing these days. This is so for several reasons. First, they must be accomplished with the existing faculty—the very ones who have benefited from the looser, fragmented one. In contrast to previous eras, reforms today cannot be accomplished by bringing in a large contingent of faculty to produce change. Second, it is difficult for faculty members, particularly senior ones, to muster much enthusiasm for yet another curriculum review. One person was heard to mutter at a conference organized by a curriculum task force, "Here we go again! This is the fourth time we've done this here." Perhaps the greatest difficulty, however, is that many colleges are in the process of reducing the size of their faculties at the very time they are seeking to forge bright and bold new instructional programs. If curriculum reform is seen as a stalking horse for retrenchment—and sometimes it is—that can doom it to a political stalemate. At best, it is a delicate process to embark on a major curriculum revision on the one hand while retrenching on the other. If it were not for the fact that so many colleges and universities have been successful in both retrenching and strengthening their curricula, one would be inclined to deny that it can be done.

The key to successful curriculum change is faculty development. The faculty can revitalize the general education of students if they are willing to learn how to do so. Part of this learning process is negative; that is, a sound contemporary curriculum cannot simply spring from the autobiographical experience of individuals. While any individual can design an ideal course of study, the trick is to get the best curriculum that all can agree to; individuals must not be so strongly adamant about curricular principles that they cannot be subjected to critical analysis, modified by new evidence, or compromised for the sake of larger goods. Those faculty who approach the curriculum task in the spirit of true believers must come to adopt a more open-minded approach that permits learning to occur.

Most of the learning, however, is positive. Members of a curriculum task force typically discover that there is an extensive and useful literature on curriculum reform. Other institutions have addressed the same problems in various and informative ways. Studies of their students, faculty, and curricular configurations are valuable, and analyses of the mission, heritage, and character of these institutions provide useful clues to effective instructional programs. The task force must educate itself and thereby become the primary resource for the education of the rest of the faculty. While most faculty who are involved in curricular change learn a lot, those who are most involved—the faculty leadership—learn the most.

Faculty development is not only essential to devising and approving a new program, it is perhaps even more critical to its implementation. Faculty must design new courses, learn new subjects, and see old subjects in a new light. Ideas for courses must be generated, refined, tried out, evaluated, and modified. Large numbers of individuals must be enticed, encouraged, or pressured into making the changes dictated by the new curriculum, sometimes after having voted against the proposed changes. This, too, is a difficult and time-consuming process, but it cannot be short-circuited. Curriculum reform, at its best, involves education rather than power politics. It involves educating the faculty and shaping their collective will rather than settling for political trade-offs among entrenched individuals and blocks.

Perhaps the most common step to strengthen the general curriculum is to emphasize writing as a generic skill. Effective writing involves far more than accurate spelling and correct grammar. It is one of the primary means by which ideas are formed, sharpened, refined, and expressed. A number of colleges are responding to this renewed emphasis on writing by requiring students to take more courses in their English departments. Yet, there is reason to question the adequacy of this solution; students who complete freshman English and do not write much for the rest of their college careers may actually regress in writing ability! Writing, like a muscle, will atrophy unless exercised repeatedly. There is a need for students to continue to write, to get critical reactions, and to revise their best efforts. For that reason many colleges and universities are adopting the approach known as "writing across the curriculum." Although there are many variations in the application of this approach, it usually requires students to do a substantial amount of writing in courses spread throughout the curriculum, whether in general education or their major fields of specialization.

DePauw University in Greencastle, Indiana, for instance, determined that all its students should have repeated experiences not only in writing but also in speaking and mathematical reasoning. The faculty established the requirement that, in addition to the usual subject matter requirements, all students would have to complete a specified number of each of these skill-intensive courses. To develop these offerings, the college assembled a small group of faculty members to determine general standards of achievement and to establish guidelines for designating a course as skill intensive. It recruited faculty members from a wide variety of academic areas who were willing to incorporate substantial writing into their courses, and held special workshops to help them. The workshops included experts on the intellectual development of college students and specialists on the design of courses, as well as subject matter scholars. The end result of combining these various perspectives was a battery of courses that carry out the intent of this portion of the curriculum. Of course, follow-up meetings, sharing of "war stories," mid-course corrections, and occasional outside consultants helped to nurture the enterprise until it was able to stand on its own.

Helping students to achieve computer literacy is another common goal in curricular revisions. It is a truism that students will be at a severe disadvantage if they are not familiar with the computer, although there is disagreement about precisely what kind of familiarity and expertise they need. At one extreme, about a dozen institutions require students to own computers. A more common pattern is to require some minimal degree of proficiency. Hamline University in St. Paul, Minnesota, for example, assumes that *all* students should (1) be familiar with the basic operations of the computer and have some knowledge of hardware, software, computer terminology, and potential applications; (2) have first-hand experience in using existing programs and applications in a few areas, such as word processing or spread sheets; and (3) consider some of the social consequences of computer usage, such as the implications for privacy, security, and societal life. A special course that has been taught by faculty members from the mathematics, education, and English departments has been developed to serve these purposes. Students who want to learn programming can take courses in BASIC and Pascal languages, but even in those courses there is a component dealing with the values and social implications of the computer.

The problem that Hamline, and most similar colleges, faced was the lack of faculty expertise. The solution that it adopted was to draw faculty from various departments, assist them in learning about computing, and shift a portion of their teaching responsibilities to computer literacy. Faculty members from the mathematics and physics departments have taught the programming courses; faculty members from education and English have taught the general literacy course; and two directors of Academic Computing have come from physics and education. A mathematician served as project director of a grant from the Exxon Education Foundation to help faculty members from throughout the college develop computing abilities and incorporate modules into their courses. Building on this foundation, the faculty approved a new requirement involving computer usage in courses beyond the first-level ones. This action builds on a literacy approach and leads to more extensive usage and more intensive study than has been possible heretofore. This pattern of evolutionary curricular change through the development of faculty is a common one.

In addition to the skills we have already discussed, curriculum revisions are incorporating substantive new knowledge. Two areas that cut across a host of academic disciplines are global perspectives and gender considerations. In the recent past, these kinds of interdisciplinary study have been concentrated in specialized programs such as area studies or women's studies. The problem with this approach is that the programs function as ghettos for the converted. The great bulk of students have no contact with these particular offerings—only those most sympathetic to, and sophisticated about, each area are drawn to them. But reports from the Association of American Colleges urge a different strategy. The association's *Toward Education with a Global Perspective* (1981) declared that "the first priority is to implant a strong international dimension into the core of general education requirements" (p. 4). It continued, "The curriculum should be expanded to introduce students particularly to non-Western cultures." Another report by the Association of American Colleges (1982) recommends "mainstreaming" women's perspectives by incorporating recent research on gender into appropriate courses.

One of the pioneers in mainstreaming women's perspectives is Wheaton College in Massachusetts. It has introduced the study of women into all courses where faculty members believe that research on women is relevant. Of course, for a faculty member to make an informed judgment about this matter he or she may have to learn more about such research, much of which is recent. In order to bring this information to the attention of faculty, the college sponsored a conference to raise key issues and suggest avenues for action. Several departments followed up by reviewing the scholarship on women in their domains, collecting and evaluating relevant materials, and developing plans to incorporate the new material into courses. An intensive workshop was later held to feature the new scholarship on women by leading scholars in various academic areas; participants were given a stipend for purchase of books and reports on feminist scholarship related to their interests. Several faculty members visited other colleges and attended special conferences; in addition, the college invited consultants to visit the campus and held a student essay contest to solicit ideas about women in the liberal arts. With the assistance of a faculty advisory committee, many faculty members are developing, testing, and evaluating new curricular materials. This approach is similar to that in which faculty members are encouraged to learn about other cultures so as to incorporate these new ideas into their courses.

A resurgence of interest in values is a central part of today's curriculum reform movement. Value education is problematic because there are no moral experts and no universal standards of judgment; furthermore, there is more than a little suspicion that teachers may inculcate some particular set of values. Yet it is apparent that while values may be purged from education, they cannot be ignored in life. The absence of explicit study of values and of the give-and-take among individuals with differing moral stances may leave students ill equipped to deal with the value conflicts they are sure to encounter in life. Several colleges are seeking to help students become aware of their own values, understand alternative value schemes, and consider the value implications of knowledge or of their own behavior. The inclusion of values is yet another attempt to restore wholeness to undergraduate education.

While there are many examples of this change, St. Andrews Presbyterian College in Laurisburg, North Carolina, is particularly illuminative. It has instituted a new two-semester senior requirement called "Human Choice and Global Issues." This consists of interdisciplinary courses that provide students with an opportunity to effect a synthesis of skills, knowledge, and values, and it thus serves as a kind of practicum in decision making. The first semester focuses on a series of situations in which decisions are within the students' immediate realms of control or influence—personal, family, or community issues. The second semester focuses on national and global issues, such as world hunger, international terrorism, or nuclear weaponry. In order to reflect the multiplicity of legitimate perspectives on any of these issues, the course is taught by open-ended methods, such as simulations or the case method. But how to staff such a course? St. Andrews adopted, as a part of its new curriculum, a staffing policy that affirms the obligation of *all* faculty to teach in the general education program. Each faculty member normally teaches one course in the core, such as the course described, as well as one more in the breadth component. The college provides special assistance for those faculty members teaching "Human Choices," including opportunities to share the planning of the specific issues to include in the course, resources for understanding various aspects of each, and training in using the case method of instruction.

The final illustration about the application of faculty development to achieve curricular change pertains to the development of integrative learning. One of the main problems with the undergraduate curriculum is its fragmented—even disjointed—quality, and many colleges have sought to foster greater coherence through such mechanisms as freshman seminars, upper-division interdisciplinary courses, and senior capstone courses. Whatever the specific mechanism, all must come to grips with the dictum of Jonathan Smith, former dean of the college at the University of Chicago: "Students should not be expected to integrate anything the faculty can't or won't." The simple truth is that integration of knowledge among students is not likely to occur unless it is structured as a central portion of the curriculum and modeled by the faculty. How can that be accomplished, particularly among faculty who are above all specialists?

One answer to that question is provided by Pacific Lutheran University in Tacoma, Washington. Dissatisfied with a curriculum revision process that simply made modest changes in a distribution scheme, faculty members organized to see if they could devise an integrated, alternative way of meeting these requirements. A group of thirty-two participated in summer workshops that were described by the faculty director as an "exercise in creative humiliation. . . . we learned to understand each other's jargon, share concerns about our teaching more openly, and learn from carefully chosen consultants some of the existing options for interdisciplinary curricular structure and teaching methods. Trust levels and cooperative behavior were heightened. Participation in these workshops was linked to the creation of team-taught minicourses immediately following the workshops, using the information and skills [gained] in the week-long experience. The reinforcements thus provided gave faculty some confidence in attempting new instructional techniques and evaluative reaction from hundreds of students. The experience was thoroughly successful because faculty development was tied to specific tasks of curricular change" (Huber, 1977, pp. 160–161). Eventually a set of four sequences, each with two interdisciplinary courses, were devised for what is formally called the Integrated Studies Program but is known among students as the "hard core." This program has involved nearly half the faculty since its inception, and it has undergone dynamic revision in light of changing intellectual interests of the students and participants. But one thing remains firm: All new faculty must participate in an interdisciplinary workshop prior to teaching in the program. The reason? "Far from being a 'frill' or 'fad,' we have found this kind of in-service learning and sharing among peers to be one of the most potent methods of dissolving the national and institutional barriers to educational integrity and coherence" (Huber, 1977, pp. 160–161). Here is a fitting conclusion to this discussion: The many techniques of faculty development can be applied to change the curriculum. Indeed, efforts to change the curriculum without conscious attention to the development of faculty have dubious prospects.

Redefining Liberal and Professional Education

A quiet revolution has taken place on college campuses during the last fifteen to twenty years, namely, the shift in balance of power from the liberal arts to the professional fields. Historically, the liberal arts faculty were the dominant force; and although they prepared graduates to enter the established professions of clergy, law, teaching, and medicine, they did not take too kindly to less traditional professions. Liberal education was regarded by many as morally superior to professional education, which tended to take a more narrow focus, to place more stress on technique and applications at the expense of ideas and theory, and to prepare graduates for specific jobs. This ideology was guarded by faculty members in the arts and sciences, and they held a comfortable majority. Students enrolled in liberal arts disciplines tended to be both more numerous and more able, at least as defined by the usual measures of grades and test results. The primary connections between these separate faculty cultures occurred when the liberal arts disciplines provided "service" courses to students studying in such practical fields as business, engineering, or agriculture.

In recent years these categories have become jumbled, even reversed. Students have spurned the liberal arts for professional courses of study; they have left English for journalism, economics for business, and biology for nursing and a host of new allied health fields. New specialized programs were created to provide education for a variety of occupations, and the faculty members who were hired to staff them have become the new majorities on many campuses. Students in some of the newer fields are not only more numerous than in the liberal arts but also of better quality; they see more opportunities to exercise their intellects and imaginations in the professions than in academic disciplines and careers. In many instances the professions are now providing "service" courses for liberal arts majors; institutions as different as the University of Maryland and Hamline University offer concentrations of business courses for students with liberal arts majors. In short, faculties are in the process of redefining the understandings and relationships between liberal and professional education.

On the one hand, for example, the professions are increasingly coming to see that a liberal education is a necessary ingredient to the effective practice of law, medicine, and so on. An official from the National Institute for the Humanities has commented that it recently had awarded more grants for professional ethics programs than for any other kind. Courses in business ethics, medical ethics, legal ethics, and journalism ethics are all becoming an integral part of professional education. Similarly, courses dealing with at least the rudiments of history, social institutions, professional relationships with clients, and the like are being inserted into many professional training programs. The University of Minnesota College of Business Administration recently increased the number of liberal arts courses it requires from ten to nineteen. These include five courses in written and oral communication, three in mathematics, two in science, three dealing with the individual and society, three in language, literature, and artistic expression, and three in international issues and cultures. The program aspires to produce a broadly educated manager who can adapt to changing circumstances. Rather than produce what the former dean David Lilly calls "narrow-gauged number crunchers," the new program, it is hoped, will yield graduates who can take the long view and provide the leadership to keep businesses productive and vital.

On the other hand, however, just as the professions are reaching toward the liberal arts, many of those involved in the liberal arts are making bridges to the workplace. Thus, several studies have confirmed the practical value of the liberal arts by showing that they provide, if not training for a single job, a broad base of preparation for many jobs. This conclusion is documented by alumni studies (Bisconti, 1980), studies of elements in career success (Beck, 1981), economic analysis of human capital investment (Mohrman, 1983; Bowen, 1977), surveys of employers (Warren, 1983), and testimony from chief executive officers, politicians and other leaders. All these studies confirm the practicality of the liberal arts. The goals of a liberal education—effective writing and speaking, critical thinking, problem solving, the ability to work independently, getting along with other people—are, in large part, career-related skills. In this sense, all the curriculum revisions discussed earlier are part and parcel of enhancing the career relevance of the liberal arts.

A second aspect of the matter is that some liberal arts colleges are now doing more to make connections with the world of work. Experiential learning, service learning, internships, practicums, travel study programs—these are all steps taken by some institutions to give students an opportunity to make connections between the classroom and the workplace. Humanities internships were a pioneering venture when established by Scripps College about a decade ago, but now many other colleges have some version of this mode of learning.

Yet a third major initiative by some liberal arts colleges is to strengthen their career counseling and placement operations. Liberal arts graduates generally require longer to locate the first job than do their professional counterparts, their first jobs are likely to fall considerably short of what they may have been expecting, and they may have to make two or more moves in order to locate positions that are challenging and rewarding. But soon the advancement opportunities for liberal arts graduates surpass, on the average, those of more narrowly trained individuals. This means that students need more career counseling and assistance to get established in the workplace. Institutions as varied as Carleton College and Montana State University are seeking to balance careers and liberal learning in this fashion. The upshot of all this is that the relationship between liberal and professional education, as well as between liberal education and careers, is being redefined. On the basis of what is happening at a number of pioneering institutions, this process of redefinition will be a long one, but it will probably bring all three areas closer together than they have ever been. Here, as elsewhere, faculty development is a key in effecting changes.

Recruiting and Serving New Student Clienteles

Changing demographics are causing major shifts in the clientele of many colleges and universities. Unless an institution happens to be one of the few that do not face declining enrollments, it is no doubt trying to determine just how to adapt. There are only a few options. One is to do nothing and simply react to whatever changing enrollments may bring and reduce programs and staff accordingly. Although this approach has few serious defenders, it is the route adopted de facto by many institutions in that they have not taken positive steps to devise an alternative. A second approach is the one discussed earlier, namely, to establish educational priorities, create a new vision for the institution, revitalize its instructional program, and charge ahead with confidence and enthusiasm. The disadvantage of this approach is that it takes vigorous and farsighted leadership, a leap of faith, and enormous amounts of energy to change a college's direction. The success stories discussed in this volume stand out from the crowd precisely because they are among the minority who have managed to pull off this kind of institutional renewal.

Recruiting and serving a new clientele are not easy solutions, but they are the directions taken by still other colleges. Several colleges have added vocational programs that are designed to appeal to today's career-minded student body. These range from medical and dental technology through all the business specialities, including computer-related fields. Although institutions usually hire new faculty with credentials in the vocational fields being added, these faculty are often supplemented by some who retrain from related specializations. More than one small college has found itself transformed almost overnight from essentially a liberal arts college to a trade school with a liberal arts emphasis. The resulting conflicts among faculty and staff over educational philosophies, political views, professional activities, and social relationships can be monumental. To accomplish such a shift without tearing apart the fabric of the college requires a great deal of attention to faculty and staff development. If faculty and staff are not strong proponents of the change at the outset, they will have to get behind it after the fact. If not, the institution will suffer a split that may never heal.

Other colleges are seeking to fill their classes by reducing admission standards. In Minnesota 52 percent of the high school students go on to some form of postsecondary education, but these come mostly from the upper portions of their graduating classes. If colleges are to expand the college-going rate among traditional age youth, they will have to recruit increasingly from the lower ranks. And, in fact, this is why the ability levels of entering students have declined in many institutions. One state university with an aggressive recruiting effort found 20 percent of its entering freshmen writing at the ninth-grade level or below. This poses enormous challenges to provide effective instruction at the college level. Of course, open admissions institutions, such as community colleges, have been dealing with this problem for some time. Institutions can educate low-ability students, but special steps are needed if the open door is not to become a revolving door. The faculty and staff must play positive roles if students who have not succeeded in schools in the past are to succeed in the future.

Some colleges offer special orientation and support services to high-risk students. Others have established learning resource centers, where students may secure assistance with writing, mathematics, study skills, tutoring, counseling, and other problems. Some have established "early warning systems" to identify academic problems when they have the best chance of being resolved. In addition, workshops are held on cognitive styles to help faculty members adapt lessons to students through use of more concrete and specific reasoning styles, and theories of student development are discussed. All these steps help faculty and staff understand the needs of those underprepared for college-level work and take steps to give such students a fighting chance.

Unless there is a comprehensive approach to adapting institutional practices to the new clientele, however, the chances of success are not great. Miami-Dade Community College has launched a massive program to raise its educational standards as a necessary step to keep the open door open. All new students take placement tests in reading, writing, and computation. Those who fail—about 60 percent of the freshmen—must take noncredit courses in basic skills. Further, students who earn below a 1.5 grade point average are either put on probation or suspended. Students on probation may take only a limited number of courses, and they must take one "intervention" course in remedial studies, study skills, or career counseling. Suspended students may return to college on probation after one term; if their grades are still not satisfactory, they are dismissed for at least a year. Further, the curriculum requires all students to take five specially designed interdisciplinary courses as part of their studies. These practices are noteworthy in that students are expected to perform at a desired level; and the college, the faculty, and staff are committed to helping students achieve at that level.

Finally, other colleges have tapped the growing adult education market. Whether by enrolling adults in regular courses, offering special courses in the late afternoon or evening hours, expanding a continuing education college or program, creating a new entity such as Memphis State's New College, establishing special weekend or evening colleges, or mounting off-campus programs, many colleges are seeking to make up for the loss of traditional age students with older adults. For many it is working. Indeed, it sometimes works so well that the new population changes the character and tone of the college.

As anyone who has taught adults knows, they are a different breed of student. They have much more life experience than eighteen-year-olds and are eager to share it. They have many demands on their time from job, family, and community involvements, and they have high expectations for their educational investments. They are used to dealing with institutions and may be expected to express criticisms if they are dissatisfied. They may have specific goals in mind, such as improving their work skills, that are more practical than those of their younger counterparts; they may be less patient with theoretical or abstract ideas that do not apply to their circumstances. Faculty members must be cognizant of these differences and prepared to offer adults the brand of education they need and want. In the Twin Cities new weekend colleges at the College of St. Catherine and Augsburg College are growing at a rapid rate; as is New College at the College of St. Thomas. At least a portion of the success of these endeavors can be attributed to the selection and training of faculty members to deal with this new constituency.

Developing the Faculty as a Collective

The foregoing discussion rests on the assumption that development of individual faculty members or particular groups of them can renew a college or university. As valuable as these individual approaches may be, however, they are not sufficient to meet the challenges facing many institutions of higher learning today. The vitality of the faculty as a collective is assuming greater importance. Hence, additional concepts and strategies are being developed to preserve vitality in college faculties during a time of retrenchment.

A college facing a declining enrollment future has several needs. It must come to grips with the difficult issue of *reducing the scale* of its faculty. Since even the best forecasting models are not very reliable, a college must *maintain flexibility* in its staffing pattern, so that it can adjust in the case of greater than expected drops in enrollment. Because there is a graying of the faculties in many institutions, leaders must try to *achieve a balance* between senior and junior members. And because faculty are often overconcentrated in fields of declining student interest, colleges must be ready to *shift resources* to fields of high student demand. Neither faculty development concepts deriving from professional development, instructional improvement, and organizational effectiveness nor their particular applications in curriculum revision, realignment of professional and liberal education, or development of programs for new clientele are of much help in shaping the structure of a faculty. But additional concepts and strategies to address these needs are being developed by academic and financial administrators as well as by faculty leaders.

What are some of the means used to meet these goals? One of the most difficult tasks is coming to grips with the realization that the college will have to reduce the size of the faculty. A number of avoidance mechanisms are typically used to delay the day of reckoning: "We may be able to buck the enrollment trend." "Last year's drop was less than we thought, so we may get by without cuts." "This faculty works hard, and we can't reduce it." "We have cut as much as possible without destroying the instructional program." Despite these and other rationalizations, many institutions have already been forced to face the reality of reduced enrollments and/or reduced state appropriations. Almost all institutions will have to make hard decisions, and the only questions are when and how they will come to grips with the problem.

Three guidelines for dealing with reduction in scale are quite clear. Experts agree on a number of fundamentals (Mortimer, Bagshaw, and Masland, 1985; Bowen and Glenny, 1981), and several institutions have put them into effect. First, it is better to anticipate the issue and to engage in hardheaded planning than to be brought up short and forced to deal with a serious problem in a crisis atmosphere. The longer one waits, the more one's options are limited. Second, although across-the-board actions (hiring freezes, spending freezes, reductions in staff and program budgets) are the easiest to impose, they are the least likely to position the institution well for the future. They weaken all portions of the institution indiscriminately; and since retrenchment is expected to be the order of the day for a decade, they will force an institution to make even harder decisions in the future when all of its units will be weaker. The recommended way is to make selective reductions in areas that are least essential to the long-term health of the institution. Third, it is difficult if not impossible to make personnel decisions apart from a consideration of their impact on instructional programs. It is preferable to review programs and to establish priorities as a part of the retrenchment activity. Despite the growing agreement on these principles, however, they are often violated in practice.

Achieving flexibility in faculty staffing is as important as it is difficult to effect in institutions that are becoming "tenured in." Mortimer, Bagshaw, and Caruso (1985) report from their study of chief academic officers that tenure limits exist at over a quarter of both private and public institutions. Sixty percent of the private and 71 percent of the public institutions reportedly raised standards for achieving tenure within the last five years. Institutions adopt these strategies to preserve whatever flexibility in faculty staffing they may possess. Also, institutions increasingly employ term contracts to permit them to adjust to an uncertain future. And there is a greater use of part-time faculty at some colleges to fill gaps without long-term personnel commitments. But all these measures have unfortunate effects: They reduce the stability of the faculty, weaken the commitment of faculty to the institution by making their employment status less permanent, and foster a greater degree of turnover. However, these disadvantages may still be better than the alternatives, especially if the majority of the faculty can gain a greater sense of security and confidence in the welfare of the college.

Because many faculties are tilted toward the upper ranks and there is little mobility, it is difficult to secure new blood. Sometimes cutbacks are concentrated among the young, untenured faculty whose salaries are relatively low; thus, the savings gained by terminating a position at that level are reduced. A set of related mechanisms are therefore coming into play to create openings among senior tenured faculty. These rely on inducement strategies except in those cases where colleges are willing to simply lay off tenured faculty by claiming financial exigency or at least emergency. Early retirement is one such device that offers faculty members the opportunity to depart before the legal retirement age of 70. Such programs may offer severance pay, continued contributions to the retirement fund, payment of Social Security, and continuation of health benefits and other perquisites. Some faculty members prefer to enter retirement gradually, and colleges are making it possible for them to decrease their work loads without suffering a loss of retirement benefits. Some institutions prefer a more direct approach and offer to buy out the contracts of selected faculty; Michigan State University in 1981 reached such an agreement with approximately 100 tenured faculty members. These strategies may be hard to implement because of the substantial initial costs, but over a short period of time they pay handsome dividends in financial terms, to say nothing of the gains in educational and human terms. Often these devices permit individuals to get out of situations in which they feel trapped, and they often create a better balance in faculty ranks.

It is necessary for many institutions to find ways to shift faculty resources from areas of declining student interest, such as the arts and humanities, to areas of high demand—for example, business administration and computer studies. Retraining is one obvious strategy, although more difficult and less successful than one might at first expect. Retraining is most successful when it involves a move to an adjacent field, from mathematics to computer science, for instance, rather than from music to sociology. (Unfortunately it is often the weak instructor who is offered retraining, and there is little reason to think that he will be more effective in a secondary field that he knows even less well than his primary one.) But even if this device is limited in the numbers of faculty members affected, it can be a useful element in an overall program. Another approach is to assign faculty members from one department to teach in certain other departmental or interdepartmental programs. For example, Hamline University assigns certain faculty members in foreign languages to teach freshman English sections, and a new freshman seminar program offers the opportunity for faculty in undersubscribed departments to teach in it. Introductions of more flexible assignments can enhance what sociologist Rosabeth Kantor calls the "opportunity structure" on a campus;

these possibilities are limited only by the imagination and capabilities of the individuals involved.

Some institutions also have programs that allow faculty to explore careers beyond the campus. As already noted, midlife crises are common, even among successful faculty members, when they realize that they have many more years of the same job to look forward to. Yet it is difficult for a faculty member to abandon the security of his or her present position and chart a new direction. Thus, some colleges are assisting faculty members with career counseling and are helping them to locate short-term employment opportunities and explore alternative careers. The college may guarantee that a faculty member's position will remain open if, after a trial period, the alternative does not work out; it may supplement the faculty member's salary during the leave; and it may keep benefits such as health insurance and retirement contributions in place.

In conclusion, faculty development is one of the keys to renewing both individual faculty members and the institutions of which they are a part. Indeed, it can lead to a fundamental reassessment of the relationship between individuals and institutions. Many faculty may feel that they are pitted against their college and that they need to be better supported, but faculty development may help them realize that their own welfare depends on a strong and successful institution. Similarly, leaders of institutions sometimes act as though people don't matter, and faculty development may help them realize that the institution can be only as strong as its faculty and staff. The self-interests of both individual faculty members and colleges and universities are intimately intertwined, and some institutions have managed to restore this sense of mutuality, in spite of—perhaps because of—hard times.

The example of Furman University in South Carolina may illustrate the point. During the period from 1975 to 1978 the university launched a process of institutional planning that involved all departments in making analyses and preparing long-term plans. Near the conclusion of that work the university established programs for the development of midcareer and younger faculty members. The faculty development programs were designed by faculty members and implemented primarily by means of a faculty steering committee. The midcareer faculty were asked to prepare plans for their professional growth, within the context of future plans for the university and the various departments. Individuals made analyses of their strengths, weaknesses, opportunities, and threats. They then proposed specific plans to foster their own growth; and requested support to carry out these plans. The steering committee reviewed the proposals and funded them wholly or partially. The program for young faculty was designed to better orient them to the teaching profession and to acclimate them to the university. The new faculty were paired with senior colleagues and worked on a variety of mentor-novice projects dealing with instruction. A cadre of faculty in-house consultants was selected and trained on a variety of teaching concerns, such as applied learning theory, teaching methods, and classroom observation and feedback. The university sponsored a series of lectures, seminars, and workshops on topics of common concern and made small grants available to assist individuals in improving aspects of their instruction. An evaluation of the faculty development program, which was funded by grants, was very favorable, and the faculty came to expect that the university would provide funding to continue the program. The president made a commitment to secure an endowment for this purpose, and the program continues with some modification today. The professional development of faculty and the long-range planning of the university go on hand in glove, and Furman is in a good position to take on the hard times that are ahead. It is a lesson that other institutions should not neglect.

References

Association of American Colleges. *Toward Education with a Global Perspective.* Washington, D.C.: Association of American Colleges, 1981.

Association of American Colleges. *Liberal Education and the New Scholarship on Women.* Washington, D.C.: Association of American Colleges, 1982.

Beck, R. E. *Career Patterns: The Liberal Arts Major in Bell System Management.* Washington, D.C.: Association of American Colleges, 1981.

Bisconti, A. S. *College and Other Stepping Stones: A Study of Learning Experiences that Contribute to Effective Performance in Early and Long-Run Jobs.* Bethlehem, Pa.: The CPC Foundation, 1980.

Bowen, F. M., and Glenny, L. A. "The California Study." In L. Leslie and J. Hyatt (eds.), *Higher Education Financial Policies: States' Institutions and Their Interactions.* Tucson: Center for the Study of Higher Education, University of Arizona, 1981.

Bowen, H. R. *Investment in Learning: The Individual and Social Value of American Higher Education.* San Francisco: Jossey-Bass, 1977.

Carnegie Foundation for the Advancement of Teaching. *Missions of the College Curriculum: A Contemporary Review with Suggestions.* San Francisco: Jossey-Bass, 1977.

Clark, S. M., and Lewis, D. R. (eds.). *Faculty Vitality and Institutional Productivity.* New York: Teachers College Press, 1985.

Gaff, J. G. *Toward Faculty Renewal: Advances in Faculty, Instructional, and Organizational Development.* San Francisco: Jossey-Bass, 1975.

Gaff, J. G., and Justice, D. O. "Faculty Development Yesterday, Today, and Tomorrow." In J. Gaff (ed.), *Institutional Renewal Through the Improvement of Teaching.* New Directions for Higher Education, no. 24. San Francisco: Jossey-Bass, 1978.

Group for Human Development in Higher Education. *Faculty Development in a Time of Retrenchment.* New Rochelle, N.Y.: Change Magazine Press, 1974.

Huber, C. E. "The Dynamics of Change: A Core Humanities Program." *Liberal Education,* May 1977, pp. 159–170.

Mohrman, K. "Liberal Learning Is a Sound Human Capital Investment." *Educational Record,* Fall 1983, pp. 56–61.

Mortimer, K. P., Bagshaw, M., and Caruso, A. *Academic Reallocation: A National Profile.* University Park: Center for the

Study of Higher Education, Pennsylvania State University, 1985.

Mortimer, K. P., Bagshaw, M., and Masland, A. *Flexibility in Academic Staffing.* ASHE-ERIC Research Report No. 1. Washington, D.C.: Clearinghouse on Higher Education, George Washington University, 1985.

Nelsen, W. C., and Siegel, M. E. *Effective Approaches to Faculty Development.* Washington, D.C.: Association of American Colleges, 1980.

U.S. Department of Labor. *Occupational Outlook Handbook.* Washington, D.C.: U.S. Government Printing Office, 1984.

Warren, R. G. *New Links Between General Education and Business Careers.* Washington, D.C.: Association of American Colleges, 1983.

8

Students: A Thoughtful Approach to Recruitment and Retention

Richard Moll

A close friend of mine is one of several vice-presidents of a major American corporation. As a result, he drives a very large and sedately gaudy Oldsmobile. "Big Buicks and big Oldsmobiles are the image-level cars of our vice-presidents," he tells me. "I wouldn't dare enter the parking lot with a Cadillac or a Mercedes unless I was in the top executive office. This car-level concept, of course, filters down. You don't sport a new Thunderbird if you are a Chevrolet-level worker."

We can sigh with dismay at this story, but it is not news that America is image conscious and image driven at every turn. The true and proven quality of a product or even of an institution of higher learning often plays a subordinate role to image when a choice must be made by a buyer, a client, or a student. In higher education, at any rate, this notion is confirmed each May by high school seniors across the land who pick colleges

164

and universities that are not necessarily the best for their individual needs but are, instead, the most prestigious of the colleges admitting them. One does not turn down Harvard to attend Bucknell, one does not turn down Bucknell to attend Allegheny—and so it goes, even though Bucknell and/or Allegheny might be the better match for the individual student who needs a particular major or a certain campus environment or a special form of personalized college training.

In undertaking research recently on public colleges and universities, I was surprised to find students so very unhappy at some of the most famous state universities in America. But almost all said they would not dream of transferring, despite their unhappiness, for fear of the repercussions of forgoing the diploma of a famous-name institution. They seemed convinced that their own happiness and satisfaction were not so important as the prospect of holding a prestigious degree when entering the job marketplace or applying to graduate school. "Image" was considered all-important.

Oddly enough, however, the public image of a college or university often does not match the self-perceived mission of the institution. This should cause alarm in the public relations office, not to mention among the faculty committees that endlessly discuss and debate the college's central mission—provided, of course, that they are even aware of the inconsistency. Consider Vassar, for example, where I worked as director of admissions in the late seventies. Much of the nation still thinks of Vassar in terms of parasols and white gloves and as a school that caters to a female social elite. Even though Vassar has been coeducational for nearly twenty years and is now 40 percent male, the public still giggles when a male appears in a Vassar T-shirt. Few people know of Vassar's historic involvement in social action, particularly in feminist movements, nor is there general awareness of its high academic standards and program flexibility. In other words, the public is little aware of Vassar's *self*-perceived mission.

Once a public image has been established in America, it remains set unless there is an ambitious, self-conscious campaign to change it. A college has to face this phenomenon squarely and approach public relations accordingly. For some colleges, of course, image versus mission is not a problem, but for a multitude of others it is. For the latter, both admissions and student retention can suffer because a college's level of self-confidence is closely related to its image. Image affects the morale of the faculty, of the administration, and certainly of the student body. If an institution is publicly perceived to be "in trouble" for financial reasons or because of internal disputes or poor leadership, prospective students and their parents will beware. And the same is true for students already enrolled; going home for Thanksgiving or Christmas vacation only to hear negative comments about one's home institution raises doubts that often translate into thoughts of transferring to another school.

None of the consequences of a particular image need be permanent, however. More important, an institutional image itself need not be permanent. But far too often internal disputes over an institution's mission consume faculty, administrative, and student energy, while its external image is completely (and naively) overlooked. Since the outsider's view of a college or university can mean more to institutional health than internal perceptions and priorities, someone must jar the institution into a recognition of reality. Often the responsibility for this falls by default to the admissions office. But that responsibility, given all its potentially uncomfortable consequences, is too often carefully avoided by the admissions director and, therefore, by the institution as a whole.

The admissions office is the voice of the institution to the public, particularly to the huge quasi-sophisticated public that often invents and sets images. The admissions office also has the opportunity to bring back to the campus messages of institutional image, good or bad, that have been received. Serving as the eyes and ears of the college is obviously not the end of the admissions office's mission regarding public perceptions. It must also chart a plan to alter any off-the-mark images that may exist. Recruiting a student body offers an excellent means of accomplishing the aims of such a plan.

Recruiting Students: Some Guidelines

"Recruitment" has a bad name. The army and navy can do it, but a good college or university should not have to. Well, that concept affronts history. Some of the institutions that are strongest today in image, admissions, health and student retention have been quietly and effectively recruiting for years. Harvard provides a good example. I remember starting an ambitious student recruitment effort at Bowdoin College in Maine in the late sixties. We first targeted the state of Maine itself and found, to our alarm, that it would be very costly and difficult to match Harvard's extensive recruitment in that large but underpopulated area. Obviously, Harvard was not recruiting because it needed more students or more able students. Instead, the nation's oldest college was aggressively spreading the word that one need not be at the top of the social ladder or valedictorian of one's high school class to think of going to Harvard. The institution was interested in diversifying its student body geographically, socioeconomically, and ethnically, as well as in academic majors. And Harvard, be it noted, launched this extensive recruiting effort years ago. Other Ivy League institutions have followed suit, but rarely as aggressively as Harvard.

On the other side of the fence, the so-called Seven Sisters thought that "recruitment" was a dirty word and have condescended to engage in that activity only very recently. Their student bodies show the result. Although these seven eastern colleges remain quite selective and deserve their superb reputations, they have had more difficulty than their brothers in the Ivy League in shedding old elitist images and diversifying their freshman classes. Had their admissions efforts not been essentially restricted to girls' private schools and affluent suburban high schools, the results for them in this era of demographic change might have been decidedly different. Given predictions for a sharply declining college-going population in America between now and the mid 1990s, no institution can afford to bypass serious consideration of its public image, and all must begin to practice creative recruitment. The two march hand in hand.

A recruitment campaign, however, cannot be conceived and launched by the admissions office alone. It must be a cooperative effort shared by the entire college family, with approval and enthusiastic support from above. The top authorities of the institution must acknowledge the need for and importance of a strong recruitment effort. And support from the top cannot be just a matter of encouraging words; money and manpower must be allocated for the effort. The various branches of the university family can then be made aware of the campaign and become involved in its planning.

A few comments regarding my current institution, the University of California at Santa Cruz (UCSC), seem appropriate here. UCSC was born in the mid 1960s, and achieved overnight enrollment success. It enjoyed instant prestige because of its University of California label, its choice to remain small and to emphasize undergraduate study, and its incorporation of the educational idiosyncrasies of the times: no grades, flexibility, academic experimentation, personal freedom. While that mission and image were right for that particular moment in history, the American public soured on this liberal concept within a decade. After the university experienced an alarming drop in applications and freshman enrollment, a new chancellor decided that considerably more resources must be allocated to the admissions effort. An aggressive national search was launched for an admissions dean, a new admissions office near the front of the campus was opened, tour buses were purchased, and the publication budget was greatly increased, as was staff for all areas of the campaign.

Soon after arriving in Santa Cruz as the new dean of admissions, I assembled representatives of the administration, the faculty, the public relations office, the alumni, and the student body to discuss the disparity between the university's mission and its image. Public perception of UCSC has clearly grown out of line with the self-perceived mission of the institution. It was decided that we could only convince the public of the focal points of our institutional mission by emphasizing the school's basic attributes, so we settled on six words that captured the Santa Cruz story: "undergraduate" (93 percent), "hybrid" (of public resources and private tone), "atmosphere" (created by the spectacular coastal location and the residential college system), "traditional" (the liberal arts program), "rigorous" (required comprehensive exam or honors project) and "selective." These basic UCSC concepts have now been repeatedly drummed into the ears of prospective students, their parents, and their high school counselors. Happily, tangible results are apparent in both the size of the applicant pool and what one hears in the rumor mill.

Our experience at UCSC suggests that an effective way to launch a new student recruitment effort is through a three-day retreat off campus. All groups can enter the discussion of institutional mission versus public perception, agreeing on the institution's basic tenets and assessing how far the public is from recognizing them. The admissions professionals can then outline a campaign to translate the reality of the institution to the public, and the program is under way. But all parties must realize that the effort *must* get launched—it cannot wait until every member of the staff, faculty, and alumni has totally agreed on the finer points of the mission. There comes a time when the external admissions effort cannot wait for unanimity to be achieved at home. (The admissions office can and must play a key role in bringing about near-consensus among members of the university family.)

Planning strategies for the recruitment campaign need not rely solely on internal resources. Successful admissions directors in the nation are often available as consultants, and there is a growing library of articles and books on marketing and student recruitment. Some important contributors in the field to date are John Maguire, recently dean of admissions at Boston College; William Ihlanfeldt, an experienced admissions director and now vice-president of Northwestern University; and William Elliott, vice-president of Carnegie-Mellon University of Pittsburgh. Reports of the College Entrance Examination Board, as well as the American College Testing seminars on marketing and recruitment, are particularly helpful.

Publications, of course, play a key role in the recruitment effort and in altering an institution's image. Today, with too

many zealous admissions officers badgering students in the cor-
ridors of high schools, school authorities are becoming more
and more reluctant to pull students from classes to attend college information sessions. There is, as a consequence, a greater
recruitment effort through the mails. And, although a "viewbook" or catalogue may never prove as persuasive as a role-
model representative of an institution, admissions publications
today are of key importance.

At the same time, however, it is politically painful to create admissions literature on campus because there is rarely more
vigorous argumentation and posturing within the college family
than in the preparation of an admissions viewbook that sym-
bolizes a statement of, and commitment to, institutional mission. Many admissions directors thus find it more comfortable
to assign the task to an outsider; and, happily, the result is often
a publication that is fresh, imaginative, and objective. Using an
outsider, institutional staff and faculty and students can still
have their say: Representatives of the college promotional company visit the campus to conduct extensive interviews, to attend classes, and to try to understand the campus "tone." While
the writing may be done miles away from the institution,
themes are made publicly appealing, graphically interesting, and
are sent for final approval to appropriate campus committees
and individuals. For institutional peace of mind, this seems to
me the best course to follow. Perhaps there are institutions
whose members would find this exercise a joy and who can put
forward their cause in writing and graphics with professional
flair. But beware: The market is very competitive, and a good
student may receive cartons of college mailings late in the junior
year and early in the senior year of high school. To be noticed,
an institution's mailing must be dramatically appealing, honest,
and persuasive.

Once the new publications are in production, the college
family must organize itself for the opening of the campaign.
First, the admissions staff. Although all admissions staff members will be expected to make presentations to students and parents on campus and to visit secondary schools, each should also
have a special area of responsibility. For example, one can oversee the alumni/admissions effort; another might organize the

admissions/secondary school activities (the scheduling of school visits, special seminars or lectures for counselors and students, campaigns to attract outstanding scholars, and so on); another can be assigned on-campus admissions activities such as tours and interviewing programs that include periodic group informational sessions and seminars with faculty. A larger staff can, of course, become much more specialized, but the areas mentioned are basic ones.

All other units of the college family must also be organized for the admissions effort, while recognizing that each group has its own assets and liabilities.

1. *The faculty.* Faculty members are often distrustful of admissions officers and feel that they themselves could accomplish the enrollment job while ensuring that academic respectability is at the same time kept intact. Although their ideas regarding admissions are always well intentioned and articulately expressed, faculty members sometimes have problems translating words into practice. Too often faculty do not know the full institution as well as they know their own discipline and department; too often faculty offer to travel and volunteer time beyond what proves to be realistically possible; too often faculty are out-of-touch with the basic public relations approaches that are effective with parents; and faculty too often are fearful of "popularizing" the institutions's serious message, not acknowledging that many in the prospective admissions audience read *Reader's Digest* rather than *Harper's*.

In my view, faculty members can best serve as on campus consultants for outstanding student prospects who are interested in particular disciplines. They can also serve as speakers at special seminars for prospective students and parents when accompanied by admissions officers who can make certain that the faculty message is complementary to, and consistent with, the admissions campaign. It is the faculty, of course, who set admissions policy through faculty admissions committees, and I believe that faculty are best used at this policy-making level. Their performance as recruiters is too erratic and unpredictable for assured success. They can click with the unusual student, but often not with the group.

2. *Alumni.* Alumni are invaluable to a strong admissions

recruitment campaign, provided they are not given a completely free hand. Their zeal to assist their alma mater is frequently unmatched but should not go unchecked. Too often alumni are quite willing to share the good news regarding the college they attended rather than the college that exists today. Indeed, the institution may have changed considerably since the year they graduated from it. Alumni enthusiasm is taken more seriously by candidates and parents than the alumni themselves often realize. As a result, the alumnus or alumna must be prepared to say, "I don't know," if indeed he or she doesn't know what the faculty-student ratio is, what computer facilities are available, what fraternity and sorority life is now like, and so on.

Now that a cautionary word has been introduced, it is important to underscore the positive contribution that well-organized alumni groups can make to the admissions effort. Once again, some of the Ivy League colleges can be role models for us all. The Brown, Dartmouth, and Yale alumni, among others, are marvelously well organized to assist the admissions cause. And so are some of the alumni groups at the larger, more prestigious state universities: the University of Michigan and the University of California at Los Angeles, for example. A professional admissions team can come to town like a Billy Graham evangelism movement, stirring up emotions and presenting the good news, but too often it must leave before student commitments are made. At this point alumni can enter and be irreplaceable in their effectiveness. If alumni can remain in contact with local students after admissions officers leave town by giving receptions or making goodwill follow-up phone calls, everyone gains: The family of the candidate feels the university "cares," and the university is gaining a new loyalty. But a fine line must be drawn. Some alumni are overzealous in their campaigning, and turn students and parents off. Again, training can help alumni learn how to draw the line between recruiting and pressuring candidates.

The institution that can afford it should bring key alumni recruiters to campus at least every other year. (Often these alumni will be willing to pay for transportation themselves if the university or college picks up the other costs.) Once on campus, these recruiters can attend classes, meet professors and staff at receptions, and examine "test" admissions cases with the professional admissions staff. The key recruiter can return home and convey the news to other alumni volunteers, and the campaign is off to an honest, well-informed start. One of the most effective contributions the alumni can make is follow-up on students who have just been admitted and must make up their minds which college to attend. Often this is a difficult choice for a student and his or her family. A simple human gesture by an alumnus—a phone call or home visit—can make all the difference in the final decision. Every strong admissions recruitment campaign needs the cooperation of well-organized and well-informed alumni in the field.

3. *Parents.* At UCSC, we are not old enough to have many well-established alumni with permanent addresses. Although we are getting a fledgling alumni support group started for admissions, we have also turned to parents of current students. We are finding that parents are not only enthusiastic but extremely well-informed regarding the institution as it is today. They carry little emotional baggage regarding alma mater "as it was" and somehow feel that their own child is well placed if they can convince other students to become enthusiastic about the same institution. Parents of current students are the most underutilized members of the college family in today's recruiting efforts, but they can be a most valuable resource.

4. *Students.* Undergraduates have a credibility that others of the college family do not have. Prospective students naturally identify with young people of their own age and station. If currently enrolled undergraduates are interested in the admissions campaign *and* are willing to undergo minimal training, they can be a most effective force. Indeed, it is often the students who complain most about the food or the large classes while on campus who become zealots regarding the institution when unleashed in their hometown high schools. And their zeal, like that of the alumni, can often know no boundaries when they encounter a student they would like to convince to enroll. Undergraduates, above all others, will stretch truths about an institution to convince others to attend it. Nevertheless, their enthusiasm, their tireless energy, and their comradery with pros-

pects—not to mention their knowledge regarding the institution's current environment and offerings—can prove to be a strong resource.

Many colleges now have well-trained student tour guides, who are able to effectively share their enthusiasm with prospective students. Also, more and more institutions are hiring and training outstanding college seniors to be admissions office interviewers. We hired "admissions fellows" at both Bowdoin and Vassar with positive results. To become an admissions fellow, after an extensive selection process, meant achieving one of the highest honors at these colleges. Seniors seemed pleased not only to be of service to their institution but to have an opportunity to add an important new dimension to their resumés. In contrast, ad hoc student recruiting during college vacations in hometown high schools seems less rewarding and uneven in effectiveness. But well-organized and well-trained students *can* be a most compelling element of the college family for admissions purposes.

All colleges and universities have distinct images that can dictate admissions health and enhance the confidence and satisfaction of their enrolled students. The first goal of an institution must be to *understand* its public image, uncomfortable as that knowledge may be, study the relationship of that image to the institution's true mission, and plot a recruitment campaign accordingly. It is fashionable today for the recruitment campaign to "sell" rather than "tell." But students are becoming wise to admissions gimmickry and yearn for a more academic, serious, and truly personal college representation. When freshmen classes were easier to come by, in the fifties and sixties, admissions officers consistently used "tell" strategies. The winners of the upcoming era may be those who return to that style and mentality.

A Plan for Retaining Students

The more an institution keeps in touch with an enrolled student, the better the chances of retaining him or her for the full college duration. At point of entry, colleges should systematically conduct controlled individual interviews with first-year and new transfer students to discuss their expectations. Different students matriculate with extraordinarily different expectations of the same institution, partly because of that institution's public image and partly because of rumors heard from high school friends and counselors, parents, alumni, and others. There is no better time for an *institution* to take a clear look at itself than when discussing image versus mission with new students. And the student, of course, benefits most. If the student's expectations are realistic, the mutual experience is almost certain to be a positive one.

We must realize, however, that teen-agers do dramatic turnarounds in college regarding vocational priorities, academic majors, and personal values. Helpful and important as the at-entry interview can be, it is only a start. Someone at the college must methodically keep up with the individual student as his or her priorities change to make certain that the institution can and will respond to these changes. Often students do not realize that an institution can accommodate their new as well as their old priorities. Too frequently undergraduates consider transferring to another institution when their priorities change. Dissatisfaction and/or alteration of goals and needs can be talked out at the home college. But too few colleges have advisory systems that prevent students from falling between the cracks during periods of personal change.

We must also face the traditional needs and idiosyncracies of the teen-age years. UCSC consistently errs, it seems to me, in mistaking undergraduate students for graduate students. Even though our faculty would like to think that teen-agers can become holistically academic and nontraditional in their enthusiasms and loyalties (foregoing sports events, fraternities and sororities, and so on), I question if that is possible for a large group of students. UCSC has an unfortunately high attrition rate for undergraduates even though institutional priorities seem ideal in terms of an academic emphasis closely tied to issues of social conscience. But something is missing—institutional loyalty, school spirit, an emotional attachment to the place. Does this kind of loyalty develop only by rooting for winning scores and/or attending the big dance? One would hope not. But in the absence of traditional collegiate activities, an institution must find *substitutes* to build loyalties. UCSC has not stumbled upon the right formula yet. Perhaps we have simply failed in maintaining individual contact with our students, discussing with them the values that attracted them to Santa Cruz as new students and reviewing with them how institutional tenets might relate to their own maturation. Whatever an institution's mission or style, retention of students depends on personal, continued contact with individual undergraduates. Many colleges and universities have superb faculty advisory systems on paper but little real follow-up to make certain the systems work.

Today, a strong student body comes as the direct result of a self-conscious, ambitious, and well-organized admissions recruitment campaign that calls on the talents of all members of the collegiate family. An objective analysis of collegiate mission versus image is an essential exercise before the campaign begins and as the campaign continues. But as much care must be expended in keeping as in enrolling students. Collegiate advising systems must be as personal and as well-orchestrated as recruitment efforts. The two are inseparably linked.

9

Resources: Management for *Colleges*, not Businesses

Robert H. Atwell
Madeleine F. Green

This chapter would not have been written twenty-five years ago; then, the business side of colleges and universities was not particularly conspicuous or important to the higher education community at large, and presiding over growth and plentiful resources posed a different and happier set of administrative problems from those we face today. Declining enrollments, decreasing state appropriations, inflation, and the rest of the well-known problems now buffeting many colleges and universities had not yet appeared on the horizon, and so institutions and their leaders could concentrate their efforts on issues associated with a growing and prosperous enterprise.

Historically, management in higher education was the province of treasurers and business officers, not deans or presidents. The latter neither needed nor cared to be preoccupied with resource management except in the most general way. And indeed, by the very nature of the enterprise, higher education defies being managed. The absence of a bottom line, the ambiguity of purpose and outcome, and the nature of the academic culture make colleges and universities intrinsically hard to manage (Green, 1981, p. 12). But times have changed, and the academy's historic resistance to management and its tradition of amateur managers have been challenged by a new managerial ethos that has emerged to coexist with the old value system.

Financial and human resource management, as well as strategic, short-term, and long-range planning, were born of hard times and constant preoccupation with making ends meet in academe. Recent years have brought rounds of budget cuts for many, if not most, institutions. Some weathered the early years of declining enrollments by cutting budgets in such a way that all parts of the institution bled equally, others by performing radical surgery on some programs to preserve and nurture others. Private institutions stepped up their fund-raising efforts, and some public institutions began development efforts for the first time. Many small private colleges have cut back as far as they can and now face the prospect of limited new dollars from foundations, corporations, and alumni. And so they have become increasingly aggressive in their quest for new sources of income and students.

Ventures aimed at increasing the resources of an institution or making maximum use of existing resources are receiving increasing attention and legitimacy. Institutions are selling and leasing their land and buildings, using them on Saturdays and weekends, and forming profit-making subsidiaries that will allow them to enter into business ventures. In the financial aid arena, colleges are becoming lenders, subsidizers of loans, bond issuers, and, in general, sophisticated financial aid managers. But where is this new wave of businesslike behavior taking higher education? Are there some institutions that can adapt, reach out, and seize opportunities better than others? If the dangers of the antimanagement ethic were stasis, resistance to change, and obsolescence, what are the dangers of the new entrepreneurial age and of the neoconventional wisdom that tells us that for a college to act like a business is not all bad?

Trade-offs in Financial Management

Any discussion of sound financial management in times of scarcity will turn on three basic courses of action: retrenching, using and reallocating existing resources for maximum effectiveness, and generating new income. At any given point in time, some combination of all three strategies will be deployed, with the emphasis shifting according to evolving circumstances.

Every important financial decision reverberates throughout an institution. Putting resources in one area will mean that dollars are not going somewhere else. In accounting, as in financial management, the principle of trade-offs will prevail. Trade-offs, or "alternative ways of investing the same amount of money" (Dickmeyer, 1981, p. 8), are a key concept in charting a course among the three basic strategies (retrenching, maximizing and reallocating resources, and increasing income) and in decision making within those three broad options.

Cutting the Budget for Short-Term Solutions. Reducing expenditures is the first response to hard times. Across-the-board cuts are the most frequently taken first steps. These measures typically include deferral of maintenance costs, hiring freezes, reduction in student support services, travel reductions or freezes, and postponement of equipment purchase and maintenance. Every effort is usually made at this stage to preserve the integrity of the instructional budget. Other strategies often adopted at this point include attempts to make certain activities self-supporting, such as radio and television broadcasting and continuing education operations (Hyatt, Schulman, and Santiago, 1984, p. 2). Concurrent measures are often taken to generate revenue, either through raising tuition fees or through one-time charges. In the early stages of its budget crisis, Michigan State University, for example, imposed a $20 registration fee surcharge and laid off all but essential personnel for two and a half days.

Budget cuts inevitably "cost" the institution, either in the short or long term. In the very worst case there will be year after year of budget cuts without sufficient thought as to how

far the mutilation has to go or whether there will be anything
functional or attractive left for students when it is all done. The
dispiriting effects of this approach are obvious—demoralized
and underpaid faculty, a physical plant in disrepair, and inadequate staffing throughout the institution.

Even if instructional budgets have escaped direct blows,
the cuts made elsewhere will inevitably affect the quality of academic programs and morale. Hyatt, Schulman, and Santiago
(1984, p. 7) have cogently summarized the adverse long-term effects of reductions in support units, cuts in student services, deferral of equipment purchases, reductions in library services,
and postponement of plant maintenance. Thus, reduction of
support units may hamper the institution's ability to comply
with state reporting or audit requirements and may consequently damage the institution's reputation and ability to attract outside money. Cuts in student services damage the quality of life
and may ultimately make the institution less attractive to students. Deferral of equipment purchases has a direct impact on
the quality of research and instructional programs and will also
limit the institution's ability to compete for grants and students. Similarly, inadequate library services and shrinking collections limit the college's ability to provide proper support for
instruction and research. And finally, deferral of physical plant
maintenance may mean inadequate facilities for instruction and
research, exposure to legal liabilities resulting from accidents or
injuries, and larger expenses down the road to compensate for
the cumulative neglect.

If the financial crisis persists after the first round of
bloodletting, more profound cuts and serious reallocation are
in order. At this stage, the involvement of faculty and constituent groups is important, and representative committees are
usually set up to guide the process. The foundation of this process is a clear definition or redefinition of the mission and goals
of the institution; programs are typically evaluated according to
their centrality to the mission, their quality, and their cost.
This stage is characterized by efforts to bring income and expense into long-term equilibrium through budget cuts and program eliminations and ultimately through the generation of ad-

ditional income. The Stanford Budget Adjustment Plan was a highly successful effort to accomplish those goals. The project was rooted in careful planning projections, an open approach to the various university constituencies, and a high degree of consensus. Such efforts are usually accompanied by ever larger capital fund drives designed to raise extra money for renovating buildings and restoring reserves depleted by past deficits. The focus is on achieving equilibrium in the annual operating budget.

Undue concern with the operating budget, however, may lead institutions to some erroneous conclusions and unwise decisions. As Peck has so cogently stated (1984a), and as Howard Bowen has always argued, fund accounting segments our thinking about the resources of an institution. For example, an institution that runs a $200,000 deficit during a year when the value of its endowments rose by $2 million—either through skillful investing or by additional gifts—will be viewed as having had a bad year. By the standards of the corporate world, however, that institution had a very good year. Similarly, an institution that spent a $2 million unrestricted gift to balance the budget may pride itself on being in the black when, in fact, it acted irresponsibly in the trade-off between the present and the future. This excessive preoccupation with the short-term bottom line that has characterized American business—often a point of criticism when contrasted with the long-run orientation of Japanese business—is also true of colleges and universities.

To summarize, the rigidities of fund accounting point out the trade-offs between the balance sheet and the current operating budget. A balanced operating budget may be achieved at the expense of the longer-term health of the institution; and, conversely, a deficit in the short term may be less significant than some real gains in the financial stability of the college. While budget cutting fulfills short-term needs, it may have dangerous implications in the long run. Five, ten, or twenty years later, institutions will be faced with the considerable cost of undoing some of the damage done to shore up the college in the short run.

Maximizing and Reallocating Existing Resources. Getting the maximum return from existing financial and human resources is a canon of good financial management even in the best of times. In hard times, it is crucial. Many institutions have worked diligently to streamline administrative structures and procedures. Improved cash management techniques have enabled institutions to avoid using credit during the cash-poor summer months. The wise financial officer pushes the system to the limits by delaying the payment of bills and collecting payments as quickly as possible. Investments in computer technology should produce savings in administrative, library, and even instructional costs; investments in energy conservation should yield similar long-term savings in utility bills.

Since salaries account for as much as 75 percent of some institutional budgets, the careful management of human resources is essential. Many colleges are retraining faculty to serve in high-enrollment areas. A widespread example is the mathematician turned computer scientist. Humanities professors may be deployed to staff the many sections of composition classes. In addition, faculty members are being eased out through a variety of early retirement programs or programs designed to help them make a career transition before retirement. Other workers, too, can enhance institutional effectiveness. Chowan College in North Carolina began using its own staff of highly skilled crafts workers to perform construction and renovation projects, thereby saving considerable sums on wiring, air conditioning, and landscaping (Hunt, 1984, p. 52). In other cases, it turns out to be less costly to contract out services such as trash removal or custodial services than to maintain a permanent staff. Frugality, inventiveness, and, in some cases, a willingness to invest in the short run to benefit in the long run are the principles that guide the maximum use of existing resources; no institution can achieve its optimum financial health without careful attention to this area.

Reallocating existing resources within the institution has become a much-discussed and highly important technique of good institutional management. Colleges and universities now find themselves forced to decide in which areas they want to invest. No college does everything equally well; and when resources are limited, decisions must be made as to which areas and programs to nurture and build and which to eliminate or not to improve. The trade-offs in the reallocation process are obvious and persistent. A decision to utilize institutional resources to supplement external student aid will mean lower faculty salaries, less equipment purchased, and lower maintenance standards. A decision to channel a larger proportion of institutionally funded aid dollars into merit-based aid is a trade-off by which needy students may get less money, resulting in a less diverse student body. A decision to feed the business and computer science programs may starve the humanities faculty. And so on.

An extensive program review process is invariably the basis for reallocation decisions. Institutions are in a better position to respond to requirements for cuts and reallocation if this process is already in place and is an ongoing activity. Such was the case at the University of Washington, where the first review was initiated by President William P. Gerberding when he came to the university in the summer of 1979. Each dean conducted a series of program reviews to pinpoint problems, strengths, and goals. When the first round of budget cuts came in April 1980, the groundwork had already been laid. A university-wide review process was instituted when the second round of cuts were ordered.

The longer-term reallocation and realignment strategies may result in redefinition of the institution's mission. This recognition dominated reallocation at Michigan State University, which affirmed that its mission needed to be more narrowly defined and that it could no longer afford to continue all its current programs. Decision-making parameters included the principle that faculty salary increases had to be sustained so that Michigan State could continue to be competitive with peer institutions. With decreasing appropriations, that decision would eventually have to be paid for by additional budget cuts.

The University of Michigan began its reallocation efforts before the budget cuts hit. In 1977, a "priority fund" was created to achieve budget flexibility. Dollars were freed up by an annual "tax" on all base budgets; anticipated savings through this system were to yield $1 million, $1.3 million, and $1.5 million in three years. In 1982, a new five-year, $20 million dol-

lar reallocation plan was introduced; funds freed would be reallocated by the central administration to high-priority areas.
Under this plan, $5 million were captured for reallocation into
faculty salaries in the summer of 1982, and a year later $4 mil-
lion were reallocated into special adjustments for faculty and
staff, instructional equipment, and graduate financial aid
(Hyatt, Schulman, and Santiago, 1984, pp. 76–86).

Thus, reallocation of funds among academic programs
and priorities is a key strategy to cope with financial difficulties. The more severe the situation, the more institutions must
choose among worthy causes. Though the process is inevitably
painful and wrenching, many leaders observe that their institutions have profited from the experience. Hard scrutiny of the
quality of programs, along with institution-wide discussion and
review of institutional priorities, is a salutary exercise for many
institutions. There are important lessons to be learned from
reallocation.

Not all reallocation decisions involve academic programs.
Unfunded institutional aid (unrestricted dollars spent on aid)
is a large budget item for private institutions, representing as
much as 15 percent of the education and general expenditures.
Unfunded aid is simply a discounting arrangement, so prevalent
that only about a third of the students in the independent sector pay "the sticker price" listed in the catalogue. Monies spent
on unfunded aid, or put another way, revenue not collected
from students receiving such aid, are dollars that cannot be
spent elsewhere. Monies spent on merit-based aid are unavail-
able to needy students. There has not been much systematic
analysis of the growing trade-off between need-based and non-
need-based aid. The use of institutional funds for the latter has
been growing very rapidly and is obviously in competition with
the need-based system. While the financial aid profession is well
aware of the problem and is nearly united and often doctrinaire
in its opposition to merit-based aid, those concerned with recruiting able students are increasingly favoring expenditures on
merit-based aid.

Any decision to invest funds, whether in financial aid,
computer courses, or faculty salaries, must be evaluated in

terms of the costs and benefits of other alternatives. A clear sense of institutional mission and short-term and long-term goals must inevitably undergird these decisions.

Increasing Income: Collegiate Businesses. The last ten years have brought forth unprecedented new efforts by colleges to generate additional revenues. It is in this area that entrepreneurial administrators flourish—seizing new opportunities as they arise and creating new programs and ventures that will enhance the revenues flowing to the institution.

As with budget cutting, there are discernible stages in an institution's efforts to generate additional revenue. Obvious measures are levying a one-time surcharge, as Michigan State did, increasing gifts, and raising tuition. In taking the latter course, an independent institution must be careful not to price itself out of its current market and must determine the point at which price resistance will cause a falloff in enrollments. Also, with each increase in tuition, institutions must consider how much additional financial aid must be made available both for enrolled and prospective students. Stepped-up annual giving and capital campaigns are also time-honored ways to improve the short-term and long-term budgetary picture. Public institutions, too, have started intensive fund-raising efforts, and many now have thriving foundations. At the University of Idaho, a response to austerity was to achieve an increase of 20 percent for each of the last five years of private giving to the university foundation. Michigan State University raised $9 million through a number of small capital campaigns.

But the greatest challenge over the past decade has been the development of new sources of revenue, rather than simply augmenting the old ones. Diversifying revenue sources has a twofold attraction: First, it provides more income, and, second, it decreases dependency on any single source, such as tuition. Colleges are now looking to their existing resources to enhance their revenues. Land, buildings, equipment, human resources, and programs can all be used to make money for the institution. And almost every college and university has found a few ways to put these resources to better use in generating revenue. Buildings can be rented or leased to local business and community groups, or a portion of the entire college given over to special summer activities such as camps and meetings. Equipment that is not constantly in use may be rented or loaned to other groups in exchange for other services. Programs for working adults can be brought to local businesses and employers, or faculty can take on the task of providing training to their employees. The list of innovative approaches to using these institutional resources is vast (Hunt, 1984).

But as institutions get into more complex ventures, especially in real estate, they run into the problem of jeopardizing their not-for-profit status if they generate more than 15 percent of their income from "nonrelated" sources. One alternative is to form a partnership with the for-profit private sector. Another is to form a separate corporation to own the taxable assets. The advantages of forming a subsidiary corporation or of acquiring a for-profit partner are several: Both strategies preserve the not-for-profit status of the institution; both give the college access to equity financing; and both allow for a flexible, risk-taking management style that is more compatible with the management of business ventures than is the usual collegiate style. O'Neil (1984) indicates that those colleges that have been successful in such development ventures have all established separate corporations to conduct their entrepreneurial activities.

This is all new and difficult territory for most colleges. New kinds of business expertise and legal advice must be brought into the college, and presidents may find themselves in a frightening new territory where the stakes are high. The road to diversification and income enhancement is strewn with danger, for instead of making money, institutions may lose it. Colleges and universities have a long tradition of losing money on bookstores and food service; and inexperience in a sophisticated financial or commercial arena may produce even worse results. Perhaps more significant is the danger that administrators and boards will be distracted from the central mission of their institutions and will "[diversify] out of education" (O'Neil, 1984). Here, the trade-off may be between the energy directed toward the educational enterprise and the attention required to tend to new business ventures. O'Neil sees the danger point "when the investment vehicle begins to require the active attention of a board of trustees and senior college administrators." He goes on to say, "We found that in real estate ventures —especially those that go wrong—attention to the investment becomes all consuming and college affairs are left to drift. Without intending to, college administrators find themselves managing a real estate development rather than an educational institution."

Trade-off analysis needs to take place as institutions assess the feasibility of some of the more aggressive ideas for better utilizing resources. The seemingly beneficial result in one area may be accompanied by damage in another. One of the lessons of Japanese management for American business is that an obsession with the annual or even the quarterly report to stockholders can severely compromise long-term modernization and viability. Governing boards that insist on annually balanced budgets may so impoverish an institution that it has little or no appeal to future generations of students. By the same token, of course, the institution has to survive in the short run to enjoy the fruits of some brilliant planning for the future.

Boards need to realize that presidents are transitory (with an average incumbency of about seven years) and must be more concerned with the current operating budget than with the longer-term balance sheet. Boards must recognize that their longer-term ownership of the institution is to some degree in conflict with short-term survival. Trade-off analysis must point to an equilibrium of the short run and the long run, as well as to a balance between the college as a business and the college as a college.

A Question of Leadership

The management of financial and human resources flows from the leadership. Charting a successful course for an institution, in hard times or good, is ultimately a question of leadership and good management. Institutional leaders must provide direction for a college, whether into new areas or along its current course. No two leaders or observers of leadership behaviors agree completely on the characteristics of an effective president or administrator. Individual personalities, institutional history and circumstances, and a host of other factors will determine effectiveness in any given situation. Indeed, the concept of "situational management," widely accepted in the management world, posits that managerial style and behavior will vary with the nature of the followers and the task at hand. The same group may exhibit one set of behaviors faced with one situation, and an entirely different set in another situation. A faculty overhauling a curriculum in an atmosphere of consensus will behave quite differently than when recommending a series of budget cuts. Different leadership will be required in each situation.

What kind of leadership has the current climate called forth? Two related trends have emerged: one recognizing and legitimizing the managerial and entrepreneurial elements of leadership, and another calling for more decisive, less facilitative leadership. In an article on the entrepreneurial college presidency, a keen observer of managerial strategies and leadership in small colleges posed the question: "What makes some small private colleges thrive in spite of enrollments under 2,500, modest endowments, and limited geographical impact?" (Peck, 1983). To answer it, he studied nineteen "invisible colleges." Peck's findings have more to do with leaders' *approaches* to resource management than to particular strategies or techniques. He discovered that the successful colleges approached the future in a manner that was "informal, intuitive, and opportunistic" (1983, p. 18). Presidents rely on "intelligence" or the pulse of the campus more than on data. According to Peck, "the small independent college is an entrepreneurial enterprise, and its leaders are entrepreneurs in the best classical sense" (p. 19). He hastens to add that not all parts of the institution nor all its activities are or should be entrepreneurial in nature; the successful entrepreneurial president must always keep the fundamental mission of the institution in mind.

Nonetheless, the entrepreneurial president focuses on the external environment and looks for opportunities presented by that environment. He or she relies on intuition to make decisions in ambiguous or unpredictable circumstances and is willing to take risks. Not surprisingly, entrepreneurial leaders are strong and assertive, and "the feeling of 'top-down' administration pervades the small college not so much by the exercise of autocratic power as by an exercise of will" (Peck, 1983, p. 22).

The myriad pressures of internal and external constituencies that tie presidents' hands, as well as the bureaucratic constraints that leaders face, have produced a new vision of more powerful and decisive leaders. Fisher (1984) sees weak leaders as sorry characters, battered by the forces of boards, legislatures, accrediting agencies, and others into being "mediators," "support mechanisms," "chairs," "managers of human resources," "apostles of efficiency," "energy maximizers" (p. 16). He buttresses his call for powerful leaders by citing such well-known commentators on the presidency as Joseph Kauffman, David Riesman, Frederic Ness, and Richard Cyert, who describe the many forces that weaken the presidency and who posit the need for courageous new leaders. Fisher states unequivocally, "Without towering presidents, men and women of ability and courage, the problems of the immediate future will become more serious" (p. 17). He places high value on charismatic leadership and has concluded that "the three principal conditions for charisma are distance, style, and perceived self-confidence" (p. 43). He believes in cultivating the presidential mystique, in always making it clear that the president makes the final decisions, and in working to enhance and preserve presidential authority.

It is not surprising that the current climate, ranging from uncertainty for some institutions to siege mentality for others, has spawned a new version of the "take charge" leader. Adversity often breeds the wish to find a savior, a heroic individual who can make the bold and difficult decisions, and a prescription for a vigorous leader who can cure the institution's ills. And indeed, the more perilous the situation, the more the collegiate community needs and welcomes strong leadership. Walker (1979) asserts that "university communities are more tolerant of seemingly high-handed administration when the university is faced with threats from inside or outside" (p. 19).

Keller (1983) agrees that, in difficult times, organizations "tend to look toward a center, to be more tolerant of strong leadership" (p. 55). It is noteworthy that both authors use the word *tolerate*; authoritarian rather than collegial leadership is fundamentally alien to the academic culture and value system.

Walker (1979) in particular eschews the "muscle" view of administration as misguided and ineffective. Administrators who see themselves in heroic terms, according to Walker, apply a pathological hierarchical model to university administration. The university operates, he continues, like a "political democratic community" (p. 8), and leaders can lead only with the consent of the governed. According to this model, leadership in the real world of administration consists of full and equal partnership in the operation of the university. Walker is not convinced that the great old-time presidents were the giants that we now imagine. He cites the writings of William Rainey Harper, Robert Hutchins, and Charles W. Eliot on the limits of presidential power. Walker does note, however, that "it is perfectly reasonable to assume that university presidents did, indeed, exercise more authority in earlier days" (p. 22), and he points to the greater homogeneity of faculty and student bodies and the significantly smaller size of colleges in times past.

Walker's skepticism of the leader as savior is echoed by Toffler in *The Third Wave,* who cites the danger of the "messiah complex" (cited by Kauffman, 1984, p. 10), the misguided belief that the "right" leader can save us. The recent writings calling for stronger presidential leadership have made the sacred values of collegiality and consultation less important, action oriented, and decisive. While no one has come out and flatly stated that the president should rule and collegiality be damned, the emphasis has clearly shifted. But is this newly rediscovered assertive leadership the wave of the future, the answer to the inertia and traditionalism that prevent many institutions from adapting creatively to trying times? We doubt it.

Again, the concept of trade-offs is useful in considering the kind of leadership best suited to the current climate of uncertainty and stringency. The heroic leader may be able to stabilize an institution in the short term, perform the radical surgery needed to prevent it from going under, or transform it into a different, more viable college. But the price may be the alienation and confusion of students, faculty, and alumni and other external constituents. When the crisis has passed, the leader will inevitably have to pay attention to the frightened and demoralized faculty who were not fully part of the rapid change process. Crisis and rapid change do not lend themselves to extensive collaboration and planning; they are too time consuming and unwieldy. But to ignore those traditions and the need for self-determination is to threaten the ability of the institution to continue to plan, adapt, and move forward as a body.

Managing "through people, rather than through structures" (Peck, 1983, p. 20), a healthy preoccupation with "productivity through people" (Peters and Waterman, 1982, p. 14), in short, viewing human resources as the most valuable ones are central to effective college leadership and management. Decisive leadership need not be autocratic. Peck talks of "top-down" administration by the force of will of the president and of the necessity of a strong "strategic vision" (1983, p. 22). At the same time, he notes that presidents in successful colleges appear to perform more as "collaborators, facilitators, consensus makers," and incentive providers than as creators (p. 22).

Clearly, however, there has been a reaction against collegial leadership, and leaders under stress may be tempted to move an institution singlehandedly. If they attempt to do so, however, they may well damage the long-term health, morale, and value system of the institution. Peters and Waterman (1982) cite a business chief executive officer's prescription for organizational success: He observed "that a leader's role is to harness the social forces in the organization, to shape and guide values. He described good managers as value shapers concerned with the informal social properties of organizations. He contrasted them with the mere manipulators of formal rewards and systems who dealt with only the narrower concept of short-term efficiency" (p. 6).

Maccoby (1981) also stresses the long-term dimension of effective leadership. "Technical skills may be necessary, but all leaders must be able to articulate goals and values" (p. 31). In his study of six successful leaders, he found that they share the following "attributes of the new social character: a caring, respectful, and responsible attitude; flexibility about people and organizational structure; and a participative approach to management, the willingness to share power" (p. 31). Maccoby, in fact, seems to be describing the classic college president.

The rush for new students and new resources and the pressing need for institutional leaders to effect change before it is too late can cause administrators to forget that they are first and foremost educators and that their institutions are not businesses. The dilemma is real: Colleges will not survive unless they are businesslike, but they will not be colleges if they become businesses. A confusion of means and ends is all too common. Chief executives absorbed in entrepreneurial ventures not directly related to whether students are learning and teachers are teaching may find themselves with successful shopping centers but empty dorms and dispirited faculties. While colleges can become more businesslike in some respects, they must beware of trying to conduct themselves like businesses. Colleges and universities are low-consensus organizations, with strong differences within each collegiate community about curriculum, governance, and often purpose. Businesses, in contrast, have higher organizational consensus about fundamental goals, although there may be disagreement on means and strategies.

The need for abundant communication, "selling" of ideas, and respect for institutional values and traditions are not unique to colleges and universities. The new gurus of business management are espousing many of the principles of management that have historically been honored by colleges and universities. Perhaps we have instinctively known what we were doing. The test that faces us now will be to continue the best of an older style of collegiate management while borrowing and adapting the strategies of businesses.

References

Benezet, L. T. "Do Presidents Make a Difference?" *Educational Record,* 1982, *63,* 10–14.

Chaffee, E. E. "Successful Strategic Management in Small Private Colleges." *Journal of Higher Education*, Mar./Apr. 1984, pp. 212–241.

Dickmeyer, N. "Financial Policy Making and Planning." In R. H. Atwell and M. F. Green (eds.), *Academic Leaders as Managers*. New Directions for Higher Education, no. 36. San Francisco: Jossey-Bass, 1981.

Fisher, J. L. *Power of the Presidency.* New York: American Council on Education/Macmillan, 1984.

Green, M. F. "The Paradox of Leadership Development." In R. H. Atwell and M. F. Green (eds.), *Academic Leaders as Managers*. New Directions for Higher Education, no. 36. San Francisco: Jossey-Bass, 1981.

Hunt, S. (ed.). *New Sources of Revenue: An Ideabook.* Washington, D.C.: Council for the Advancement and Support of Education, 1984.

Hyatt, J. A., Schulman, C. H., and Santiago, A. A. *Reallocation: Strategies for Effective Resource Management.* Washington, D.C.: National Association of College and University Business Officers, 1984.

Kauffman, J. F. "Profile of the Presidency in the Next Decade." *Educational Record*, Spring 1984, pp. 6–10.

Keller, G. *Academic Strategy: The Management Revolution in American Higher Education.* Baltimore, Md.: Johns Hopkins University Press, 1983.

Maccoby, M. *The Leader: A New Face for American Management.* New York: Simon & Schuster, 1981.

Martin, W. B. "Adaptation and Distinctiveness." *Journal of Higher Education*, Mar./Apr. 1984, pp. 285–295.

O'Neil, J. P. Letter to the authors, Aug. 31, 1984.

O'Neil, J. P., and Grier, P. M. *Financing in a Period of Retrenchment—A Primer for Small Colleges.* Washington, D.C.: National Association of College and University Attorneys, 1984.

Peck, R. D. "The Entrepreneurial Presidency." *Educational Record*, 1983, *64*, 18–25.

Peck, R. D. "Entrepreneurship as a Significant Factor in Successful Adaptation." *Journal of Higher Education*, Mar./Apr. 1984a, pp. 212–241.

Peck, R. D. "The Entrepreneurial Business Officer." *Business Officer,* Oct. 1984b, pp. 31-34.

Peters, T. J., and Waterman, R. H., Jr. *In Search of Excellence.* New York: Harper & Row, 1982.

Walker, D. E. *The Effective Administrator: A Practical Approach to Problem Solving, Decision Making, and Campus Leadership.* San Francisco: Jossey-Bass, 1979.

10

Alverno College:
Toward a Community
of Learning

Sister Joel Read
Stephen R. Sharkey

Alverno is a Catholic liberal arts and professional college for women located in Milwaukee, Wisconsin. It is in that broad category of institutions that, according to some educational experts, are either maladapted to our times and headed for quiet extinction or doomed after great struggle to a noisy fiscal collapse. Indeed, Alverno *is* sitting in the heart of the so-called Rust Belt, and the number of eighteen-year-old women who might be recruited by the college is dwindling. At Alverno, we do not have a huge computer center, high-tech laboratories, wealthy alumnae, a large endowment, or a winning athletic team. What we do have, however, is a successful place of higher learning, one that works and even flourishes.

Here, we want to analyze those factors that have made possible or encouraged Alverno's dynamism, as well as those that have sometimes threatened its survival. Our basic thesis is that Alverno has been making and is continuing to make itself *a community of learning* characterized by (1) an increasing awareness of and responsibility for its primary mission as a teaching institution, (2) widespread involvement at all levels in designing and implementing both curricula and organizational structure, (3) and innovation grounded in ongoing research and self-evaluation. Like any essentially dynamic community, Alverno has had its share of both consensus and conflict. The college's success lies in the fact that most faculty were doing what they enjoyed doing and were good at doing—namely, teaching. Moreover, the energy engendered by competition for resources could more often than not be used to generate new ideas or strategies, and it was thus directed forward toward the collective future rather than backward onto old sectarian disagreements. The faculty's commitment to creating a better educational process for women produced and sustained this forward-looking thrust. But the important questions to ask here are: How did this whole process unfold, and what use might other colleges make of the lessons we learned?

The specific curricular and organizational outcomes of the process described here are organically tied to Alverno's particular context. This is significant, in part, because of the meaning that the term *institutional planning* has taken on here. Our "plan" consisted of an emerging, shifting, but very widespread consensus about what questions needed to be addressed when, by whom, and with what resources. This contrasts quite sharply with the image of a "plan" as some master agenda developed and imposed by a select group of administrative experts who are solely responsible for directing change in the institution—an agenda against which "progress" by others "lower down" is periodically checked. We had no such specialists planning *for* others, or testing theoretical models of pedagogy for their universal applicability. Alverno students, faculty, and staff were all involved in a gradual unfolding of change based on their responses to their own particular environments. In the beginning they shared not much more than an urgency to *do* something and perhaps the rudiments of a vision of the future. But this vision was consciously and regularly modified, along with the definition of the means needed to achieve it. People at all levels

planned not for but *with* each other to meet their own perceived needs. What may be transferable from our experience at
Alverno, then, are some ideas on encouraging innovation and
critical thinking among colleagues across an institution and
spanning its hierarchy—in short, some ideas about *how* to
change, not simply about what to change.

Inquiry and Opportunity: 1969-1971

In the late 1960s Alverno faced a series of turning points
in its history that demanded that faculty and administrators re-
consider their understanding of the college's mission: "higher
education for women." The college was an outgrowth of three
institutions of the School Sisters of St. Francis, which were
originally established to prepare members of the order for the
community's work in teaching, music, and nursing. By the early
1950s these separate institutions had been successfully merged
into a liberal arts college, which quickly received formal accreditation. The college occupied a new physical plant, but its small
number of students were at first almost all still members of the
religious order. By 1968, however, enrollment had grown significantly to about 1,500 full-time equivalent students, and lay
students outnumbered their religious counterparts for the first
time.

At this point, the parent order decided to admit women
into the community only after they had completed college
work—thereby nullifying the purpose for which the college had
been created. Enrollment precipitously declined, and the fiscal
position of the college was seriously weakened. As a response,
in this same year the board of trustees reorganized itself to include laypersons and, upon the retirement of the incumbent,
selected a new president, Sister Joel Read. The board gave her
the explicit mandate to initiate a radical self-examination within the college, to question its very identity as an institution of
higher learning for women.

The need for change pressed both from within and from
without. Internally, for example, several faculty who had been
involved in the fledgling women's movement since the early

1960s had increased their awareness of the directions that women's education would have to take to better prepare them for new career and life roles in society. Many students, too, were expressing concern about the relevance of Alverno's program to their interests and needs. Both faculty and students felt that the quality of learning in the classroom could be improved.

Externally, the college faced potentially serious competition in its environment. Greater Milwaukee, with a population of roughly one million people at the time, supported two other Catholic women's colleges, two major universities, a nationally known engineering school, and several professional schools. The three women's colleges were, at least in 1968, virtually indistinguishable from one another in the public eye; and further, Alverno had not established a significant recruiting base in regional high schools. Incoming students tended to be increasingly nonresident commuters. Though we had had older "returning" women since 1960, we had just begun to recruit them. These were both new groups for the system to accommodate at the time.

In the face of such challenges, what was Alverno to become? Faculty and students formally opened a dialogue about this in September 1969. This dialogue not only increased their awareness of the problems and prospects of American education but set in motion a college-wide exploration of alternatives to Alverno's quite traditional course structure and requirements. Throughout the year discussion continued, not least because there was time officially allocated for the faculty to assemble on a regular basis. The leadership also made every effort to focus debate on themes of self-evaluation and renewal. Such regular collaboration had its roots in part in the communitarian traditions of governance among the religious faculty; that general approach was broadened and defined in new terms so that both religious and lay faculty could participate.

A particularly important and successful component of this process was the Faculty Institute, a sort of abbreviated conference with a theme related explicitly to the teaching mission. This, too, had a long history. And it was this vehicle that was to be important for consensus building throughout the 1970s. By

1970 this end-of-year session was augmented by a somewhat briefer institute session in January and, later, with one in the early fall. These institutes always involved college- and department-level discussions and frequently included special colloquia featuring nationally known educational critics and innovators as well. This is still the case today.

Early in the 1970–71 academic year, as part of the continuing dialogue on mission and the curriculum, the president and dean posed the following set of basic questions to the college community:

- What kinds of questions are being asked by professionals in your field that relate to the validity of your discipline in a total college program?
- What is your department's position on these?
- How are you dealing with these problems in your general education courses and in the work for a major in your field?
- What are you teaching that is so important that students cannot afford to pass up courses in your department?

For the rest of that year faculty in their respective disciplines met regularly to hear each department explore its contribution to undergraduate education. Rather than a specific plan, faculty generated a set of new questions from the institutes and meetings. A consensus gradually emerged that the key issue in higher learning was not what students should be exposed to and asked to reproduce but what students should be able to do with their lives as a result of having gone to college. What are the specific observable outcomes of a good liberal education? What is the relationship between liberal arts and professional programs in respect to outcomes? And how can faculty better teach for these outcomes? By May 1971, faculty had identified four broad "goals" of the educational process, namely, problem solving, communication, valuing, and involvement.

This set of goals would serve as the central organizing framework for creating a new curriculum based, first, on outcomes rather than on exposure to a particular range of content and, second, on an attempt to integrate theoretical with applied learning. By concentrating on a few bottom-line questions, faculty accomplished a breakthrough and were able to reframe their definition of higher learning. This was for them an exciting and significant milestone.

It is important to note that while such conceptual developments were occurring, faculty and administrators were also taking some very concrete steps to improve the college's learning environment and its relations with the urban community and to support the curricular innovation. Organizationally, for example, the board of trustees authorized a management study covering the entire institution and set forth its first five-year fund development campaign. The faculty created a senate to help oversee its welfare; and the administration, cognizant of the particular needs of women students, created the Research Center for Women, a campus baby-sitting service, and a career development office.

Some initial experiments to test different approaches to teaching were attempted, often by taking risks. Two examples might be interesting here, one that occurred very early in the process of rethinking Alverno's curriculum and one that came somewhat later. First, back in 1969 and 1970 the faculty were discussing change in terms of how to revise the general education program to give it more coherence and integration. The English department devised a plan whereby it would no longer offer the standard "required" course in composition and instead would help any faculty member who so desired to teach writing skills in their particular courses. It spearheaded the adoption of a college-wide policy that required each student to submit three papers for approval to both her major department and the English department. This plan more widely distributed the faculty's responsibility for producing articulate students, as well as increased the student's opportunities to perform. Though perhaps shocking at first, and certainly more demanding for everyone, the new policy on writing did begin to promote greater accountability among faculty outside the English department for teaching communication skills. More importantly, it provided a taste of the new roles faculty and students would be shaping for each other. Such policies as this helped the faculty to see that it was possible to focus an educational program on the development of particular skills.

The second example was the creation of an off-campus internship program that over time would become a required component of every major the college offered. The faculty sought here to provide each student with the chance to learn in a nonacademic setting by experientially testing what she got in the classroom. In 1969–71 the experiential approach to learning was not yet very widely practiced in the United States. And further, though organizations like the Consortium on the Advancement of Experiential Learning would later argue that experiential learning was most meaningful when spread across a curriculum, what few experiments there were in this regard around the country tended to remain "pocketed" inside particular departments or programs. Alverno faculty were aware of this problem and sought to avoid it from the start by including an experiential learning goal in all department-level mission statements.

Looking back, we can identify the spirit of interdisciplinary dialogue and debate as having been critical to the college's ability to survive. This took many forms, such as those we have already noted, but also included what is usually categorized as "evaluation." For example, in 1971 all faculty and staff were requested by the academic vice-president to submit their personal assessments of the strengths and weaknesses of both the college as a whole and their individual areas. Practically everyone did this in a spirit of frank appraisal and hope for the future, and a synthesis of the main themes was openly discussed. Significantly, such activities revealed early on the powerful commitment people shared to the teaching mission, from which no great deviation was ever really considered. In an atmosphere of crisis, faculty and staff were thus expressing a basic desire to go with their strong suit rather than to concoct a new mission as a way to capitalize on some perceived marketing trend. The signal was so clear that it gave the college's leadership, from the trustees to department coordinators, an unambiguous focus for program development. Further, the custom of open communication provided a way to air conflicts, impelled leaders to define their roles in more facilitative terms, and encouraged those who expressed either ideas or gripes to act on them in some systematic way, since everyone was in the arena together. An important latent consequence here was the decentralization of leadership throughout the faculty as a whole. While not every faculty member was cut out for leadership, the overall tendency did serve to strengthen the ability of the faculty to become self-moving.

But this is not to say that there were no problems. Faculty and students were both worried about the future of the college. Quite simply, they wondered if it would even survive. We had to confront and overcome the tendency of some faculty, particularly in departments with few students, to respond defensively to their anxiety by guarding the program requirements that seemed to "guarantee" the safety of their turf. In this very fluid period, administration was sometimes ineffective; increased meeting time and paper work, as well as poor planning, produced high levels of stress. Perhaps most importantly, the college had to deal with contradictory public images. On one hand, Alverno was seen by some people in the region as "merely a girls' school" or a "convent." On the other hand, it was just as often seen as "radical" and a hotbed of feminism, because it was making conscious efforts to implement educational programs with the specific needs and problems of women in mind. Our external communications efforts at this time, especially those intended for the general public, were neither very systematic nor very successful at helping others recognize who we were and understand what we were attempting to do.

New Approaches to the Curriculum: 1971–1973

In the initial stages of change we often sought out consultants and colleagues from other settings who seemed to have had more concrete experience in dealing with the kinds of questions we were raising than we ourselves did. But by the end of the 1970–71 academic year, we realized that there were no real experts on outcome-oriented education. We would have to become our own experts and our own laboratory, and create our own means for securing external resources to support the effort required to teach and learn at the same time. Alverno thus entered a period of intense self-education, but one in which the "curriculum" had to evolve as the participants went along. The mission was clear: to develop each student's abilities and verify that learning had actually occurred. But the college was still essentially set up as a classical liberal arts institution with professional programs such as nursing and music that were focused on mastery of content. We became increasingly aware that much of this needed to be changed and made more consistent with the renewed and clarified mission of the college.

Pursuing the practical implications of our central idea, we set out to modify the criteria and procedures for allocating staff time, determining individual work responsibilities, and organizing work groups, so as to better account for and encourage our own development as teachers, leaders, and collaborators. And within the classroom, faculty tried more strategies analogous to the revised writing requirements described earlier, in an effort to encourage students not just to memorize content but to develop particular cognitive and affective skills in a self-conscious way.

Tracing the ripple effects of our shift in basic approach to the curriculum was quite exciting but also, at times, overwhelming. Any misgivings that we may have felt, however, did *not* obstruct our process, because there never was a precise "that" to which we were aspiring or against which we felt we should compare our performance. There never was, as we observed earlier, a master plan of development. *Planning with* each other meant adopting a very pragmatic view: We held together as a community around a daily routine of *trying* ways of solving the concrete, immediate problems that resulted from looking for better ways to teach, on the assumption that solutions could probably be found in the long run. At its best, leadership in such circumstances meant facilitating the process of problem solving, coordinating activities, keeping people focused on the mission, and anticipating needed resources. The best plans emerged where this approach to leadership prevailed. When leadership failed, as it sometimes did, it was because individuals did not have the requisite abilities or because they imposed agendas too unrelated to the emerging thrust of the institution.

It must be said that recasting the meaning of teaching did tend to threaten faculty identities, forged as they were in a more traditional environment. Emotion sometimes got the better of analysis, and some faculty members felt the tension more strongly than others. Faculty experienced a conflict between their commitment to achieve depth in a particular discipline and their commitment both to collaboration across disciplines and to teaching for "general" outcomes. They positioned themselves all along a broad "content versus process" continuum. Perhaps this effort would have failed had not most finally agreed that this was, after all, another false dichotomy, a product as much of personal anxieties as of professional commitment to a particular literary and cultural heritage. The resolution of this dilemma came when, after considerable discussion, faculty agreed to define the student not as a repository of data but as a user of meaningful information to make decisions in her life. Specific courses could thus be viewed not as *sine qua non* elements of an educational package but as opportunities, to learn and demonstrate certain skills needed to better control one's life.

Once past this hurdle, faculty were able to design a full ability-based curriculum of eight distinct outcomes, an expansion from the earlier four "goals." They defined each ability in developmental terms, that is, as holistic characteristics of the person. At the same time, they employed explicit criteria for measuring the student's successful performance and narrative evaluations of her progress. To accomplish this, the faculty spent a great deal of time brainstorming and planning; the program framework thus went through several versions. In this period an academic task force was created by releasing four faculty members half time so that they could coordinate much of the work. But about thirty other faculty members representing every department were also designated to serve on a curriculum committee, and everyone participated in regular discussions. The question of how to evaluate student performance was particularly troublesome, since we sought to tap cognitive and affective abilities that would generalize across settings, and our research into testing revealed that most academic evaluation did not go beyond certain beginning levels of the cognitive domain. After further research and debate, we identified the framework of *assessment,* which focuses on evaluating how a student applies learned skills or information across a range of concrete situations. Assessment became a keystone of program development.

It is important to note that the program the faculty agreed to was stated in tentative terms, was to be phased in incrementally, and was set for review after both faculty and students had some practical experience to refer to. With these stipulations the faculty decided that the freshmen entering in the fall of 1973 would be admitted under the new requirements and that older students would be "grandmothered" out. This decision frankly required a certain leap of faith on the faculty's part. One current faculty member, recalling for us the climate of this period, remarked that there were times when it seemed that her colleagues would never move off dead center: "In 1973 we didn't really *know* we were ready to admit students to this new curriculum," she said. "In fact, if we had waited until we were all ready, we would still be working on perfecting it. The 1973 decision to admit students, then, was both an act of leadership and a gesture of faith in ourselves."

Faculty then began to prepare explanatory materials as well as new course syllabi. Meanwhile, it became obvious that outside resources were going to be crucial to support the planning and implementation of the new curriculum. In this period Alverno applied for and received one of the first large grants from the Fund for the Improvement of Postsecondary Education for institutional renewal, plus various smaller grants to subsidize specific projects; and it also received an unanticipated Ford Venture Grant. The college organized new offices for development and public relations. Integral to the new model of measuring student effectiveness was an Assessment Center, created with the help of executives from AT&T. This center, along with a now more fully functioning off-campus experiential learning program, helped establish links between "school"

and "life" at various institutional levels. There was a great sense
of focus, direction, and exhilaration but also an awareness of
how much work all these developments were going to require
over the long haul.

Years of Change and Effort: 1973–1977

If up to now most change was internal to the college and
rather unobtrusive, during this period the college "went public" in many ways. Also, these were years of just plain hard
work. Since at all levels goals were being defined in rather un-
conventional ways, faculty had to invent new criteria for effectiveness and new measures of accountability but express them
in such a way that they could be communicated meaningfully
and credibly to others. If parents of potential students, foundation executives, or accreditation team members looked closely at what we were doing at Alverno, would they understand
our aims and could we show them concrete results to justify all
our efforts to teach more effectively? For that matter, would
we be able to communicate our goals and strategies effectively
to our own students?

We all felt a strong obligation to live up to our vision of
education. Though most of us within the college were convinced of the merits of our effort, we were also aware that at
some point we would be asked to demonstrate whether it was
all actually working. This sense of accountability would presently be translated into a formal office of research and evaluation,
which got its start with a major National Institute of Education
grant, but faculty were involved in such activity from the start.
In short, we needed "intelligence" about the system, so verifi-
able mutual responsibility, explicitness, and accountability became central issues in the institutional culture.

To complete the implementation of the program, a new
administrative structure was required. Its first feature was a
two-dimensional mode of academic organization; that is, the
college was organized by traditional discipline divisions, such as
fine arts or behavioral sciences, and also by interdisciplinary
competence divisions responsible for developing each identified

outcome, such as analysis or social interaction. Most faculty had an appointment in both a discipline and a competence division. Each dimension generated its own academic requirements that students had to meet and that faculty struggled to integrate within their courses. The second feature was a mechanism for monitoring student growth in the new curriculum; this involved institution-wide collaboration with the newly organized office of research and evaluation to gather both quantitative and qualitative data. The third feature was a system for acculturating new students and faculty to the comparatively more proactive roles they would play within Alverno. New offices were opened to deal with such student services as orientation and basic skill development. A standing faculty development committee was created to coordinate new staff orientation and plan the regular institutes.

These three features—the two-dimensional organizing principle, the gathering of data through research, and the socialization functions—often made for a very hectic and complex situation. Both students and faculty were coping with new and often transitional procedures for record keeping, working with new educational outputs (such as videotaped group assessments or off-campus internship performance evaluations), and trying to evaluate the whole process at the same time. Students and faculty alike usually entered Alverno from traditional backgrounds and had to adapt to the narrative, criterion-based forms of evaluation that had replaced grades, as well as to teaching strategies that went beyond lecturing. Some with little sympathy for the outcomes framework and low commitment to the group process of disciplinary reformulation said "we told you this would be a waste of time," withdrew, and/or failed to live up to their responsibilities. But most managed to adapt to the prevailing atmosphere of complexity and ambiguity.

In such a difficult time leadership was crucial; fortunately, the new dean selected from within the college proved particularly adept at managing conflict and helping individuals identify their own inner resources. Despite the frustrations, there was a high degree of internal solidarity. Illustrating this is the almost universal and immediate support that the college received from its members when a small group attracted local press coverage of their dissatisfactions. This created a minor furor that played on the already contradictory public image of the college.

Reflecting back, we can highlight some major successes in this period, including increased positive national attention by educators, the beginning of annual national workshops in assessment and valuing, successful reaccreditation, the graduation of the first full class under the new system in May 1977, and the inauguration of a Weekend College program. Faculty and administrators also realized that it was important to apply the same approach to evaluating their own performance as was being employed with the students; thus the faculty senate and other bodies began working out new criteria for retention and promotion based essentially on teaching ability, teamwork and leadership skills, and quality of contribution to the process of institutional change. In this area of faculty evaluation, faculty were able to learn something from having conceptualized how to help students modify their traditional, rather passive role in the educational process. All across the new curriculum students were routinely required to evaluate their own and their peers' performance by employing specific behavioral criteria. This was in line with the greater degree of responsibility they were trained to take for their own growth.

Resources at Alverno were still precarious, however, despite the influx of some major grants and increased tuition from a growing enrollment. Salaries and benefits were comparatively low. The administration felt that it was crucial to solidify the resource base, improve staff compensation, and support ongoing growth. The college thus expanded its development campaign and took advantage of its national exposure to broaden its faculty pool, hiring new members from all over the country. These conditions set the stage for the next phase of change.

Clarification and Refinement: 1978 to the Present

At this point the ability-based curriculum was conceptually well defined and could be understood in principle without much difficulty by both students and professional educators. But the language we created to describe it had tended to become specialized, and the logistical intricacies of implementing it could be confusing and downright contradictory. Some pieces of the program were better developed than others; some departments had a better handle on applying it than did others. New faculty could easily feel overwhelmed by the nuts and bolts, while remaining committed to and even enthusiastic about the basic theme of teaching for outcomes. The fundamental problem continued to be ensuring that the actual practice of teaching and assessment reflected the intended curricular design and, conversely, that the design meant something meaningful. The learning process, as a theory, had its fascination from various angles, and it required the faculty to keep refining their ability to deal with the question, What is the difference between what currently happens in the classroom and what could be happening? This meant we had to improve our monitoring of actual student performance, so that the program would remain grounded in students' experience and thereby take best advantage of their real potential.

Thus in the late 1970s faculty began working on a new set of questions. Essentially these questions were: How can the logistics of managing two dimensions of requirements be made less confusing for both faculty and students? Can requirements be made simpler, perhaps even more "elegant"? How can faculty communicate their ideas in simpler, clearer ways, using less technical language? How can we better apply our outcome-oriented approach to effectively discuss broader intellectual and social issues on campus? What decisions can we make about refining the program with the data we have now accumulated that we could not make before? Faculty discussed these concerns on a regular basis, as well as in the quarterly institutes, whose special programs and symposia reflected current needs. For example, during the late 1970s and early 1980s a standing faculty committee on assessment gave many workshops on how to improve assessment instruments, how to use community volunteers with practical experience in a field as co-assessors, how to improve the design of a syllabus, and how to create better criteria for evaluating student performances—to name just a few

major topics. All these suggestions were put forth with the intent of helping faculty better translate their technical ideas into
living educational experiences.

In the late 1970s, the college received a major grant from
the U.S. Department of Health, Education, and Welfare as part
of its Advanced Institutional Development Program. These
funds enabled individual faculty members to refine their particular ideas and join with others to forge new institutional links.
For example, several departments worked together to create a
behavioral sciences center; the natural science departments col-
laborated to reorient their laboratory practicums around the
framework of investigative learning; the arts and humanities departments developed a new interdisciplinary structure for general education, both to conserve resources and to present a
more integrated approach to the appreciation of culture. During
several institutes faculty responsible for these and other similar
projects asked their colleagues for their views on possible
changes and sounded out their plans. They also brought in colleagues from outside the institution. During 1980, for example,
William Perry (Harvard) led an extended workshop on developmental approaches to teaching and learning, and David Kolb
(Case Western) led another on how to use experiential learning
theory both inside and beyond the traditional classroom. The
year 1981 saw a major emphasis placed on Alverno students as
women facing new problems and challenges in the 1980s. In
short, clarification, convergence, synthesis, and simplification
became dominant institutional values, as could be observed in
such phenomena as consolidation of departments, improved
internal and external communications, and the emergence of
faculty interest groups, such as on creativity or peace studies,
that were not direct and necessary outgrowths of the technical
program development.

The tradition of internal dialogue continued. While exchange of syllabi, assessments, and other learning materials had
long been common, the process was stepped up, and clearer criteria for evaluating their quality evolved. Resources improved
as an expanded board of trustees generated more gift revenue
and more grants were won. Salaries and benefits became less of

a problem. Since the college had a head start on its competitors for nontraditional student markets, it weathered fairly well the downturn in traditional age student populations, and the student body became more diverse. Alverno's program continued to enjoy national prominence, and its representatives traveled around the country as speakers and consultants. Some difficulties persisted then and continue into the present. For example, faculty need to refine their efforts to reach and motivate students of very different backgrounds, ages, and aptitudes. As they learn more about assessing performance, they need to keep reexamining the criteria whereby they judge what students do. Faculty also need to find creative ways of designing assessments of complex abilities, such as critical thinking. An even greater problem is the growing gap between incoming faculty and more experienced faculty—the gap in their respective facility with an ability-based program. Efforts are of course being made to deal with all these difficulties.

Future Approaches and Old Problems

Visitors often remark on how much time faculty spend talking about the important problems, how much energy they have devoted to solving them, and how much they seem to be enjoying themselves, above and beyond the moments of fatigue. They wonder how they might "take a piece of all this" back to their own institutions. "How did you do it?" they ask. For a long time we failed to grasp the meaning of the question; we assumed people were interested in a chronology of events, and so we would launch into a history of the last fifteen years at Alverno. But as our efforts brought us into close working contact with faculty and administrators from colleges around the country, we came to appreciate the real question, which might run something like this: "Given the typical characteristics of college faculty members, how was it possible for yours to design and implement a college-wide program?" By "typical characteristics" was meant, for example, that faculty view themselves primarily as scholars and specialists in their disciplines or professions and only secondarily as educators. Also, faculty value their own and their colleagues' individual autonomy too much to subordinate it to an institutional thrust. And above all, faculty are extraordinarily sensitive about the traditions surrounding liberal education and would be very cautious about instituting major changes. Because we agree that these descriptions do indeed characterize faculty in general, and in fact constitute the very strength of a college faculty, we must ask how these characteristic faculty strengths operated at Alverno to facilitate curricular change rather than impede it.

One major difference between the pursuit of excellence as an educator and as a scholar is in resources. Faculty who aspire to excellence as educators must discover or create their own form of excellence; mentors are not as available as they are to someone who aspires to excellence in scholarship. At Alverno, the necessary reliance by faculty on their own collective experience in the educative process has been one of the most significant factors in their developing a sense of expertise, indeed of pride. When an individual has to rely on her own and her colleagues' experiences, she is in the same position as when an individual moves beyond her mentors to create her own theoretical position. It is creative and elating, and our faculty thrive on those moments of professional autonomy.

An important step the faculty took has been the development of a new synthesis in undergraduate education—a synthesis that is premised on the realization that students do not necessarily aspire to follow them in mastering an academic specialty. They have thus had to discover the meaning that their fields might have for students aspiring to many different professions or life-styles. Almost ironically, the necessity of making one's field meaningful to such a broad and diverse audience actually requires a greater mastery of and facility with the essentials of that field than when one is addressing mostly specialists or future specialists. One can never take clarity and relevance to the audience for granted. The large nontraditional student population at Alverno thus actually becomes an intellectual advantage.

Finally, faculty simply found that by collaborating they could enhance each other's individual strengths and make better use of the academic context. As autonomous academics, college faculty share with many other professional groups a preference for individual responsibility, a desire to imprint their own creative stamp upon their work, and a latent suspicion of the effect that too much peer collaboration will have on their personal autonomy and creativity. It is surprising, therefore, to many of our colleagues across the country and at times also to ourselves that we embarked at all on a venture that involved—indeed required—faculty consensus on major curricular changes and sustained collaboration across disciplines. What helped initially was that our faculty were aware that the education of students results from the total thrust of the institution, involving not only its mission but its resources, admissions policies, and array of support services. Faculty-student interaction is just one part of the whole system. Much of the change we instituted resulted from group creativity, which in turn produced an exhilaration that became part of the institutional ambiance.

Further, the fact that all faculty had to master some aspects of such broad fields as developmental psychology, assessment design, creativity, and communications skills provided considerable satisfaction and challenge to them. Faculty also spent countless hours debating the meaning of higher education in today's world. To judge the changes they made in traditional liberal arts education, they used yardsticks that are, in fact, quite time honored, even ancient: "Can our students think critically, express themselves effectively, respond with depth to esthetic forms, and develop a meaningful philosophy of life?" We fanned the desire to do *something*, gave people the time to do it, and rewarded them for honestly evaluating their own efforts, squarely confronting what was not really working.

Our problems at Alverno are the familiar ones that many colleges often face: enrollment dips, fears emerging from uncertainty, slow decision making, overwork, lack of money, ineffective management, and poor communications internally and externally. But few of us at Alverno are bored, and our agenda for tomorrow is full because we developed early on—and supported with a regular budget allocation—a mechanism for researching and evaluating our success at meeting our mission. It gives us quick feedback on our strengths and weaknesses and shows us areas that need to be developed. The college has recently completed a seven-year longitudinal study of its students, one of the few of its kind in the country, and there are plans for more of this type of analysis. The spirit of inquiry and exploration continues to prevail at Alverno, enriching and invigorating the teaching and learning experience. And the ideal of community inherent in Alverno's tradition since the college's inception continues to strengthen our endeavors.

The following publications are available at printing cost from the Alverno Institute, Alverno College, 3401 South 39th Street, Milwaukee, Wisconsin 53215, or call (414) 647-3966: *Liberal Learning at Alverno College* (1976); *Assessment at Alverno College* (1979); *Nursing Education at Alverno College: A Liberal Arts Model* (1979); *Valuing at Alverno: The Valuing Process in Liberal Education* (1980); *Analysis and Communication at Alverno College: An Approach to Critical Thinking* (1984); and *Careering After College: Establishing the Validity of Abilities Learned in College for Later Careering and Professional Performance. Final Report to the National Institute of Education, Overview and Summary.* (1984).

11

Bradford College: Curriculum Reform and Institutional Renewal

Paul Byers Ranslow
David Charles Haselkorn

Bradford College is a private, coeducational, four-year liberal arts college located in northeast Massachusetts. Its seventy-acre, parklike campus is set in the Bradford section of Haverhill, Massachusetts, from which the college takes its name. In 1984, the college enrolled 422 students. Although modest by most comparisons, this figure is close to the historic high for the institution and represents a 5 percent increase over the previous year's total. Moreover, the enrollment gain was achieved against the backdrop of a 2.3 percent decline in enrollments at private liberal arts colleges across the nation. Equally significant, the freshman class entering in September 1984 was academically stronger than its predecessors, for the enrollment gain was built upon a 29 percent increase in applications, enabling admissions officials to be more selective than in previous years.

Nineteen eighty-four was significant for the college not just in terms of its favorable enrollment trends. As college officials and faculty led new students through a carefully designed freshman orientation program, they could look back upon an exhilarating (and exhausting) two and one-half years in which, together, they had

- formulated a new mission for Bradford College as a four-year practical liberal arts college;
- developed and implemented a new curriculum based upon that mission;
- increased enrollment;
- increased the size of the applicant pool and the quality of admitted applicants;
- attracted new faculty members from several of the nation's leading higher education institutions;
- increased the rigor of the academic program and upgraded student academic standards;
- strengthened institutional governance and enhanced the professional status of the faculty;
- moved from a red-ink budget to a healthy bottom line;
- increased foundation support dramatically;
- launched the largest capital campaign in the college's history; and
- received considerable national recognition for their accomplishments.

In sum, 1984 was something of a watershed for the institution, which, like many other small private liberal arts colleges across the country (the so-called invisible colleges), had been consigned to a fate of decline and extinction by the conventional wisdom in academe. In sharp contrast to the doom and gloom predictions, Bradford is thriving—not just surviving. A look at its recent (and not so recent) history will show how its success has been achieved.

A Look Back

The college began as Bradford Academy, one of a number of coeducational academies that found fertile soil in early nineteenth-century New England. Thirty prominent citizens of the parish of Bradford met in the spring of 1803 to establish a school "for the purpose of promoting piety, religion, and morality, and for the education of youth in such of the liberal arts and sciences as the trustees . . . shall direct." Drawing students from all over New England, the young academy helped prepare many of them for college and many others directly for positions in society. Graduates became teachers, lawyers, doctors, and missionaries.

In 1836, however, Bradford chose to devote itself exclusively to the education of women. But instead of simply offering the then standard program of embroidery, painting, and domestic arts, Bradford began offering women a diploma for college-level study. By then the academic program combined the classical curriculum with modern subjects, which had begun to form part of higher education in the late eighteenth and early nineteenth centuries. These included natural philosophy, modern languages, and debate. By 1902, the academy had started to offer "advanced course work" for those "special" students interested in teaching. The school became Bradford Academy and Junior College and set in motion the curriculum additions that would soon cause it to abandon its academy status altogether.

In 1932, the former academy became the first junior college in New England to be accredited by the New England Association of Schools and Colleges. Flourishing as a junior college for women, the college for nearly forty years had an established identity as one of the three Bs—Bennett, Briarcliff, and Bradford. It was, in other words, one of the most prestigious two-year women's colleges in the country. But by the late 1960s danger signals began to appear on the horizon that would presage a decade of drift and decline for the college.

First, like small colleges in the United States generally, almost "all women's colleges were relatively impoverished" (Jencks and Riesman, 1968, p. 305). This economic situation was exacerbated for two-year private women's colleges such as Bradford. Their alumnae often transferred their college loyalty either to the senior college or university from which they had received bachelor's degrees or to their husbands' alma maters. Second, two-year colleges were traditionally denied access to some of the significant sources of funding for four-year colleges, particularly foundation and research monies. Finally, in the late sixties and seventies, the growth in public community college enrollments began to impinge on Bradford and other elite private schools, and to put added pressure on these tuition-driven institutions.

Although some research (Cole, 1972; Keezer, 1969) identified certain benefits in having women study in a community that was not male dominated, the move toward coeducation during the sixties was a strong one, resisted by only a relatively small group of women's colleges throughout the country. Against this backdrop and without much debate, according to faculty who were at the college at the time, Bradford opted for coeducation in 1971. When the fall term began in 1972, there were nine males in attendance. Later that same year Bradford became a baccalaureate institution. Again, this major change met with little resistance from faculty and alumni.

The decade of the seventies was a difficult time for Bradford. The transition from a two-year to a four-year college, coupled with the move to coeducation, created complex problems. The fact that the transition from a two- to a four-year institution was not accompanied by concomitant changes in administrative policies or instructional resources compounded the problems. One faculty member described this period as one in which Bradford "essentially [operated] a four-year college with a two-year curriculum." Lack of curricular planning was also evident in the proliferation of faculty-proposed majors and the inevitable turf battles that ensued.

The turmoil that this created on campus contributed to a further decline in enrollment. In 1971–72 the college enrolled 326 students; by 1975–76 its enrollment had declined by 20 percent. Further indications of the decade-long turmoil at Bradford are easy to find. For example, although the size of the faculty declined, the number of courses offered rose from 119 in 1967–68 (for a student body of 423) to 151 nine years later (for only 261 students). In 1975, the New England Association of Schools and Colleges expressed concern because only 19 percent of Bradford's faculty held doctorates (Martin, 1984, p. 32); moreover, the faculty narrowly resisted a drive to unionize in 1981. Adding to all these difficulties, unbalanced budgets since 1968 had left Bradford with an accumulated deficit. Bradford ended the 1981–82 academic year with a deficit of over $175,000 and an endowment of barely $2 million. Finally, the physical plant, although considered complete and in fairly good condition, had accumulated $500,000 in deferred maintenance.

In fairness, there had been some improvements made at Bradford during the 1960s, mostly in the area of campus renovations. However, the on-campus struggle of the 1970s, following on the heels of the physical expansion of the college, had greatly increased the college's difficulties. The decade can most accurately be described as a period in which Bradford was searching for an educational model that would permit the college to adhere to its liberal arts mission, retain its traditional emphasis on education and service, and continue to serve the educational needs of its students. However, the decade ended for Bradford with no solution in sight. By 1980, faced with a blurred mission and an uncertain future, the college was adrift.

Nationally, higher education entered the new decade in very similar straits. The baby boom that had buoyed enrollments since the sixties began to deflate. Demographers warned of an impending "baby bust." Enrollment decline spelled retrenchment at most institutions. Rising costs and high inflation added to their woes. By 1980, the consensus was that higher education had definitely entered an era of adversity. Colleges and universities were forced to readjust their sights and reevaluate their ways of thinking. But Bradford's response to the new environment was, in some respects, unique. Instead of adopting a crisis management mentality, the college seized the opportunity to install new leadership, reassess its instructional mission, clarify its institutional goals, strengthen its academic standards, and reform its administrative procedures. The resignation of the dean in the spring of 1981, followed by that of the president one year later, set the stage for a dramatic period of institutional renewal.

Rebuilding Bradford College

This process began with the hiring of a new academic dean, Janice Green, in 1981. Prior to coming to Bradford,

Green had taught at Tufts University and had served for five years with the Massachusetts Board of Higher Education, where she was vice-chancellor for academic affairs. It soon became evident to her that many of the internal difficulties that had beset Bradford in the seventies were the result of poorly defined and, in some instances, inappropriate and inconsistently applied personnel policies and practices. Green was able to instill confidence in the faculty by involving them heavily in curricular matters on campus while offering strong academic and administrative direction. Under her leadership, the faculty was restored to an appropriate role in academic planning, policy making, and governance.

Equally significant, in 1982 the college selected Arthur E. Levine to be its new president. Levine, a widely published sociologist and former senior fellow with the Carnegie Foundation for the Advancement of Teaching, was an expert in curricular issues and institutional reform. He brought to Bradford a clear vision for an educationally distinctive liberal arts college, formulated during ten years of research in higher education. Convinced that a small liberal arts college could remain vital, Levine used the long selection and interviewing process that he had to undergo as a candidate for the presidency of Bradford to propose a unique new mission and curriculum for the college.

Thus, in 1982, Bradford promulgated a clear and coherent statement of its mission and embarked upon a major curricular review and reform to reflect that mission. Levine had identified five key challenges facing undergraduate education:

1. The need to enhance student communication skills;
2. The need to rethink general education, or the learning that should be common to all people;
3. The need to provide students with better career preparation;
4. The need to reaffirm the importance of ethical values and social concerns;
5. The need to respond to changing demographic, financial, social, and technological conditions.

Although these challenges were common to most institutions of higher learning, Bradford's own recent experience of curricular drift and enrollment decline suggested that a coherent response to each of these challenges could be a first step toward institutional renewal. The faculty and trustees agreed. So enthusiastic were the faculty that in October 1982, just two months after Levine arrived on campus, they unanimously endorsed the blueprint for a practical liberal arts college that Levine had brought with him, signaling a new phase in the institution's history.

A Curricular Blueprint

The Bradford Plan for a Practical Liberal Arts Education (as it has come to be called) seeks to provide students with a high-quality liberal arts education and at the same time prepare them practically for life after college. Its goals are (1) to educate students about the existing society of which they are a part and (2) to teach them the higher-order intellectual skills and knowledge necessary to live in that society in an autonomous and socially beneficial manner. Implicit in the plan is a vision of the educated person, a vision true to the historic ideals of both the liberal arts and Bradford College.

Seven principal elements combine to form a sound, sequential, and coherent program of study:

1. *Communication Skills*—All students are required to become fluent in the two fundamental human languages: words and numbers.
2. *A Core General Education Curriculum*—Students are asked to study those subjects that underlie and give insight into the common human experience: groups and institutions, human heritage, ethics and values, arts and esthetics, global perspectives, and work and leisure. Seven specific courses make up the general education core. They are required of all students.
3. *Freshman Inquiry*—At the end of the first year, each student is required to prepare an essay examining the fresh-

man experience and discussing future academic plans. The
paper is defended before a panel composed of faculty, administrators, and another student.

4. *Comprehensive Major*—All students are required to study a
    broad-gauged interdisciplinary major in one of five areas—
    humanities, human studies, creative arts, management, or a
    student-created major.

5. *Practical Minors*—Students are offered clusters of four or
    five courses in such useful skill areas as computers and writ-
    ing or in such practical theme areas as public administra-
    tion, arts management, or gerontology.

6. *Internships*—Student internships in the junior year combine
    with the core general education course on work to provide
    experience at a job that connects theory to practice. Fac-
    ulty internships allow instructors to spend a winter or sum-
    mer break applying their knowledge and skills in the world
    outside academe. Internships are also available for commu-
    nity professionals—individuals with notable accomplish-
    ments in the nonacademic world—that allow them to spend
    a week on campus working on a project of interest to them
    and to share their results with the college and local commu-
    nities.

7. *Senior and Junior Projects*—As the capstone to a Bradford
    education, all seniors are asked to formulate a question,
    work that question through to a conclusion, and produce a
    major project. As preparation in the junior year, they go
    through the same exercise as part of a group—a faculty
    member poses the question and a class develops an answer
    together. Members of the class present the finished project
    to the college community. A week of intellectual celebra-
    tion—readings, speakers, films, theater, performance, music
    —is planned to coincide with the junior project exhibit and
    freshman inquiry.

With its accent on practical education, the Bradford Plan
is clearly responsive to the times. It is designed to meet student
and parental vocational concerns in the context of the liberal
arts, where enrollments are now plummeting. Nationwide, over

the past fifteen years, enrollments in the liberal arts have fallen by more than a third while attendance in professional subjects such as business administration has grown by more than 50 percent. The authors of the Bradford Plan—for the faculty soon became the driving force in its development—are confident that the rigor of the program and the skills that it seeks to teach will make graduates quite desirable from an employer's point of view, and thus will make the liberal arts more attractive to prospective students.

A great deal of effort was required to transform the Bradford Plan blueprint into a curricular reality. Following its approval, the faculty curriculum committee met weekly throughout the fall and spring semesters of 1982–83 to design and work out the details of the new curriculum. Individual faculty and groups of faculty were asked by that body to develop new courses and the other elements of the curriculum. The approval process varied widely from class to class—some courses were approved by the curriculum committee on the first presentation; others required several submissions and a good deal of negotiation. The faculty worked on the plan without release time or additional compensation throughout the academic year and summer of 1982–83.

In January 1983, a full-day faculty workshop on the Bradford Plan was held to review preliminary course proposals, and the following month a college-wide convocation considered the new curriculum and its consequences for Bradford. In March, meetings were held with students on every dormitory floor to explain the plan and answer their questions. A series of very well attended faculty development lunches and evening symposia were scheduled throughout the year. All college publications were rewritten to reflect the new curriculum. Meetings were held with alumni in twenty cities and with parents on campus to explain Bradford's program and plans. By September 1983, about two-thirds of the Bradford curriculum was in place. By fall of 1984, the program was 99 percent complete. It is required of all freshmen who entered Bradford during or after the fall semester of 1984, and optional for all students enrolled prior to that date.

Results on Campus

There is also no mistaking the enthusiasm of the faculty and students for this curricular revision. It represents a curriculum "with direction and vision," as a longtime faculty member observed. "It will encourage students to remain in the liberal arts plus add practical values," she concluded. Another faculty member who had been at Bradford for almost twenty years added: "We used to dream without substance here. This plan represents the first realistic and solid attempt to address the problems of a college this size in attracting students and offering them a good education." A graduating senior commenting on the plan in the student newspaper noted, "Everytime I read about the Bradford Plan, or learn about it, I get very excited and wish I were a freshman again."

However, from the standpoint of the plan's impact on the campus, its most important aspect may be the extent to which it has unified the college community and helped focus its energy on achieving a central mission. This sense of harmony extends as well to faculty-administration relationships, which are acrimonious on so many other campuses. One senses at Bradford more than the usual good feelings associated with a president's "honeymoon" period. One faculty member summed up this way the feeling that many others share: "With the new administration we feel more secure." Further, she states, for the first time there are "a president and dean who have presented us with an intellectually valid and cohesive plan."

A good indication of the administrators' positive attitudes at Bradford is their frequent use of "we." They have a strong sense of belonging to a team, and most attribute this feeling to the president. They like Levine's casual, relaxed style, but more significantly they appreciate his reliance on their participation in administrative decisions. On his arrival, Levine formed the president's cabinet, which includes the director of admissions, the vice-president for administration, the vice-president and academic dean, the vice-president for college relations, and the dean of students. The president actively seeks the advice of this group to chart institutional direction within the context of the college's practical liberal arts mission.

As president, Levine seems to be mirroring much of the style of management outlined by Peters and Waterman (1982) in their bestselling *In Search of Excellence*. Peters and Waterman identified participatory management as a common element in some of the most successful companies in the United States. These authors also pointed out that the leader's role is to be an "orchestrator and labeler." A leader must "make meanings" by shaping action into an enduring commitment to a new strategic plan. Through his articulation of the Bradford Plan, Levine has performed this task admirably.

Bradford College now has a commonly understood direction for the first time in the recent history of the institution. The plan appears to have had this positive impact on the campus community for basically three reasons. First, the plan centers on precisely what the college always felt it was, a liberal arts institution. The board of trustees and the faculty of the college could see that clear continuity in the new curriculum even as they refocused their efforts to meet the new educational challenges. Second, the turbulent recent history of the college left it clamoring for strong leadership and a reasonable direction. Finally, the plan's adoption took place within a context of growing faculty empowerment. Changes in academic and administrative policies gave faculty ample opportunity to participate fully in the renewal process. Despite the extreme burden it places on the faculty, this participation has contributed to the sense of "ownership" critical to successful institution-wide reform.

Administrative Changes. While the new curriculum was being formulated, the college began to deal affirmatively with the administrative and fiscal gaps left over from its transition from a two-year to a four-year institution. Among the improvements that it can now point to are:

- development and implementation of policies, criteria, and procedures for faculty evaluation;
- development and implementation of a faculty rank and promotion system; establishment of a faculty committee on promotion;
- development and implementation of a faculty salary schedule linked to criteria for rank and promotion;

- introduction of multiyear contracts for faculty holding the rank of associate professor and above; development and implementation of a faculty contract form;
- development and implementation of a maternity/paternity leave policy;
- development and implementation of procedures for consideration of faculty grievances;
- development of policies and procedures designed to encourage and support faculty development;
- creation of a faculty manual; and
- establishment of an administrative advisory committee to enable elected staff representatives to meet regularly with senior college administrators to discuss policies and procedures, fringe benefits, and so on.

Perhaps above all, Bradford can point to a strengthened faculty. As of May 1984, 44 percent of the forty-three active Bradford faculty members held doctoral degrees. All those not holding doctorates had earned master's degrees considered terminal in their fields—the master of fine arts or master of business administration, for example. The advanced degrees earned by Bradford faculty come from some of the most prestigious institutions in the Northeast, including Brown, Boston College, Boston University, Princeton, Cornell, and Tufts. In addition, some Bradford faculty have received degrees from large and well-respected state universities such as Iowa, Kansas, North Carolina, New York, Oregon, and Wisconsin.

The new administration also put far greater stress on strategic planning in setting institutional priorities than had previously been the case at the college. For example:

- Five-year budget and enrollment planning was instituted; projections are now examined and updated semiannually, using the most informed assumptions and data available.
- The senior administrative team (college cabinet) meets weekly for several hours of planning and problem-solving discussions.
- Each summer the senior team holds a three-day off-campus

retreat for evaluation of the previous year's activities and formulation of specific goals and tasks for the coming year as they fall within the purview of each administrator. These goals are reassessed at the end of each semester. Senior administrators are held accountable for meeting their goals.

- Day-long faculty retreats are held prior to the beginning of each semester for discussion of and workshops on critical issues.
- Faculty committees are actively engaged in planning in areas of curriculum, faculty affairs, academic standards, library development, and student life.
- Monthly meetings of all department heads permit not only exchange of information but strategic planning that involves several departments.
- Open meetings of faculty and staff are held annually. These "frank discussion" sessions provide a forum for the exchange of information, ideas, and concerns. The sessions are particularly helpful because they allow the administration to communicate fiscal priorities and constraints to the college community, as well as to explain the administrative procedures that have been developed to control the allocation of resources.
- The president annually delivers a "state-of-the-college" message to faculty, administrative, and staff groups to ensure that each member of the community knows and can question the decisions that have been made, and how and why they have been made.

Improving Bradford's Financial Position. Bradford's new administration has also steadily sought to improve the college's financial position through greater budgetary control and enhanced fund-raising efforts. As a result, since 1981 the college has been operating under balanced budgets. The $175,000 deficit that the college had accumulated by 1981 had been whittled by 60 percent to just over $70,000 by 1984. The $500,000 deferred maintenance requirement had been reduced by 40 percent. Moreover, during the last two years, Bradford has enjoyed increases of 48 percent and 10 percent, respectively, in the amount of institutional income realized from endowment investment; and with a $5 million endowment drive that began in the fall of 1984 the institution hopes to increase its investment base.

While much of the credit for these accomplishments must go to the budgetary vigilance of Peter Freedman, vice-president for administration, college officials like to stress that the management improvements they have made cannot be divorced from the college's new mission. According to Levine, "A well-defined mission provides the best basis for institutional management. It dictates priorities and produces a daily tool for decision making. It defines the relationships among programs, budget, development, admissions, publications, and other campus operations."

His position is upheld by recent research by Chaffee (1984) that has shown that of two groups of colleges in the seventies faced with increasingly difficult environments, the most successful were those whose adaptive strategies flowed from a clear articulation of mission. Certainly, in view of the dramatic impact that the Bradford Plan has made in the financial condition of the campus, as well as in staff morale, there are few at the college who would take issue with Levine's thesis.

Strategic Planning

Colleges are distinct cultures, not just organizations. As such, they are held together not only by interrelated functions but by shared meanings. At Bradford, shared meanings take precedence over the latest fads in enrollment management, marketing, and fund raising; and this may be one of the secrets of the school's success. It is also an area where Levine's strengths as an institutional leader are most in evidence. Of course, the Bradford Plan has helped create this shared sense of mission and purpose or "subjective consensus" (Peck, 1983) that is vital to any institutional reform. This has enabled the institution to move in a commonly understood direction. As a consequence, Levine and his colleagues are able to concentrate much of their energies on strategic planning and institutional advancement.

And in three areas that have been crucial to the college's turn-around—recruitment, development, and public affairs—the college has pegged its efforts on effectively communicating the value of its new curriculum.

Admissions and Financial Aid. Bradford relies on tuition and fees for three-fourths of its income. Consequently, admissions receives a great deal of attention in the strategic planning sessions of the president's cabinet. In addition, the four-person admissions staff at Bradford emphasizes the Bradford Plan in virtually all activities designed to attract the interest of prospective students. Not only does the Bradford Plan receive first-page attention in the catalogue, but the college's "viewbook" (admissions recruiting publication) focuses almost exclusively on the plan.

Bradford also makes extensive use of the College Scholarship Service's recruitment materials. With an 18 percent response rate (compared with an 11 percent response rate nationally), as many as 10,000 inquiries may be generated after the "Greetings from Bradford" letter is sent. This first letter and a follow-up sent to nonrespondents (which has yielded as many as 1,000 additional inquiries) both have an informal and friendly tone. The director of admissions, Greg Polakow, believes that an informal approach is more effective than the "stuffy" ones used by many other institutions. The Student Search Service is expensive (this year Bradford will spend about $18,000 on it, including printing, postage, and the cost of purchasing the names), but the cost of under $2 per inquiry seems reasonable when compared with the cost of having a staff member travel to meet with prospective students.

Even so, Bradford relies heavily on visits to high schools. Despite some research that argues against its cost effectiveness (Ihlanfeldt, 1980), Bradford's admissions director feels that, while the college is still in the process of becoming more visible, printed materials cannot yet take the place of a well-trained admissions officer. The admissions staff travels a combined total of twenty-five weeks a year in an attempt at more face-to-face meetings with students, parents, and secondary school counselors. In addition to visiting areas where Bradford has traditionally attracted students (public high schools in the Northeast), the admissions staff has also targeted new areas, specifically the Southwest (including California) and the Southeast.

Bradford officials clearly recognize that financial aid to students is an important aspect of the admissions package. In 1981-82, the student aid expenditure at Bradford was $353,000, or 10 percent of institutional expenditures. In the 1982-83 budget, over $650,000 was spent on student aid (an increase of 85 percent), representing 16 percent of the college's expenses. The Financial Aid Office sends out "quick response" forms to give potential applicants an estimate of how much financial aid they are likely to receive if they apply and are admitted. In addition, those students who are admitted and qualify for assistance are sent their financial aid package along with their letter of admission. According to Polakow, it is in Bradford's best interest that the students and their parents know what financial help is available to them as soon as possible.

The results to date have been encouraging. Over the past two years, enrollment has risen by 9 percent. Last year the inquiry pool rose by 46 percent while the applicant pool increased by 29 percent, which meant that there were between four and five applications for every new freshman admitted. Today, much of the admissions effort is targeted toward increasing the inquiry pool, which would allow Bradford to become even more selective.

Development. Since adopting the plan, the college has spent considerable time cultivating corporate and foundation sources able to provide grant monies. The relative success of Levine's efforts (along with those of his vice-president for college relations and the assistant to the president, who is the college's principal grant writer) is evident in the awards that Bradford has received over the past two years. Foundation support rose from $400 in 1982 to $300,000 in 1983-84. Grants have been received from the Exxon Education Foundation ($125,000), Jessie B. Cox Charitable Trust ($75,000), Ford Foundation ($35,000), Fund for the Improvement of Postsecondary Education ($52,000), National Endowment for the Humanities ($51,000), Atlantic Richfield Foundation ($25,000), Surdna Foundation ($100,000), and several others. This has been the result of a conscious, determined, and ongoing effort at Bradford.

Neither Levine nor Freedman sees the future financial health of Bradford tied exclusively to the attraction of grant funds. Rather, they look upon grants received as supplements to the college's other income sources—supplements that allow Bradford to pursue programs or activities that it could not otherwise afford. Equally important, these funds have added the imprimatur of the nation's leading educational philanthropies to the college's endeavors. Such endorsements provide added fuel to the college's development programs (alumni giving, annual fund, capital campaign, and so on) and public relations programs.

Recently the college has embarked upon a three-year, $5 million capital campaign to increase the size of its endowment. It is designed to reach personally the Bradford family of some 8,000 alumni in thirty-four geographic areas. By the spring of 1985, (six months into the campaign), the college had raised 50 percent of its goal. College leaders are confident that the momentum and enthusiasm that the Bradford Plan has generated will help put them over the top by campaign's end.

Public Relations: Improving Bradford's Visibility. Bradford has been favorably featured in numerous articles in the public media since its adoption of the Bradford Plan. As in the case of the college's successful grants program, this is the result of an intensive effort by Levine, his assistant, and the college's public relations staff to gain attention for the college. Articles mentioning the college have appeared in the *New York Times, USA Today,* the *Boston Globe,* the *Christian Science Monitor, Newsweek, U.S. News and World Report,* and the *Miami Herald.* News stories have run on the Associated Press and United Press International wire services, and Levine has been the subject of numerous television and radio interviews.

Presentations have been made on Bradford and the Bradford Plan at professional meetings (for example, at the College Board, the Association of General and Liberal Studies, and the

Association of American Colleges) by Levine, the academic
dean, and members of the faculty. Nor has the professional literature been ignored, with *Change, Liberal Education,* the *Journal of Cooperative Education,* the *National Forum,* and the
Chronicle of Higher Education being just a sample of the journals in which articles have appeared about Bradford or by Bradford authors. Levine and his colleagues have also taken the
Bradford message around the country, speaking before business
and community leaders, parents, school principals and superintendents, guidance counselors, and so on. Key education leaders also receive regular mailings on the college. In 1984, Bradford's improved public information program received an
honorable mention in the annual Case awards for college public
relations offices.

In addition to these attempts to make Bradford more
visible to the general public, much effort has gone into bringing
Bradford alumni up-to-date on the college. Soon after becoming
president, Levine traveled around the country to meet with
groups of Bradford alumni, many of whom had all but lost contact with the institution. He also was especially careful to maintain contact with those graduates who had been consistent supporters of the college. Levine sees the 8,000 living alumni as a
potentially strong base for the financial support that will be crucial to Bradford's growth. Moreover, the alumni are continually
kept informed about the progress the college is making, and this
effort has been helped by an expanded edition of *Bradford
Now,* the alumni newspaper published three times a year.

In sum, much of the success that the college has achieved
can be ascribed to effective communication on and off campus.
Beyond making technical improvements in its publications and
public information programs, Bradford's leadership has understood the fundamentally interrelated nature of each of the college's activities. This translates into an ability to use the college's increased visibility to benefit admissions efforts, fund
raising, faculty recruiting, and general morale on campus.

The overall strategy that Bradford College employs is a
simple one. By clarifying its mission, the college has been able
to capture the imagination and support of both the campus

community and important constituencies beyond the campus. The Bradford Plan for a Practical Liberal Arts Education has become the linchpin of a coherent, institution-wide strategy for advancement. As a result of this well-defined, widely understood mission, Bradford has emerged from the anonymity of its "invisible college" status and is beginning to play a national role in higher education. With Levine as its principal spokesperson, Bradford's practical liberal arts curriculum is gaining the college both visibility and acclaim. But the college community realizes its job is by no means complete. Faculty groups are presently developing a new and much-needed major in the natural sciences, a four-year honors program, adult and summer programming, and an expanded instructional role for the computer. Ongoing evaluation of the new curriculum is also a key agenda item. Thus, Bradford's recent successes have bred new challenges.

Whether or not the college can continue to build on its achievements depends on many factors, not the least of which is today's unforgiving environment for small liberal arts colleges. However, the momentum the college has built, the strides it is making to improve academically and financially, and the cohesion its new mission has created on campus have given the Bradford community a new confidence in the future.

References

Chaffee, E. E. "Successful Strategic Management in Small Private Colleges." *Journal of Higher Education,* Mar./Apr. 1984, pp. 212–241.

Cole, C. C., Jr. "A Case for the Womens' Colleges." *College Board Review,* 1972, 42 (2).

Ihlanfeldt, W. *Achieving Optimal Enrollments and Tuition Revenues: A Guide to Modern Methods of Market Research, Student Recruitment, and Institutional Pricing.* San Francisco: Jossey-Bass, 1980.

Jencks, C., and Riesman, D. *The Academic Revolution.* Chicago: University of Chicago Press, 1968.

Keezer, D. M. "Watch Out, Girls." *The New Republic,* 1969, *161* (11).

Martin, P. "A Step Inside the Circle: Bradford College 1968–1975." Unpublished paper, Harvard Graduate School of Education, 1984.

Peck, R. D. *Future Focusing.* Washington, D.C.: Council of Independent Colleges, 1983.

Peters, T. J., and Waterman, R. H., Jr. *In Search of Excellence.* New York: Harper & Row, 1982.

12

Hood College:
A Decision to Be Different

Martha E. Church

Taking a firm decision to launch a college for women that would be different from those already in existence in the latter half of the nineteenth century, the pastors of the Potomac Synod of the Reformed Church of the United States founded the Woman's College of Frederick (Maryland) in 1893, with the full expectation that women would not only work in the home but would also enter professions outside the home. (At the turn of the century, of course, the helping professions appeared to be the only ones women might possibly enter.) The founders of the Woman's College of Frederick organized the curriculum so that all students would benefit both from taking foundation work in the liberal arts and from electing a major that either built upon one of the liberal arts or sciences or provided professional preparation in such fields as early childhood education and home economics. The founding president, Joseph Henry Apple, not only set the academic and moral tone of the college but raised the necessary funds to educate and house the college's growing student body.

In the early days of the college, Apple encouraged an alumna of its antecedent institution, Frederick Female Semi-

nary (chartered in 1839), to make several substantial gifts to his
fledgling women's college. Margaret Scholl Hood responded
with sufficient generosity to permit the purchase of land and
thus to make possible a move from the seminary's buildings in
downtown Frederick. In gratitude to Margaret Hood, the board
of directors voted in 1912 to change the college's name to Hood
College. From 1913 onward, the college's diplomas have proud-
ly carried the name of Hood. By preparing women for the world
of work, Hood College chose to be different from other wom-
en's colleges, which were preparing women to transmit the nation's culture to the next generation within the home. In the
mid 1980s, Hood continues to be strongly committed to its
original mission.

Danger Signals

During its first seventy-five years, Hood benefited from
continuity in presidential and board leadership, stability in its
academic program, infrequent turnover in faculty and staff, and
a relatively constant enrollment of slightly more than 500
undergraduate resident women. It maintained a student-faculty
ratio of eleven to one, it employed a high proportion of women
on its faculty and staff, it kept its budgets balanced, and it had
a careful building and maintenance program. It had a small but
steadily growing endowment and enjoyed tremendous loyalty
among its alumnae. Special mention must be made of the generosity of the family of Clarence Hodson, founder of the Hodson Trust, which has been and will continue to be Hood's major, long-term benefactor until 2020. Yet some of these very
strengths proved to be sources of emerging weakness. By the
late 1960s, it was evident to many familiar with Hood that the
college had begun to drift. In retrospect, the lack of vigorous
presidential leadership permitted the college to stray from its
firm sense of purpose and to become vulnerable to the rush to
coeducation among New England colleges, the stirrings of the
women's movement, and the general student unrest related to
the war in Vietnam.

By the academic year 1969–70, the college was beginning

to encounter an important danger signal—enrollment decline. It was not a dramatic decline but rather a nearly invisible, incremental decline. Enough uneasiness about Hood's future was beginning to be evident among students, faculty, staff, and alumnae, however, that the board of trustees decided to look for a new president in 1971. During this same period, the leadership of the local community college sounded a second danger signal: There was a strong possibility that a four-year public institution might open in Frederick County. Thus, the trustees took action in 1970 to admit local commuting males and to retain the residential college as a college for women. Because they took this action at the behest of the chairman of the Board of Education of Frederick County, which had jurisdiction over the school system and the community college, they did not engage in any discussion of coeducation. Rather, they took this step to protect both the community college and Hood and to provide increased services to the local community.

The third danger signal was less evident to those outside of higher education, and it paralleled actions being taken by faculty on many campuses across the nation. With Hood's academic compass somewhat askew, the faculty voted, without much discussion, to abandon all degree requirements, except for a freshman course in composition and two units of physical activity. Thus, no one seemed clear about Hood's mission, about what kind of student body it should have, or about what curricular actions it should take in response to such phenomena as the women's movement.

Beginning the Turnaround

In 1972 the trustees selected Ross Pritchard as the new president of Hood, and he immediately set out to bring the college back on course. On October 15, 1974, *The Chronicle of Higher Education* reported on its front page that Hood had 390 new students in contrast to 170 in 1973. What had happened? Pritchard and his colleagues had pursued several new strategies. To begin with, the college made use of the Middle States accreditation self-study process to reaffirm its mission as that of a

woman's college. Next, admissions consultants analyzed studies
of applicants who chose other colleges and determined that
the college was perceived as "traditional, unexciting, socially
limited, and restricted to a few strong academic areas." In response to these perceptions, Pritchard pushed hard for (1) curricular changes to increase career options for women, such as
adding career components in each academic department; (2)
more relaxed social regulations; (3) establishment of a continuing education program that would open the college's regular degree programs to students (primarily women) twenty-five
and older and provide counseling support to them; (4) development of internship programs for academic credit; (5) upgrading
of physical facilities; (6) *no* changes in fees for three years; and
(7) aggressive marketing of the college.

The college also decided to use reserves to fund curricular
changes, faculty appointments, and facility improvements. In
1972, the college had $500,000 in an operating reserve fund
and $800,000 in the plant reserve fund, both of which had
been fully used up by the close of the 1973-74 academic year.
On a temporary basis, the Hodson Trust agreed to have its major annual gifts applied to the operating budget.

Responding magnificently to these new priorities, the
faculty developed solid but innovative programs throughout the
curriculum, including new programs or concentrations in art
therapy, medical technology, environmental studies, management, special education, Latin American studies, consumer
studies, law and society, clinical psychology, recreation and
leisure studies, and social work. In addition, women on the faculty and staff worked on a variety of women's issues, including
use of more neutral language in college documents. These changes
were included in a new catalogue that carried the subtitle "A New
Dimension in Higher Education for Today's Woman."

At the president's behest and to keep a four-year public
institution out of Frederick, the faculty worked to enhance the
college's graduate program in education and developed a number of graduate programs in other areas of academic strength.
Thus, the faculty applied an interdisciplinary approach to the

human sciences, offering concentrations in administration and management, contemporary government, early childhood education, elementary school science and mathematics, environmental biology, psychology, public affairs, reading, and special education. The college also began to offer master's degrees in gerontology and community counseling and developed a master of science program in biomedical sciences in cooperation with scientists in cancer and infectious disease research at nearby Fort Detrick. These strategies brought Hood back into the mainstream of higher education, caught the attention of many colleagues at other institutions, and allowed the college to recruit and enroll better students. The decision to be different kept Hood apart from other institutions until most others decided to be "different" too.

Between the fall of 1972 and the spring of 1975, however, the faculty had become increasingly restless as they watched what they termed the "collapse of collegial governance." Budget preparation took place in the president's office behind seemingly closed doors. The fourteen persons who reported directly to the president appeared to be sparring with one another for attention and resources. Only in June of 1975 did the trustees become aware that the college budget had crossed the line from black to red in 1974. The use of reserves and Hodson monies masked this situation from most observers. In fact, the trustees, who by now had decided to replace Pritchard, learned that same month that the new president would inherit a budget $300,000 in the red rather than what they had thought would be a budget $300,000 in the black. What had happened? Short-term responses had worked, but at a cost to the morale and finances of the college. Longer-term strategies would be required to stabilize the college and complete the turnaround.

Longer-Term Strategies

As Hood's new president in 1975, I diagnosed the college's immediate needs in the following terms:

Problems	*Proposed Solutions*
1. Need for healing among faculty and staff	Return to faculty and staff participation in decision making
2. Growth without a plan	Necessity of linking planning to budgeting
3. Expenditures beyond the means of the college	Balanced budget; appropriate fee increases and belt tightening
4. Admission of local commuting males in 1970; passage of Title IX in 1972; lack of clarity of mission	Clarification of mission of the college first as woman's college and second as institution to serve local community
5. Lack of equity in salaries and need for overall improvement in salary levels	High priority for salaries in budgeting
6. Hodson Trust monies in operating budget	Placement of these sizable annual gifts in endowment
7. Organizational concerns about too many persons reporting to president	Establishment of four administrative divisions
8. Student life concerns, such as lack of key counseling services, living space, and so on	Expand services; find housing
9. Haphazard development efforts	Search for chief development officer; establishment of development and external relations division
10. Two large classes moving through the college at the same time and consequences of this for the college	Admissions and publications in need of further attention

What was most urgently needed was leadership that would build on the college's basic strengths—its mission as a women's college, its trustees, its faculty and staff, its curricular programs

and services, its loyal alumnae, and its position of respect in the
Middle Atlantic area. What were problems, therefore, could become opportunities if they were carefully documented, expli-
cated, and then addressed.

With the assistance of a broadly based Long-Range Planning Task Force, faculty, staff, students, and trustees discussed,
revised, and enlarged the college's mission statement. In November 1976, the board of trustees adopted a mission statement
that addressed Hood's role first and foremost as a contemporary liberal arts college for women and secondly as a major educational resource for women and men living in the Frederick
area. The president of Frederick Community College assured
Hood's president that its physical education department would
be available to assist its counterpart at Hood, should there ever
be a challenge related to Title IX. During 1985-86, the mission
statement will be reviewed again in light of various studies conducted in 1984-85.

Budget hearings before a budget review committee composed of elected faculty, senior officers, and student government leaders brought the college budget into the open, with all
line items except individual salaries available for review. Charts
produced and distributed annually make it evident that salary
equity has been achieved and maintained. Financial aid policies
were studied and revised so that Hood money will be distributed last, not first. Balancing the budget and maintaining salary
and wage equity continue to be the president's highest priorities
within the fiscal area.

Simultaneously, work went forward on governance issues,
staffing, student services, admissions, publications, creation of
an information base for planning, cost saving in energy, annual
giving, and meeting local educational needs. Analysis of student
transcripts confirmed the need to look at degree requirements.
So, after the faculty completed work on revamping and modern-
izing the faculty code, it commenced work in 1978-79 on a study
of degree requirements, with (1) discussions and a vote taking
place during 1979-80; (2) courses designed, voted upon, and
placed in the catalogue in 1980-81; and (3) implementation of
a core curriculum in 1981-82. The Hood faculty take pride in
these efforts and believe they have focused the curriculum on

the crucial needs of students in the 1980s and 1990s. While they are fully aware of the importance of good advising, they believe a guided curriculum will fill in gaps and ensure that skills have been learned and breadth has been achieved.

In the five-year period that ended in 1983, the college was awarded numerous major grants. For example, it received a Title III grant of $950,000 to support substantive curricular improvements, purchase of library materials, faculty development in various departments, establishment of a Learning Assessment and Resource Center, and so on. The National Science Foundation Consortium for the Advancement of Undergraduate Science Education awarded the college $250,000 to substantially upgrade its computer capacity and to establish an academic computing center. In addition, the Fund for the Improvement of Postsecondary Education gave $150,000 for expanded educational opportunities for Hispanic women; the Beneficial Corporation and the Pew Memorial Trust gave $75,000 and $100,000, respectively, for the academic computing center; the Charles A. Dana Foundation gave a $300,000 challenge grant for the Resource Management Center; the State of Maryland gave $450,000 for Hodson Science Center improvements and $200,000 for the Resource Management Center; and the Kresge Foundation gave a total of $400,000 for two different projects. Most generously of all, the Hodson Trust added $4.2 million to the endowment fund to support the Beneficial-Hodson Program for Academic Excellence, established in the fall of 1978 to provide student honor scholarships and faculty sabbatical fellowships.

The Advanced Institutional Development Program (Title III) grant provided the necessary resources (fiscal and personnel) for sound planning. On September 27, 1979, the Long-Range Planning Task Force endorsed a substantive list of *measurable* institutional goals and objectives. By 1980, the college had a draft plan that, upon revision, became the college's master plan for the period from 1981 to 1984. Reviews of the academic programs and divisions were launched in 1981. Instead of growth without a plan, the college now plans, budgets, and evaluates its programs and services against the college's mission, goals and objectives. These activities take place within the context of a comprehensive list of planning and budgeting assumptions.

While student morale has moved upward at a steady pace, faculty morale has had its ups and downs related to the college's efforts to maintain a balanced budget. Salary and fringe benefit improvements have exceeded inflation rates, but much more needs to be done in this area. Trustee morale is at an all-time high, given the leadership it has enjoyed since the early 1970s. Alumnae support has also reached new levels. Moreover, recognition of the college as a good place for women learners is signaled in major college guides: The college received the third highest ranking in *Everywoman's Guide to Colleges and Universities,* was cited in Fiske's *Selective Guide to Colleges,* and was listed as one of the seven best colleges east of the Mississippi River in a poll of 662 college and university presidents conducted in 1983 by *U.S. News and World Report.*

In short, the turnaround of Hood College was completed in just over ten years. Statistics tell the story: In 1972–73, the college had 606 undergraduate students, virtually all of them full-time residential students. In contrast, fall 1984 enrollment figures included 650 residential students, over 230 older women commuting students, and approximately the same number of traditional age commuting students. Again, in 1972–73 there were only 86 graduate students, most of them part time, and only one area of graduate study. In 1984–85, however, there were over 600 graduate students working for master of arts and master of science degrees in fourteen areas. And, as a final note, the number of graduate students is soaring in the college's recently implemented program in information and computer science, in its biomedical science program, and in its entirely restructured program in administration and management.

In his recent book *Academic Strategy: The Management Revolution in American Higher Education,* Keller asserts that Hood seized upon targets of opportunity (in adversity) and was successful in pursuing that strategy. In doing so, the college has remained true to its founding purposes: to prepare women for work in the home and for success in the world of work. The faculty, staff, trustees, alumnae, and friends believe in Hood's women students and recognize that their options now are virtually unlimited. That is the real key to Hood's success story.

13

Birmingham-Southern College: Rediscovering the Mission

Neal R. Berte
Philip A. Shirley

The history of Birmingham-Southern College began in 1856 when a new private liberal arts institution, Southern University, was founded in Alabama by the Methodist church. During the nineteenth and early twentieth centuries, the young institution experienced alternating cycles of prosperity and hardship. By the end of the First World War, Southern University and a second Methodist institution, Birmingham College, were at the point of collapse. A merger in 1918 created Birmingham-Southern College and stimulated a new cycle of growth and development that continued until the late 1960s.

During that period, a combination of circumstances—an unexpected presidential resignation in 1968, a substantial enrollment decline over several years, and prolonged deficit spending—placed the college in jeopardy. The problem was aggravated

Note: The assumptions presented in this chapter were first discussed in N. R. Berte and E. H. O'Neil, "Managing the Liberal Arts Institution: A Case Study." *Educational Record,* 1980, *61* (3), 25–33.

by the college's consideration of moving the campus to a suburban location. Public discussion of this alternative hampered
recruitment and development efforts for four years. Also contributing to the gravity of the situation was the lack of long-
term, stable leadership; three presidents served between 1968
and 1975. This disruptive pattern caused a general loss of confidence in the college and was accompanied by sharply reduced
fiscal support by the Methodist church.

When Neal R. Berte assumed the presidency of Birmingham-Southern in 1976, the years of turmoil had taken their toll.
Financial exigency had forced faculty and staff reductions,
weakened a recently adopted, innovative curriculum, created
uncertainty as to institutional mission, and caused the physical
plant to deteriorate. Campus morale was at a low ebb, and
enrollments, predictably, continued to decline. Immediate action was called for to reverse this decline.

Strategies for Renewal

A first and most important step was taken in the spring
of 1976. Berte engaged Birmingham-Southern faculty, administrators, and students in a collective reexamination of institutional mission and an analysis of internal and external factors
affecting mission. On the one hand, this study resulted in a
number of fairly standard findings. Birmingham-Southern's
problems were in general found to be the same as those of other
institutions—financial difficulties created by inflation, declining revenues, and higher energy costs; the expected decrease
over the next decade of college age youth; deteriorating facilities and high renovation costs; and the increased doubts among
Americans about the value of a college education and, most particularly, of a liberal arts education. On the other hand, however, this collective study allowed the college to establish key
assumptions on which to base both short- and long-term planning. This process of formulating assumptions relative to college
mission and future prospects was in actuality a process of self-
evaluation that continues to the present as the college's environment is monitored and responses to problems are modified as

necessary. This process involves research, planning, action, and evaluation on an ongoing basis.

The first assumption established that, despite some problems, the academic program at Birmingham-Southern was still vital and sound and had maintained standards of quality throughout the recent difficult years. This finding was supported by the assessments of external groups, which rated the college highly in comparison to other regional institutions. An additional indicator was the fact that faculty continued to receive recognition for excellence in the form of grants, fellowships, and prizes.

A second assumption affirmed that Birmingham-Southern was one of the few Alabama institutions still offering a traditional liberal arts curriculum. This fact placed the college in a special niche within the state and regional higher education community and offered a unique position upon which to build.

However, as the administration and faculty examined the changing educational environment, they recognized the need to offer expanded opportunity for study to the older, nontraditional student. They also recognized and identified the problems involved in attracting this new population: access, scheduling, financial aid, and, perhaps most difficult of all, articulation of the value of a liberal arts education to a student clientele holding different values and expectations. It was finally determined that new career-oriented courses of study, set within the framework of the liberal arts curricula, were necessary. This decision led to the implementation of majors in computer science and nursing and to the expansion of the business program, particularly in the field of accounting. More recently, a graduate management program was initiated that departs noticeably from the conventional business degree. Based on programs at Yale and Stanford, this program places emphasis on social, political, and ethical concerns, as well as on the development of analytical and problem-solving skills. Students are taught and encouraged to develop a broader perspective.

Other events helped the college narrow the gap between liberal arts and career education. In 1976, a grant was obtained from the U.S. Office of Education under Title III to develop support services for adult learners. One year later, the Kellogg Foundation awarded the college a $250,000 three-year grant to examine ways in which a small, private liberal arts college could address the demands of the world of work. Projects resulting from these two awards included a program that placed faculty in businesses for four to six weeks as visiting professors, an executive-in-residence program that brought business leaders to campus for two weeks to study and talk with faculty and students, the development of expanded off-campus learning opportunities for students in business and industry, and the offering of "work and culture" seminars for discussion of the interrelationships between the workplace and the liberal arts. The programs begun under Title III and the Kellogg grant were so successful that the college has continued many of them with funds from the general operating budget.

Each of these new programs represented a response to the need to preserve the college's liberal arts mission within a changing environment. While believing firmly that this mission must be safeguarded, Birmingham-Southern nevertheless recognized that the demands and interests of students were changing and that it must accept the responsibility of meeting those demands and interests with a strong program. In short, it was and still remains essential to find ways to articulate the relationship of a liberal education to the world of work rather than to alter the institutional mission by offering a vocationally oriented curriculum.

A third assumption adopted by Birmingham-Southern held that budget deficits would have to be dealt with immediately to avoid even more severe financial problems in the future. A corollary decision was made to eliminate budget deficits while maintaining existing faculty and staff. Ten out of seventy-five faculty members had been released in 1971 for financial reasons. It was now critical to improve faculty morale and create a positive academic environment.

Substantial physical plant improvements were also needed quickly if the college was to keep its current students, attract new ones, and prepare for a further decline in revenues in the 1980s when the projected decline in college age students would begin to take its toll. Since 1975, therefore, the college has spent over $5 million on campus improvements. Delayed plans for a new library and learning center were carried out, and the new building opened in 1976. Further expansion was completed in 1983 with the assistance of a $250,000 grant from the Pew Memorial Trust.

Major renovation projects were also completed in two classroom buildings, and a new multipurpose building was constructed to house a 1,500-seat basketball arena, athletic offices, and the headquarters of the North Alabama Conference of the United Methodist church. In the spring of 1984, the last major physical facility needed by the college was funded by a $2.6 million grant from the Olin Foundation. The Olin Computer Science/Mathematics Center is scheduled to open in the fall of 1985. This facility was designed to support Birmingham-Southern's efforts to take the lead in use of the computer in the liberal arts curriculum. At present nearly half of all Birmingham-Southern students use the computer in at least one course, ranging from English to sociology to chemistry.

Those looking seriously at the college's problems in the mid 1970s found that alumni, friends, the Methodist church, faculty, and students were willing to contribute time, effort, and financial resources to help improve the college's situation.

In order to make full use of the time and expertise that people were willing to give, ten task forces were appointed in the spring of 1976. These groups were charged to think about the future of the college and what it should aspire to become. The more than 150 people who participated in this exercise were asked to report their collective thinking in the form of specific policy and program recommendations. A report issued in August 1976 presented seventy-five recommendations. It first gave a brief explanation of the topic assigned to each task force: new learning environments, delivery systems for new clientele, support and fund raising, student recruitment, public relations and information, church relations, campus life, values clarification, career dimensions of the liberal arts, and governance. Explanation of these topics was followed by specific recommendations and a report of action taken to date relative to the recommendations.

These recommendations guided the administration in its renewal efforts over the next eighteen months, though it is interesting to note that the task forces found that approximately 80 percent of the recommendations had already been acted upon by the time that the report was published. The greatest benefit of the effort was its success in involving so many constituencies in institutional goal setting.

This organizational model was adopted once again two years later when the president appointed an All-College Planning Council of students, faculty, administrators, and alumni to help define directions for the college. The purpose of the council was to propose directions for growth—since a clear turnaround had begun and was evident in substantial increases in enrollment and revenues—and to institutionalize the planning process. Seven subcommittees were appointed: admissions, academic affairs, finances, student life, physical plant, faculty and staff, and external relations. Their assignment was to examine future growth over three time periods: short range (present to three years), intermediate (three to five years), and long range (five to ten years).

The planning council was charged with analyzing alternatives, stimulating conversations among constituent groups regarding future options for the college, and offering recommendations for growth and development. The plans and recommendations were meant to be flexible and dynamic. It was understood that before any goals and objectives were implemented, feasibility studies would be conducted. The result of the council's deliberations was the "Long-Range Plan for Birmingham-Southern College," which was submitted to the board of trustees and adopted in September of 1979.

Yet another critical assumption was adopted during this period of evaluation. The college affirmed the importance of making a definite commitment to remaining in its present location and to working with the surrounding neighborhood toward the promotion of stability and community renewal. The older neighborhood in which Birmingham-Southern was located had experienced a transition from a white to a racially mixed, predominantly black neighborhood, but it had remained basically middle class.

A series of breakfast and dinner meetings were arranged with elected city and neighborhood officials, business and civic leaders, ministers, and other community leaders. While some of these same people had been involved in the ten task forces already mentioned, it was felt that even more community interaction was needed. As a result of these meetings, the college decided to help the community with a neighborhood housing service that assisted community members in securing low-interest loans for home improvements. Birmingham-Southern then purchased a plot of land adjacent to the campus and created a small neighborhood park for community use. The college also worked with city and neighborhood officials on a major beautification project on Bush Boulevard near the campus.

A final assumption made by Birmingham-Southern was that the college must take the lead in redefining and improving its relationship with the United Methodist Church. While the church and the college were not far apart on any particular issue, there was clearly room to improve discussions between the two that would result in sharing the task of institutional renewal.

Each of the several assumptions that emerged during the mid 1970s served to guide the development of institutional strategies and tactics over the next several years, and in most cases to the present. It was realized that while many of the problems had been generated by external causes, they were compounded by the lack of a clear and shared sense of purpose, the disruptiveness of constant changes in the college's leadership, and an inadequately organized administrative structure. Strategies for the planning of institutional renewal were based on the clearer picture that the college now had of its environment and problems, on the recognized need to create partnerships with many different constituencies, and on a willingness to be flexible in management styles and responses to problems and needs.

Putting Plans into Practice

The first step in implementing these new strategies was to create more opportunities for individual learning. The interim term, adopted a few years earlier as part of the 4-1-4 calendar, provided an excellent opportunity for faculty and students to design such learning experiences. In addition, a grant was obtained from the Lilly Endowment for the development of a Contract Learning Center. The center was to sponsor "contracts" to enhance individual learning experiences both in and out of the classroom. Since 1976 the center has assisted students wanting individual learning options or individualized majors. Individualized study requires a faculty sponsor who works with the student to determine details of the contract, including objectives, a timetable, and a bibliography. Contracted courses include interim term projects, independent study, internships both on and off campus, and teaching experience. Individualized majors are designed in consultation with a three-member faculty committee. The student must in all cases complete general degree requirements of the college.

Because of the drop in enrollment during the early 1970s, faculty members were available to teach more classes than were needed. In order to make better use of faculty, an evening program was established for adult learners. But it was soon evident that the needs and problems of adult learners differed from those of the traditional college student, and a division of adult studies was created with a full-time director and two full-time assistants. A four-member team was sent from the college to a Lilly Seminar Institute, directing their attention to developing the adult program. In order to provide better support services, a grant was sought and received from the U.S. Office of Education under Title III. These services provided the support system necessary for adults reentering higher education. They stressed the importance of assessing past experiences, ascertaining strengths and weaknesses, and developing an educational plan that would enable students to achieve their goals.

To ensure that students received personal attention, strong emphasis was placed on faculty advising skills. (These skills are given careful consideration during the hiring of new faculty members and in faculty and staff evaluations.) Other actions taken to create better advising for all students included implementing a peer advising program, keeping the student-faculty ratio at about 14 to 1, and establishing a freshman seminar program. In the freshman seminar program, students spend two semesters in a class with their adviser, enabling them to develop relationships that allow for more personalized advising.

In the spring of 1976 the faculty approved a service-learning internship program. Students could now earn academic credits through off-campus learning experiences during the regular term. An honors program in general education was begun in the academic year 1984–85 to provide a select group of highly motivated students with an individualized approach to meeting the general education requirements of the college. The program enables students to develop the skills of analysis, synthesis, and integration while simultaneously achieving the more traditional disciplinary goals of general education. It offers another way of providing significant opportunities for individualized learning.

The Kellogg Foundation grant discussed earlier was also important in helping Birmingham-Southern professors to better understand how knowledge and skills learned in the classroom related to the world of work. Funds from the Kellogg grant also supported a series of "work and culture" seminars. Notable figures such as Hodding Carter, NBC's Richard Scammon, and businessman Winton "Red" Blount visited campus to help with the seminars and generate discussions of the relationship between work and its role in society. The grant also provided a program of "education and work" retreats that enabled faculty and staff members of the college to meet with the mayor of Birmingham and his staff, together with leaders in business and industry, to discuss mutual interests, concerns, and activities.

The Career Counseling Center became active in holding seminars on topics such as resumé preparation, how to select a major, and interviewing for jobs. Community members were invited to seminars on reentry into college. A career resource information center was set up with listings of job opportunities. In 1984 Birmingham-Southern began providing a career planning computer program titled DISCOVER, which helps students match their interests, skills, and values with possible careers.

One of the key components of the strategy for renewal, cited earlier, is the involvement of the various constituencies of the institution in goal setting. Certainly one of the most comprehensive of these activities was the 1976 task force. These task forces not only assisted in giving immediate direction to the college but have also served as models for several collective efforts since then. Another important element in the process of reevaluating and redefining goals for the college was a college-wide retreat held in 1977. This retreat, funded by the Danforth Foundation, provided the occasion for further refining of the goals and mission of Birmingham-Southern. Finally, in order to give constituent groups additional information and to provide a better sense of "ownership" in the college, the meetings of the board of trustees were opened up to the leadership of various campus groups. Members of the alumni association, the student government association, the faculty advisory committee, and administrators were invited to attend the meetings.

During the past years, Birmingham-Southern has sought constructive ways to strengthen historic bonds between the college and the church. Thus, in 1976 a director of church relations and chaplain was appointed to develop ways in which the college could respond to the educational needs of the church. One of the activities that helped most to strengthen the bond between the church and the college was a $1.5 million church scholarship campaign conducted with the North Alabama Conference. The campaign furnished an opportunity for individuals in the church to express their support of the college and involved church members in nominating students to receive donated scholarship money. The North Alabama Conference has continued this scholarship fund; and, in return, the president of Birmingham-Southern in the 1979–80 academic year chaired a campaign for the North Alabama Conference of the United Methodist Church to raise $4 million for ministerial salary pensions.

Two student organizations provide services to Methodist churches. The Music Ambassadors provide music ministry to local churches while Youth Ambassadors offer programs and represent Birmingham-Southern in local United Methodist churches. Birmingham-Southern professors are available to local churches through a visiting professors' program, and continuing education programs for pastors and church officials are taught on campus by the faculty of the college. Each year the college also works with the North Alabama Conference on "BSC Day" in the churches. Faculty, staff, and students volunteer their time to travel to churches across the conference to participate in services and represent the college as a way of keeping local congregations aware of the services of the college to the church. Each year the college also hosts a program called "United Methodist Youth Fellowship Goes to College" to give Methodist high school students an opportunity to visit Birmingham-Southern and learn about its educational program, financial aid possibilities, and campus life.

One of the more visible methods of reaching out to the church was the establishment of the Denson N. Franklin Professorship in Religion. The Franklin Professor offers seminars, lectures, and continuing education programs on campus or in local churches and serves on the faculty of religion.

Extending a hand beyond the Methodist Church, Birmingham-Southern set as a strategic objective the development of good relationships with the immediate neighborhood and the community at large. As previously noted regular meetings were held with community leaders and local residents. One immediate result was the development of a civic community project on seventy-four acres of land adjacent to the campus. A unique partnership was formed among the college, the city, and private business to develop an apartment complex (now completed) and a light industrial park, still in the development stages. The college also worked with community officials to have the Bush Hills neighborhood (in which Birmingham-Southern is located) named as one of six target areas for federal funding under a community development program. Again, opportunities were established for students to conduct weekly programs for residents of a nearby halfway house. Other students work as volunteers to tutor children with learning disabilities in local schools.

The president of Birmingham-Southern has also been actively involved in community projects. He served as president of Birmingham's Festival of Arts in 1981 and as chairman of the

steering committee of Leadership Birmingham, a project to promote community involvement among leaders in the area. In
1983 he served as general campaign chairman of the United Way
for a three-county area, helping raise over $10 million.

Trying not to overlook any of its constituencies, the college began a number of new programs, including a weekend for
parents to give them an opportunity to learn more about their
children's collegiate experiences, to meet and talk with professors, and to tour the campus. The college serves also as a cultural resource for the Greater Birmingham area by offering
entertainment, ballet, art exhibitions, drama, and musical events
that the public is encouraged to attend. In a related step, Birmingham-Southern began to find new ways of creating a more
positive image for itself. Administrators and faculty began accepting invitations to speak to groups throughout the state. A
President's Student Service Organization was created to present
a strong positive image of Birmingham-Southern undergraduate
students. These selected upperclass students assist in many activities, including recruitment of high school students, fund
raising, public relations, and hosting campus events.

The college also hosts citywide entertainment events and
a gala to recognize outstanding women from around the world
for accomplishments in business, medicine, fashion, politics,
journalism, and entertainment. Among the notable women who
have been so honored are Rosalyn Yalow, a Nobel Prize winner;
television journalist Barbara Walters; and actress Bette Davis.
Other events sponsored by the college include an annual writers'
conference and the Monaghan Lectureship in Economics, endowed by Vulcan Materials Company, that brings noted econ-
omists to campus for well-attended public lectures. Appearances
by Herbert Stein, Juanita Kreps, and William Allen have attracted many key business leaders to campus, thus providing a
community service while helping to create a positive image for
the college.

One of the important strategies for renewal—closely related to creating a good public image—was to secure funding for
necessary campus renovations. The first step was to survey the
physical facilities of the college with the help of an architect

and physical plant personnel and to estimate the costs of renovation. A New Hilltop Fund was created, and a small steering
committee of influential trustees and alumni assisted the president in making fund-raising calls. Over $3 million toward the
goal of campus renovation was raised. Major changes were made
in landscaping, lighting, and security, and basic maintenance
was completed. A Campus Beautification Committee of college
and community members was appointed to develop a comprehensive plan of beautification and to assist in fund raising. The
college is at present purchasing homes adjacent to the campus
in order to have more control over the esthetics of the area.
Major renovations in dormitories have created better living conditions for students.

The management of human resources also received needed
consideration. New positions were created in the president's
offices and in the areas of church relations, public relations, and
development. These appointments reflect the college's desire to
relate more effectively to its external constituencies. The new
positions and existing administrative staff were organized into
an administrative council that meets monthly to share information and discuss policy issues. Four new vice-presidencies were
also created—academic affairs, financial affairs, admissions services, and development. These four officers, together with two
associate vice-presidents and the dean of students, comprise the
vice-presidents' council, which meets weekly. The old departmental system with seventeen administrative units was restructured into six academic divisions.

The college was also selected to participate as one of ten
liberal arts institutions in a long-range planning program coor-
dinated by the Academy for Educational Development. A new
staff manual was written, and a classification system for staff
was created. Also, new personnel policies were developed for
the faculty handbook to replace a vague set of guidelines.

Faculty and staff members are encouraged to participate
in professional organizations and to attend seminars, conferences, and workshops to develop greater teaching or administrative skills. The administration has also encouraged faculty and
staff to participate in "growth contracts" in order to facilitate

personal and professional growth. The college is in the process of raising funds to match a $175,000 grant from the Mellon and Hewlett foundations to create a permanent $700,000 endowment to support institutional renewal, primarily faculty development.

Student recruitment efforts naturally became a high priority in the overall strategy of institutional renewal. The first need was to create a more aggressive marketing strategy that informed the public of the quality of education available at Birmingham-Southern. An increase in scholarships was an obvious goal, for it would mean that more students could be attracted without sacrificing quality. The college has been fortunate here. The McWane Corporation, for example, began funding the McWane Honors Scholar Award, which is now worth over $52,000 for four years of study. Other prestigious scholarships were established, providing full tuition plus supplemental grants for special educational travel and projects. The College also offers Phi Beta Kappa scholarships to top students on a competitive basis during special scholarship days held each year on campus. Scholarship days are also held for students interested in the fine and performing arts and in health careers, and during preview days students and their parents are given detailed explanations of the types and amounts of financial aid available.

A special alumni retreat is held on campus each year for alumni from key geographic areas who have indicated a willingness to assist in recruitment. They are brought to campus and updated about programs and financial aid, then asked to visit schools and help identify potential students from their area.

In all contacts with students a personal approach is emphasized. Letters, visits, and phone calls are favored over mass media—though mass media clearly can help support those efforts. Institutional publications and advertising are designed to inform the public in a tasteful manner of the college's liberal arts mission and educational services. The admissions office works closely with high school guidance counselors. The college hosts a dinner biennially for the Alabama Personnel and Guidance Association to show appreciation for their work and to update them on recent events at the college. Another direct contact with schools and churches is provided by the Birmingham-Southern concert choir and other musical groups as they tour the region each year.

Birmingham-Southern has made the securing of external sources of funding a high priority in its renewal strategy. In 1984 the college completed a long-range development campaign begun in 1979 to raise $25 million. Many foundations have responded to the needs of the College, including Mellon, Lilly, Olin, Brown, Exxon, Arthur Vining Davis, Kellogg, Kresge, Hearst, Amoco, and others. Several endowed chairs in the areas of music, business, and religion have allowed the college to attract prestigious senior-level faculty. The Methodist Hospital Board awarded a challenge grant of $1.3 million to the college's endowment, thus providing vital support to the health careers area.

To help foster a sense of belonging to the college community, the president's office sends out an annual report each summer to a number of friends of the college. In the fall, a printed annual report is widely distributed. Unrestricted giving has steadily increased from $160,000 in 1975 to an average of over $1 million each year since 1980. As a result of increased services and better communication between the college and alumni, the percent of total alumni contributing to the college has increased since the early 1970s from 7 percent to 29.5 percent. More than 300 volunteers each year serve on various boards and committees for the college. Several advisory boards have been set up to draw on the resources of the alumni and community leaders who have an interest in the college and its programs. The board of the Norton Center for Continuing Education in Business, for example, advises the college on programs that would help meet the needs of the business community. As a result, the business community has an interest in the academic program of the college and constitutes a potential source of support when capital needs arise for the college.

Other joint endeavors include participation in forming the Alabama Association of Colleges and Universities to assist in articulating the needs and contributions of both private and public education in the state. The college also joined with other private colleges in helping to successfully promote passage of the Tuition Grant Bill, which provides a tuition grant for students attending private institutions in Alabama.

Getting Results

The success of the strategies begun in the mid 1970s and continued with occasional modifications to the present is indicated in several areas, the most obvious one being enrollment. An enrollment that had dwindled to about 725 students in 1974 has increased every year since then to a fall enrollment in 1983 of 1,587 students—a number that falls within the 1,500 to 1,600 range considered optimum for Birmingham-Southern. In keeping with the college's goal of a low student-faculty ratio, the number of full-time faculty members was increased from fifty-nine to ninety-three during those same years. In order to retain those faculty members and attract new faculty, salaries have been given high priority during the budgeting process. In fiscal year 1982–83, the average salary increase was 9 percent, in 1983–84 it was 6 percent, and in 1984–85 it was again 9 percent.

Improvements in the academic program and in services to students are indicated in a number of ways—forty-seven graduates were admitted to medical or dental school in 1983, representing an acceptance rate of 80 percent of those who applied and were recommended by the faculty; 94 percent of those applying to law school were admitted. That same class of 308 graduates included a Rhodes scholar. In 1982 a student team placed third out of thirty-three teams in the International Scholastic Computer-Programming Contest, placing higher than schools with graduate computer programs. National publications such as *Changing Times, Town and Country, Money Magazine,* and *U.S. News and World Report* have cited Birmingham-Southern for academic excellence and institutional quality. A longitudinal study conducted at Wooster College by Alfred Hall that ranked undergraduate schools according to the number of graduates going on to receive doctoral degrees in research fields from 1920 to 1980 showed Birmingham-Southern with the highest percentage in Alabama and one of the highest in the South. It showed that one of five graduates earn a doctoral degree.

While academic work is the priority at Birmingham-Southern, the faculty and administration believe that athletics can also play a valuable role in the life of the campus. In 1979 and again in 1982, the college sent every intercollegiate team it fielded to the National Association of Intercollegiate Athletics (NAIA) national playoffs in basketball, baseball, and tennis, a feat no other NAIA school has managed previously. From 1982 to 1984 the basketball, baseball, and women's tennis teams each had an Academic All-American. The 1982–83 basketball squad also had a first-team All-American.

The financial health of the college has also steadily improved. Larger enrollments, increased giving, and better management procedures have enabled the college to complete its sixth consecutive year of operating under a balanced budget in fiscal year 1983–84, after several years of operating deficits. The endowment has increased to $20.4 million.

The efforts discussed earlier to involve all constituencies in evaluation, goal setting, and planning for the college have proved extremely valuable. The closer ties with city and neighborhood officials help keep Birmingham-Southern informed and involved when the city conducts beautification or development projects that could affect the college. Efforts to reach out to the business community and the United Methodist church have broadened the college's base of support and helped provide stability.

Several challenges remain for Birmingham-Southern and other liberal arts institutions. Probably the most ominous is the expected drop in the number of traditional college age students between now and the year 2000. The statistical predictions vary, but regardless of the exact figure, it is clear that educators must be realistic about the decline in the number of available students. Private institutions, with their higher costs, will suffer if they do not plan carefully. The competition for dollars between public and private schools will accelerate, and increases in operating costs are assured despite institutional efforts to curtail energy costs and make cutbacks where possible.

Liberal arts colleges must search for ways of interpreting the value of a liberal arts education to students and parents who are career oriented in their search for a college. The confusion that exists in society about the meaning and value of a liberal arts education can be a severe handicap for traditional colleges at a time when the baccalaureate degree is often judged in terms of its economic value.

Student needs and interests must be carefully monitored and responded to. Part of this response lies in relating current academic programs to career, professional, and other student interests rather than in changing the curriculum. Society is experiencing an information explosion that requires skills of analysis, synthesis, and judgment. The importance of learning and developing these skills must be conveyed to students. The successful people will be those who can learn on the job and adapt, since most people will change their place of employment —if not their job field—several times during their lives.

During the last decade, Birmingham-Southern has had to adjust not only to changes in society but to changes within the institution. The college's development was possible because of better management of existing resources, more widespread participation in goal setting and planning for the future, and a strict adherence to high standards. Birmingham-Southern completed a self-study in 1984 for reaccreditation by the Southern Association of Colleges and Schools. With a steering committee of twenty-nine administrators, faculty members, students, alumni, and trustees, this eighteen-month study examined changes and events at Birmingham-Southern since the last self-study in 1973. One of the critical points confirmed by the self-study was that risk taking, widespread participation, and a thorough assessment of the college's successes and failures could lead to a stronger institution.

The renewal that Birmingham-Southern has experienced during the past decade has provided the college with its own model for the future. This model stresses six components: widespread participation by all major constituent groups, a shared consensus of mission, a willingness to be flexible in dealing with problems, the development of partnerships with various constituent groups, an action orientation that seeks to solve problems rather than simply live with them, and responsiveness to student, community, and societal needs. In anticipating and planning for the future, colleges must meet such problems as increased competition for students and dollars, societal confusion over the value of education, and ever increasing costs with a clear sense of mission. Liberal arts colleges must proclaim the value of the liberal arts as preparation for future careers and personal success. These colleges must develop good marketing techniques. They must be well-managed institutions that stress quality and individualized attention. They must provide a special collegiate experience that is not replicated in larger institutions. At a time when a "catastrophic mentality" is evident in higher education, it is important to face the future with confidence.

If liberal arts colleges can maintain the delicate balance between institutional needs and the needs of students and society, if they can create and instill a sense of mission among their constituencies, and if they can respond creatively to the challenges and opportunities that exist, then they will survive and thrive. More than that, they will emerge much strengthened from the difficulties of the 1980s and 1990s, and they will possess a clear vision for the future.

14

Brooklyn College: Through Adversity to Excellence

Robert L. Hess

Spring 1979. As one of four finalists for the presidency, I had come to Brooklyn College by subway one day before the second round of interviews to experience what it meant to travel to that campus of the City University of New York by public transportation, to wander about the campus anonymously, and to discover what I might see and learn without the benefit of a guided tour. The business district just west of the college was run down. It was far from being a slum; but after living away from New York for more than twenty-five years, I found it distressing to see these indications of urban decay. One block away, but with no signs to indicate that it was there, was the campus.

That cool spring day I slowly walked through the college's west gate and wondered what lay ahead. Would it be an oasis of beauty (as a former faculty member, a close friend of mine, once described it), or would I find more evidence of urban decay? A broad tree-lined sidewalk led past outdoor bulletin boards bearing the ragged scraps of ten years of notices.

The trees, gingkos planted forty years earlier in accordance with a plan provided by botanic garden specialists, had not been pruned in at least a decade; low-hanging branches obscured the view of the buildings that lay ahead. To the left and the right were two "temporary" buildings of khaki-colored, rusting corrugated metal, a mute testimonial to the overcrowding of the campus that had taken place in the 1970s. The first two brick buildings I saw were clearly but incompletely marked with handsome cast aluminum letters indicating that one building was the " ibrary" and that the other was "W itehead Ha l."

The vista opened ahead, and I found myself on a large quadrangle flanked by handsome well-built brick buildings in a neo-Georgian style. At the head of the quadrangle was LaGuardia Hall, inspired by colonial antecedents like Philadelphia's Independence Hall. That once-magnificent building, the original library of the college, had obviously deteriorated. Its tower badly needed painting. Inside, I found that its monumental interior spaces had been chopped up into cubbyhole offices and classrooms. Wooden partitions painted battleship gray obscured marble columns, two magnificent Federal Art Project murals, and handsome stucco detailing, to say nothing of the impressive chandeliers. At the far end of the twenty-six-acre campus lay modern buildings constructed in the early 1970s. Subsequently I saw the results of shoddy workmanship in those newer buildings, and throughout the campus maintenance standards were to prove unacceptable.

And yet, one could perceive through the deterioration that a fine architect had had a master plan for the campus. It must once have been the most beautiful campus in New York City, although it looked so out of place here, as if it had been transplanted from New England or the Midwest. For it looked like a campus, a real campus, not just a collection of office buildings euphemistically dubbed an urban campus. The possibility of physical restoration was intriguing.

My eyes moved from the buildings to the students. Here there stood a group of black students, chatting among themselves. There, a group of Orthodox Jewish students. Other blacks were deeply engaged in conversation—in French patois, for they were all Haitians. A group in front of LaGuardia Hall twenty feet away wore the recognizable garb of Rastafarians. Other white students stood around the steps of Boylan Hall. Fifty feet beyond them was a group of Hispanic students. One could sense the tension in the air, even though there was no apparent crisis; but I had read about and remembered the college's legacy of recurrent racial confrontation throughout the seventies.

From a college classmate of mine who was on the faculty, I learned of the bitterness and demoralization of the teaching staff and of its harsh indictment of the college administration, which had received several votes of no confidence. An air of hopelessness, I was told, was what I could expect when I would be interviewed the next day. We sat in my friend's office, which he shared with several colleagues because the campus had been built with little concern for adequate amenities for the faculty. Was there only unrelieved deterioration? The one bright spot seemed to be the student union building. Its capable management had preserved an island of grace and elegance for students and faculty alike. How curious that one of the most heavily used buildings on campus showed the least signs of decay.

Mentally, I reviewed the literature and reports that had been sent to me as background materials. During the twenty-seven-year presidency of the outspoken and often controversial Harry D. Gideonse (1939–1966), the college had first gained national visibility for its academic excellence. Then there came in quick succession a series of short-lived presidential terms before my predecessor's ten-year tenure began in 1969. The college, a tuition-free institution for forty-six years after its founding in 1930, had experienced two abrupt changes of mission in ten years. Academically elitist in its admission policies until 1969, Brooklyn College, like its parent institution, City College of New York, had once been known as "a poor man's Harvard." Then after the newly organized City University of New York established a policy of open enrollment, the college doubled its size to 34,700 students at its maximum expansion in 1975. Free tuition ended in 1976—the price exacted by the state of New York when it assumed responsibility for funding City Univer-

sity's four-year colleges. Open admissions ended in 1978, also at
the state's insistence. With the reinstatement of relatively high
admissions standards, the college could now combine excellence
with accessibility. But the imposition of tuition, higher admissions standards, and the decreasing number of high school seniors had led to a reduction in the size of the student body by
almost one-half to approximately 19,000 students at the time
of my visit. Aggravating this stretching and then snapping rub-
ber-band effect were the loss of public confidence and the uncertainty generated by the changes in mission and leadership in
1969 and in 1979.

In short, since the supposed golden age of the fifties and
early sixties, it appeared that everything that could possibly go
wrong in an institution of higher education had gone wrong at
Brooklyn College.

Brooklyn College in 1979: An Assessment

Summer 1979. July 5, my first day on the job as president, with some eight weeks to establish priorities before the
start of the academic year. Every department head and dean insisted on having the opportunity to meet with me as quickly as
possible in order to explain the significance of his or her program, problems, opportunities, and frustrations.

Although the City University of New York defined
Brooklyn College as a "comprehensive college," most of its faculty and staff regarded it as a liberal arts college. In reality, it
was somewhere between liberal arts college and university in the
complexity and sophistication of its programs and the quality
of faculty, as well as in terms of its organization. Strong programs in education, in preprofessional areas such as the health
sciences, and in the fine and performing arts had long existed
side by side with traditional majors in the humanities, social sciences, and sciences. In addition to some seventy-five undergraduate majors, there were fifty master's degree programs and, in
conjunction with the City University Graduate School, five doctoral programs in the sciences. In order to cope with the scale of
operation of the 1970s, the college had subdivided itself into

more than a half-dozen schools, each with its own degree requirements. Tremendous competition for a rapidly decreasing number of students had embittered relations among the academic administrative units. As the student population declined from 34,700 in 1975 to 18,300 in 1979, the academic departments had added dozens, if not hundreds, of new courses to the curriculum in a mad mercantilistic scramble for "bodies."

The decline in enrollment had entailed massive cuts in the size of the faculty and staff. In 1975, the college had 1,418 faculty and 1,019 other employees. Four years later, the figures were 946 faculty and 778 other staff. The great inflationary pressures of the late 1970s had taken its toll on a steady-state "other than personal services" budget. No money had been provided for replacement of deteriorating equipment, and no inventory of equipment existed. The college had had little significant development effort. Its endowment was less than $350,000; gifts and contributions in 1979 amounted to only $138,466. Never in its history had there been an alumni fund appeal. Although the total budget amounted to $61.3 million, the bulk of it was necessarily committed to salaries, inasmuch as 78 percent of the faculty were tenured. In this context of severe budgetary pressures, the entire infrastructure of the college had deteriorated. A 1975 self-study pointed out the need for massive reform in both the registrar's office and the library. The City University authorities could provide little relief to the college. It was clear that there was to be no budgetary honeymoon period for me as the new president.

Despite the erosion of the college's enrollment and budget, there were immediately visible a number of potential assets —a very strong faculty, trained at the best colleges and universities in this country and abroad, including a large number of professors with national and international reputations; an enormous body of alumni that yearned for an indication that the quality of the institution had somehow or other survived the 1970s or that it could be restored; and an impressive network of political support, so important for a public institution in New York State. Finally, it appeared that the institution had nowhere to go but up—unless it was down for the count.

Brooklyn College enjoyed all the advantages and disadvantages of being part of the eighteen-campus City University system. As one of the original four older schools (City College of New York, Hunter, Brooklyn, and Queens), it drew upon a long tradition of excellence and had a proven track record. But as an urban public campus, it was expected to serve the entire community to some degree, although no funding was provided for extension activities, public service, or community service. Average salary per faculty rank was among the highest in the country. But faculty were expected to do research, and little budgetary support was given to that area. Faculty were also expected to teach well, a proud tradition at Brooklyn College, but they were saddled with a heavy average teaching load and severe remediation problems as the weakened public secondary education of New York City began to take its toll on students whose basic skills were adequate but whose general knowledge was lacking. The City University of New York was itself more a loose confederation of schools than a university. It had never resolved the problems flowing from the tension between the forces that made for centralization and those that made for decentralization.

The basic issue facing me was whether to move slowly until the lay of the land was clear or to strike fast. In fact, however, the agenda for the first year emerged rapidly: changes in administrative personnel, changes in administrative structure, administrative centralization, curriculum reform, easing of racial and ethnic tension within the student body, improvement of faculty and staff morale, and attainment of some short-term accomplishments as a means to buy time until longer-term goals could be achieved.

The Start of a Renaissance

Spring 1980. Commencement had ended on a triumphant note, symbolizing perhaps the rebirth of hope at Brooklyn College. The commencement speaker, a Brooklyn College alumnus who played a commanding role in the state legislature, reminded students of the college's part in his life and career. The alma mater written by Sylvia Fine Kaye (class of 1933) but not sung in a decade was reintroduced to the college community. So too was the Ephebic Oath. Skeptical graduates, coming at the tail end of a dozen years of social and political protest, slowly grasped the meaning of the ancient Athenian oath that summoned them to leave the city not less but greater than it was transmitted to them.

This capstone event of the academic year, the graduation ceremonies, had been preceded by two other events deliberately designed to raise campus morale and to signify the renewal of the college's quest for excellence. In October 1979, a special academic convocation had been held, with full panoply, to award Zubin Mehta the honorary degree he had been unable to receive the previous June when the New York Philharmonic was on tour. Escorted to the podium by a member of the faculty, Itzhak Perlman, Mehta praised the college for its attainments in the liberal and performing arts. The faculty, not accustomed to hearing much praise, seemed eagerly responsive to his words. Then in April 1980 came my installation as the college's new president in a week-long series of events that included not only the formal ceremony of investiture in the presence of a large number of delegates from other colleges and universities but also a series of major seminars in the humanities, social sciences, and physical sciences, as well as a splendid performance by the theater department. For the first time in years, many faculty reported, they felt that the campus had come alive intellectually. The experience of these three events confirmed for me the importance of formal ritual combined with special intellectual and creative events in helping the academic community rediscover its self-esteem.

From the vantage point of my first commencement I could look back and recall that early that first year I had made the decision to move as rapidly as possible to effectuate change, despite the risks involved in not having adequate preparation time. An intelligent and hardworking provost who was nonetheless unpopular because of his close association with the previous administration was removed, while the other two incumbent vice-presidents were quickly confirmed in office. Shortly after I arrived on campus, a notice was sent to the entire faculty requesting nominations for an acting vice-president for academic affairs. A popular faculty member was chosen, and the deans of the schools were informed that they would serve out the year but that a study of the entire administrative structure would take place and a decision on the new structure and appropriate personnel would be announced by March 1, 1980. Meanwhile, a national search for an academic vice-president produced an unpromising pool of candidates. An unknown president, a college whose reputation had suffered, a university plagued by mission and budgetary problems, and a city whose fiscal crisis had shaken the entire nation's confidence in its future—these were not exactly the elements that made for successful external searches. In addition, because my predecessor had been harshly criticized for bringing in his own people from outside, I felt that the best path for Brooklyn College would be to fill from within as many vacant administrative positions as possible.

By December a task force on structure had come in with its recommendations and urged the abolition of the administrative division of the college into schools. The creation of a unitary college was appealing, provided that a span of control and openness of communication could be maintained between the presidential and vice-presidential level, on the one hand, and the thirty-four department heads, on the other. Most appealing was the idea of abolishing an entire level of the campus bureaucracy. Deans of schools were to be replaced by nonhierarchical functional deans who might better serve the needs of the students. After conducting public hearings based on the report of the task force, I then issued my own set of proposals which called for an end to the decentralizing tendencies of the 1970s and introduced strong centralizing tendencies in their place. A new vice-presidency for development was created. Deans of undergraduate studies, graduate studies, and continuing higher education replaced the deans of the schools of humanities, social sciences, physical sciences, performing arts, general studies, and the New School for Liberal Arts. Prior to my arrival, a School for Contemporary Studies had already been phased out.

Only the School of Education, a department in all but name, was permitted to retain its previous title in order not to weaken its links with the New York City Board of Education.

Meanwhile, the college's faculty council was hotly debating questions of curriculum reform. In the aftermath of the curricular decentralization that accompanied administrative decentralization, a growing number of faculty had become uneasy about the abolition of the college's general education requirements. Concern was particularly marked among humanists and scientists who longed for greater structure, and social scientists who advocated some sort of uniform distribution requirements. In 1977, the faculty council passed a resolution calling for the establishment in principle of a core curriculum but deferred defining its contents until a committee could study the matter in depth. When the committee presented its report to the faculty council in December 1979, I faced a classic dilemma: how to be supportive of the principle while opposing the committee's specific proposal. The committee proposal, which was debated at several long and stormy meetings, called for a core of 72 hours (out of the 128 required for graduation). It was clearly a compromise among all the political forces at work. Some termed the proposal racist because it did not mandate courses in minority studies. Others found it offensive because it was cumbersome; perhaps some deliberately overloaded it in order to ensure its defeat. In speaking against the proposal, I realized that I had to exercise the greatest caution. After all, faculty prerogatives in the area of curriculum are not to be tampered with by even the most well-intentioned administrator.

In opposing the committee's report, I tried to state my concerns in the most statesmanlike fashion. The committee had deliberated long and well, but it had focused on only one aspect of undergraduate education. I reminded the faculty council that our common concern had to be both the totality and the balance of the three aspects of American undergraduate education—general education (whether a core curriculum or distribution requirements), the area of concentration or major, and the ability to experiment through a system of elective course offerings. A seventy-two-hour core threw the balance awry. Gather-

ing my courage, I indicated that we should make the most of
this opportunity for educational reform and perhaps be more
adventurous. Why not pass a resolution that all courses in any
core curriculum would have to be newly designed? More work
for the faculty, of course, but the possibility of faculty renewal
through curriculum renewal had to be appealing to the large
numbers of faculty who prided themselves on being good
teachers. A courageous faculty council voted down the original
core curriculum proposal, a disheartened committee resigned,
and a new but skeptical faculty council core curriculum committee was elected. Another year was to pass before the results of its deliberations would be made public.

It is still unclear to me whether an objective assessment
of the situation or a peculiar personal style of administration
dominated in my own thinking. As a professor of history I
strongly identified with the faculty's concern for curriculum
content and form. But as an administrator I was impatient with
the myriad facets of faculty politics. An element of personal
vanity must also have played a part. I was presiding over an
institution that was about to go through massive internal reorganization and administrative streamlining at the same time
that its faculty would be taking on the task of redesigning
lower-division education. And all of this, apparently, would
take place against the backdrop of further declines in enrollment, with concomitant reductions in budget and staffing.

Meanwhile, the institution forged ahead. When alumni
leaders expressed their dissatisfaction with the college's motto
of See and Be Radiant, adopted in 1960, their morale was
quickly raised by a decision to return to the earlier Latin motto, *Nil sine magno labore,* which was most appropriate to the
college's situation in an era of restoration—"Nothing worth-
while is obtained without great effort!"

All through my first semester, student politics were particularly volatile. There were three student governments on the
campus, one for the day session, one for the evening session,
and one for the graduate division. The largest of the three, the
day session assembly, was at that time a divisive force that
continually threatened the peace of the campus. Its two political parties, divided along racial and ethnic lines, contained the

potential to turn any small disagreement into a full-scale racial issue. The situation was aggravated by the fact that the two parties were stalemated, each having twenty elected seats. Student government leaders perceived the stakes as being relatively high—for example, $78,000 in student activity fees were generated in the fall semester of 1979 for allocation among more than one hundred competing chartered student groups. Rivalry between the two parties in the student government threatened to trigger intergroup unrest on campus.

Caught between student groups that were trying to turn the situation to their own political advantage, I froze all student accounts while the two parties were asked to prepare briefs for review by the university attorney. Since student government was a creature of the board of trustees, or so I contended, I was not going to be caught in a no-win situation between the two groups. When the university attorney ultimately supported me and instructed the students to reform their own electoral apparatus to give more balanced representation to all student constituencies, the student government took me to court. Fortunately, the attorney general of the state of New York defended me well, and the court ruled that my powers as president extended into areas far larger than those challenged by the students. The stakes had been high—the peace of the campus was involved, not to mention important areas of student and presidential power—and the ruling was critical. In its aftermath the intergroup tensions dissolved. Grudgingly, all student parties came to recognize that the college administration would be scrupulously fair in dealing with the legitimate concerns of each group. They recognized too that student politics would be tolerated only insofar as they did not threaten the well-being of the campus as a whole. Subsequently, the seasoned vice-president for campus affairs was able to move from crisis management to more directive leadership of student-related affairs.

In that first year one could also sense a change in the mood of the student body. In the aftermath of the Ku-Klux Klan murders in North Carolina, an ad hoc group of radical students disrupted a meeting between one of the departments and myself. The students persisted in their demands that the college subsidize their cause, but I stood my ground. Despite their confrontational posture, they could make no headway whatsoever, and the ad hoc group immediately dissolved, to my great surprise. Student activists who took no for an answer —a sharp contrast to the previous generation that would not even take yes for an answer.

Spring marked the formulation of final plans for the year-long celebration of Brooklyn College's fiftieth anniversary. Reluctantly, I assumed the chairmanship of the committee that had spun its wheels during the changeover of administrations. A series of short-term accomplishments that would raise faculty and staff morale now seemed possible.

June of 1980 saw the razing of the first of the four "temporary" buildings. The night before commencement the ugly outdoor bulletin boards were removed. The lawn of the quadrangle was seeded and sodded once again, and trees were pruned at last. The beloved lily pond and adjacent gardens were restored to their former beauty, thanks to the hard labor and dedication of a biology professor and his students. Flowers bloomed in once bare areas as the refurbishment of the campus began in earnest. The battle against graffiti on campus now also began to turn in our favor, as did a quiet crackdown on the campus drug scene.

Over the months I had established a pattern for involvement in community affairs. Off-campus evenings were filled with speaking engagements and public appearances three and four nights a week. On-campus days were busy with endless meetings. Task forces held public hearings about the future structure and governance of the college, while my vice-presidents and I conducted open hearings on departmental budgets as a means of coming to understand the realities facing each academic administrative unit. Each week I visited for two hours with the entire faculty of one or two academic departments. In retrospect that first full year on campus was grueling.

Implementing the Core Curriculum

Year Two and beyond. The rapid flow of events of the first year of a new college administration was succeeded by the even dizzier pace of a year-long fiftieth anniversary celebration. The symbolic and the real were intertwined in a mutually beneficial fashion that second year. In retrospect, one could wonder whether the boundaries between the real and the illusory were deliberately blurred by the rapid flow of events. At any rate, the college seemed to be moving ahead in dramatic fashion.

The highlight of the fiftieth anniversary year took place in November 1980 with a special convocation that turned out to be almost an intellectual orgy. Speakers included the chairman of the National Endowment for the Humanities, the chairman of the National Endowment for the Arts, the president of Rockefeller University, the governor of the state of New York, and a former chairman of the Brooklyn College Department of History, John Hope Franklin, who reminisced about what it meant to be the first black to hold a major position at an overwhelmingly white institution nearly a quarter of a century earlier. Partly as a result of events such as these, the faculty began to regain faith in the future of the college, although a healthy skepticism continues to be its dominant feature.

On a more practical level, the new administrative structure was functioning smoothly. By December of 1980 the faculty was again ready to act on curriculum reform. This time close collaboration between the faculty council's new committee on core curriculum and the administration led to more fruitful results. The council overwhelmingly passed a proposal that effective September 1981 all incoming freshmen at the college would be required to take a core curriculum with a two-tier set of ten newly designed courses. At the same time, the college reestablished a three-semester foreign language requirement. Wisely, the jurisdiction over these core courses was lodged not with the academic departments but with a new standing committee of the faculty council and with the provost. In addition, the president, upon recommendation by the provost, appoints the course coordinator for each of the core courses.

Superb faculty leadership and an interested college administration had cooperated for the explicit purpose of restoring academic rigor and a common intellectual experience for our students as a starting point for a distinctive college education. In one sense, the core reflected the desire of the faculty and administration alike to preserve something of the spirit that had made Brooklyn College a great liberal arts institution in earlier decades. That determination flew in the face of the pressures for vocationalism and careerism that have characterized much of American higher education in recent years. The decision to implement the core was made with the knowledge that it might negatively effect the college's enrollment prospects. The core curriculum itself, however, was not just a blind return to the past, for the new curriculum included innovative as well as traditional elements.

Since 1981 virtually every undergraduate at Brooklyn College, irrespective of his or her intended specialization, has been exposed to the new curriculum. The establishment of the core curriculum reflects the faculty's conviction—and mine as well—that priorities must be set with regard to the broad intellectual experience to be required of every liberally educated graduate of the college. The core ensures, first of all, a well-rounded education that values and promotes the qualities of independence and understanding and provides a foundation for making a rational choice of major field of study and, later, of career. Such an education, the faculty believes, can best be defined in terms of the abilities and substantive knowledge that each student is expected to acquire during the undergraduate years. Seven goals are attainable through this curriculum:

- Development of the faculty of critical thought and the ability to acquire and organize large amounts of knowledge; along with this, the ability to write and speak clearly—to communicate with precision and force
- An informed acquaintance with the vistas of modern science and a critical appreciation of the ways in which knowledge of nature and man is gained
- An informed acquaintance with major forms of literary and artistic achievement, past and present, and a critical appreciation of the contributions of literature and the arts to the life of the individual and society
- An informed acquaintance with the working and development of modern societies and with the various perspectives from which social scientists study these

- A sense of the past, of the foundations of Western civilization and the shaping of the modern world
- An appreciation of cultures other than one's own, including the diverse cultures represented in the Brooklyn College community
- Establishment of personal standards of responsibility and experience in thinking about moral and ethical problems

The core courses offer both a contemporary perspective and a solid liberal arts base. The core establishes requirements in ten areas that give the student a substantive acquaintance with the kinds of general knowledge that exist, how they were and are acquired, and how they are used in major forms of intellectual discourse. Through a sequence that is both complementary and cumulative, the student acquires a fund of knowledge and insights for cross-disciplinary dialogue. In this way, the common experience courses increase the quality of the elective area of the curriculum and add a broader perspective to the student's chosen major.

The first tier of the core curriculum consists of the following semester-long courses:

Core Studies 1. Classical Origins of Western Culture
Core Studies 2. Introduction to Art and to Music
Core Studies 3. People, Power, and Politics
Core Studies 4. The Shaping of the Modern World
Core Studies 5. Introduction to Mathematical Reasoning and Computer Programming

None of these courses may be taken until the student has successfully passed standardized proficiency examinations in basic skills (reading, writing, and mathematics). In addition, students must normally take two semesters of freshman composition. Students who do not pass the proficiency examinations must take developmental courses that prepare them for the core. Thus, one beneficial effect of the new curriculum has been to provide for the first time an effective and limited context established by the core for developmental or remedial courses. By the same token, there is no dilution of quality in any of the

core courses since underprepared students are not permitted to
register in those courses.

The second tier, taken after completion of the first, is
taught at a higher level of sophistication. It consists of the following semester-long courses:

Core Studies 6. Landmarks of Literature
Core Studies 7. Science in Modern Life: Chemistry and
Physics
Core Studies 8. Science in Modern Life: Biology and Geol-
ogy
Core Studies 9. Studies in African, Asian, and Latin Amer-
ican Cultures
Core Studies 10. Knowledge, Existence, and Values

The core curriculum adopted in 1980 proved to be the
first step in the revision not only of general education requirements but of the entire curriculum. Each year I select three or
four departments for an external evaluation as a means of reinforcing the seriousness of the need for curriculum reform. One
department after another has embarked on the tedious but
necessary task of reviewing its entire set of course offerings
and major requirements in the light of the new core curriculum. The core curriculum, not unexpectedly, provided a challenge to the entire faculty to ensure curricular coherence. Its
adoption marked the beginning of the process of converting a
faculty of highly qualified specialists into effective teachers in
a general education curriculum. A highly talented provost,
Ethyle R. Wolfe, who became vice-president for academic affairs in 1982, has supervised this process with unstinting devotion and dedication. For the first time in the history of this
always large and all too often impersonal college, large numbers of faculty members have come to know and appreciate
their colleagues in other departments and disciplines and to
work together with them in reforming the curriculum. This has
had the most salutary effect on faculty morale and institutional
commitment. An additional incentive to faculty involvement
has been my commitment that the Brooklyn College Press

would publish at least one volume (text, anthology, or other work) per course in the core curriculum. The college has further institutionalized faculty development in conjunction with curriculum development with the assistance of generous grants from the National Endowment for the Humanities, the Mellon Foundation, and the Exxon Foundation. The rewards system as it relates to matters of promotion and tenure now takes into account faculty participation in curriculum reform.

As the core curriculum took shape, so too did my overall view of the college and its mission. In the fall of 1980, the Humanities Institute, proposed in 1974 by then Dean Wolfe, was belatedly brought to life to complement the college's basic strengths in the humanities. Its charge was to serve as the primary agent for promoting intellectual and interdisciplinary discourse on the campus outside the classroom. Since then the institute has sponsored an impressive number of major conferences, seminars on the frontiers of research, lectures on topics of community concern, minicourses responsive to student interests, faculty study groups, and interdisciplinary courses. All these activities, on a shoestring budget, evoked a strong positive response from faculty, student body, and the outside community. The Humanities Institute, together with the core curriculum, proved to be a key element in the revitalization of campus intellectual life. It has been a major catalytic element in the genuine renaissance that has taken place on a campus that a few years earlier had seemed destined to drift without a sense of self or mission.

Just as the Humanities Institute is an extracurricular counterpart to the humanities curriculum, the Program on Society in Change serves in a similar relationship to the social sciences curriculum. The program's director, Bela Kiraly, aspired to organize research conferences, each of which would lead to a volume published under the auspices of the Brooklyn College Press. I recognized that the program, which came into existence in the mid 1970s, could be a means both to encourage research and to obtain national and even international visibility for the college. In 1980, delegates from abroad to the eighth research conference held at the college suggested that European scholarly bodies cosponsor with Brooklyn College a series of conferences overseas. Budgetary support from the National Endowment for the Humanities helped this to come to pass. Three years later, conferences were successfully held in Bulgaria (cosponsored by the Bulgarian Academy of Sciences) and Italy (with the assistance of the Rockefeller Foundation). The following year saw a similar set of conferences in Yugoslavia (University of Belgrade) and Romania (Romanian Commission on Military History). In June 1985, there were three such conferences, in Thessaloniki (Greek Institute for Balkan Studies), Pecs (Hungarian Academy of Sciences), and Vienna (University of Vienna); a fourth is planned for February 1986 in Paris (Sorbonne). Brooklyn College may be unique among American colleges and universities in its sponsorship of annual research conferences held abroad.

By the end of Year Two, a clear strategy of counterpart activities had emerged in my thinking. If the college could boast of strong programs in the performing arts, particularly music (a conservatory was established in November 1981) and theater, it could also take pride in the Brooklyn Center for Performing Arts at Brooklyn College (BCBC), which presents outstanding programs of guest artists. Some two dozen regional and international dance companies made their New York City debuts at BCBC in the early 1980s. Its governing body evolved from a committee of college administrators to a true board of directors drawn from the corporate world that helped sponsor its various programs. The traditional strength of the sciences was likewise complemented by the creation of an Applied Sciences Institute. Finally, the fifth area of academic programming, education and teacher training, found its counterpart activity with the establishment in 1984 of a campus high school at Midwood High School, directly across Campus Road from the college. The fivefold strategy of establishing the Humanities Institute, the Program on Society in Change, BCBC, the Applied Sciences Institute, and the campus high school yielded the practical results of increased visibility and intellectual vitality as the college turned its back on the hard years of the late 1970s.

While the college was pursuing these various strategies, it

completely overhauled its admissions, financial aid, registrar's, and recruitment offices and combined them under the leadership of an able dean of enrollment services. Until 1969 the college merely set its admission scores at a level that would yield the required number of students, since its free tuition, its high reputation, and the virtual lack of local competition ensured it of more than enough highly talented students. From 1969 to 1978 open enrollment meant merely processing vast numbers of students into the school. But with the end of free tuition and with the institution of New York State's tuition assistance program, with the college's reputation for excellence diminished by the open admissions experiment, with increased competition from other institutions, and with virtually no experience in the recruitment of students, the college needed to develop an infrastructure as quickly as possible.

Concurrently, with the assistance of alumni benefactors the college embarked on its first advertising campaign. *Pro bono* assistance from a major advertising firm, which had an alumnus as client, provided the college with a marvelous popular slogan: "If You Want to Go Far, Go to Brooklyn. Brooklyn College!" What were the college's image problems and its successes, I had been asked? This was my response: Brooklynites seem to feel that one must leave Brooklyn in order to find quality; non-Brooklynites seem to think that Brooklyn is beyond the end of nowhere. At the same time, however, please note how far our alumni have gone in life! More than five hundred are listed in *Who's Who,* some 250 of them presidents, executive vice-presidents, or chairmen of the boards of major corporations. And thanks to the Brooklyn diaspora, one out of seven Americans has a parent or grandparent who came from what was once the country's third largest city before absorption into Greater New York. At any rate, our full-page advertisement in the *New York Times* and subway posters took everyone by surprise. The impact was far greater than one could have ever hoped for in terms of the restoration of public confidence in the institution.

Early in my tenure, I also made the decision to treat this large public commuter institution in its urban setting as if it were no different from a small private residential college in terms of both human relations and, more significantly, institutional relations. A small faculty club of some sixty members was encouraged to expand its activities and, with the total commitment of the college's first lady, soon counted almost half the faculty as paid members. A strong emphasis was placed on both development activities and alumni relations.

For much of its history the college had been content to depend on municipal support for its entire budget. But the great dislocations inherent in the rapid expansion and equally rapid contraction of the institution limited its budgetary flexibility in ways that seriously hampered its ability to move forward. Hence, a new vice-president for development was put in place in 1982, and a functioning development office was systematically created. The college's fund-raising arm, the Brooklyn College Foundation, soon expanded to a board of some thirty men and women who were committed to raising funds for the college. By early 1985 the endowment approached $3 million, nine times the 1979 figure, and contributions from all sources in 1983–84 amounted to more than $800,000, six times the 1979 figure, as an annual alumni fund drive took hold. Significantly, a group of alumni pledged themselves to raise more than $2 million toward the construction of the college's first dormitory.

An equally dramatic growth in alumni activity occurred in this period. Although an alumni association was formed in the 1950s, it never received much attention from the college's administration. As a matter of policy, my tireless wife (who had worked extensively with alumni at her own alma mater) and I determined that it was in the college's best interest to build as strong an alumni network as possible. The Brooklyn-based alumni organization offered programs for local alumni, who numbered perhaps 25,000 in Brooklyn alone. Yet less than one-sixth of the local alumni were paid members of the Brooklyn College Alumni Association. Nothing had been done in an organized manner to reach the tens of thousands of alumni scattered across the country (there were perhaps 30,000 in the Northeast alone). What about Los Angeles—a kind of Brooklyn West? Or Brooklyn South, in Florida? The alumni had to be reassured that theirs was still an outstanding institution. Disaffected by the City University's policies of the 1970s, they were eager to rediscover and to reclaim their alma mater. By early 1985, some nineteen regional alumni chapters were functioning across the United States. And some 200 alumni formed a group in Israel, cavalierly referred to by some as Brooklyn East. Both the college and the alumni association are committed to increasing their support of these efforts.

The Years Ahead

Is Brooklyn College once again Brooklyn College? Certainly the college of the mid eighties differs radically from that of the mid seventies. Nor is it a replica of other earlier eras. With regard to the question of academic quality, however, the college may be likened to the legendary phoenix, risen from its own ashes, committed more strongly than ever to the principles of liberal arts education and nationally recognized as a leader in the field of curriculum reform. In November 1984, a highly publicized report by the National Endowment for the Humanities, while bemoaning the decline of the humanities in colleges and universities, cited Brooklyn College as one of three bright spots in American higher education. A spate of newspaper articles in the national press brought considerable attention to the college. This is not to say, however, that the college does not still face difficult times.

The state of New York continues to put tremendous pressure on the City University of New York to reduce the size of faculty at those campuses affected by the changing demography of the city. As a result of declining high school age populations, student enrollment at Brooklyn College continues to drop. Although the college increased its market share of the eligible college-bound public high school graduates of Brooklyn from less than 22 percent in 1979 to slightly more than 30 percent in 1984, the absolute figures continue their inexorable downward trend. In the academic year 1980–81, Brooklyn College had 13,215 full-time equivalent students; by 1984–85 that figure had fallen to 10,849. The profile of the faculty over those four years also changed dramatically. In 1980–81, there were 895 full-time equivalent faculty, 83.3 percent of whom were tenured. By 1984–85, there were significantly fewer full-time equivalent faculty (768), along with a somewhat higher tenure rate (88.7 percent).

An early retirement option taking effect in 1986 will result in a tenure rate of approximately 82.5 percent. Fortunately, the college has the services of a brilliant young vice-president for finance and administration who manages the college's insufficiently flexible resources with maximum effectiveness. A five-year plan to phase down the number of full-time faculty positions was introduced in 1981 to anticipate additional cutbacks without disrupting program quality, failing to meet student demand, or weakening the new forward thrust of the college. But because of drastic state cutbacks, the college was compelled to implement its plan in less than three years. The continuing challenge to the college is whether it can augment quality in the face of enrollment declines that might lead to budgetary instability.

To offset enrollment decline, a weekend college was launched in 1981, and vigorous recruitment efforts targeted New York City's nonpublic sector of secondary education. Brooklyn College is now atypical of public institutions in that approximately 35 percent of its incoming freshmen are graduates of Catholic and independent schools and Jewish day schools (yeshivas). Additional enrollment decline offset has also occurred spontaneously as graduate and undergraduate students from out of state and abroad are attracted to the college's conservatory of music by the reputation of Itzhak Perlman and other well-known faculty members, to its highly regarded art department by the presence of some of the city's finest artists, including the renowned Philip Pearlstein, and to the creative writing program, whose faculty includes John Ashbery, winner of a Pulitzer Prize in poetry. Other students come because of the reputation of an entire department (for example, the Department of Television and Radio) or because of a department's special program, such as the master of fine arts in performing arts management. By 1984 it was estimated that as much as 15 percent of the student body consisted of non–New Yorkers; and the college, with strong alumni support, began seriously to contemplate the prospect of constructing its first dormitory.

Additional offsets to enrollment decline have been sought through rapid expansion of graduate offerings to New York City teachers, between 30 and 40 percent of whom received at least one of their degrees from Brooklyn College. "Two-plus-two" articulation agreements for Brooklyn College preengineering students concluded with both the Polytechnic Institute of New York and Pratt Institute should also attract significant numbers of new students to the college. I have also given efforts to improve articulation with major feeder community colleges a high priority.

Since 1979 new programs have been added: bachelor of arts programs in Caribbean studies, journalism, and religion; a bachelor of science degree in broadcast journalism; bachelor of fine arts programs in art and in theater; master of arts degrees in Judaic studies, liberal studies, and political economy; master of science degrees in broadcast journalism, physical education/psychosocial aspects of physical activity, and physical education/sports management; a master of fine arts program in television production; and doctoral programs in geology and in computer sciences. Most significantly for future enrollment prospects, in January 1985 the college obtained from the City University Board of Trustees approval of a bachelor of science program with a major in business, finance, and management.

The stresses and strains of the budgetary situation have not always had happy results. The college's affirmative action program was set back ten years as a result of budget cuts. An inability to add faculty other than in the highest priority areas meant that two departments had to be eliminated when their faculty fell below a critical mass because of the budget crunch, and their programs were merged into other departments. Within this challenging budgetary environment, however, some of the most interesting experiments in faculty redevelopment have taken place. A relatively large number of faculty (nearly two dozen) willingly acquired the skills to teach introductory courses in computer science. Indeed, enough of them did this so

that *all* sections of computer science at the introductory level
are covered by such faculty. This enabled the college to utilize
its regular computer science faculty for the development of a
first-rate major that is now competitive with the very best in
New York City and the metropolitan area.

The most visible improvement at Brooklyn College is its
now well-maintained campus. The state of New York has responded generously to the college's physical rehabilitation
needs. New slate roofs and new windows are being installed on
the original buildings around the quadrangle. LaGuardia Hall,
no longer desolate, houses an elegant Brooklyn Room where
faculty may meet socially. The ugly partitions in LaGuardia
Hall have been removed, and its monumental spaces have been
restored. The Federal Art Project frescoes now look down upon
a restored main reading room. Plans are under way for a permanent home in LaGuardia Hall for the three-year-old, very successful Museum of the Borough of Brooklyn at Brooklyn College.

All four temporary buildings are now only a memory. Art
department students designed and constructed a handsome deck
over the concrete slab of the first building razed. The concrete
foundations of the other three structures are soon to be removed and new landscaping added. Letters are no longer missing from the signs identifying our buildings. Students still con-
gregate around the quadrangle, but more often than not the
groups are multiracial and polyethnic. The business district has
begun to show some promising signs of improvement. At major
intersections, signs now indicate the direction to Brooklyn College. The immediate neighborhood of the college has been considerably spruced up by homeowners and absentee landlords
who see the college as an asset to the neighborhood, and the
Midwood section of Flatbush is benefiting from the overall revival of the borough of Brooklyn, just as Brooklyn has benefited from the strong comeback of the city.

There is much unfinished business. The college has found
no effective panacea in remedial and developmental education
to the underpreparation that characterizes too large a section
of the college's incoming freshman class. Federal funds under

Title III have enabled us to experiment with a number of approaches, including an interesting application of Latin for developmental learning. But the college has yet to find a means to reduce the 33 percent attrition rate among lower-division students. Peer counseling in the writing center, computerized learning centers, a department of educational services, remediation efforts in the English and mathematics departments, all have been tried but without definitive results. An early attempt to provide the campus with a sharper urban focus and to involve the college directly in city affairs through an Institute for the Study of the Borough of Brooklyn failed. The undergraduate program in urban studies remains underdeveloped, despite its very considerable success in placing student interns in state and local government agencies. The college still has to develop an integrated academic and career-counseling and advising system appropriate for a new generation of students. Although mandatory academic counseling is in place for most core curriculum students as part of the registration process, it still falls far short of addressing student needs. That bit of unfinished business will be given a high priority in the college's next five-year plan.

Presidential leadership, often outspoken and always direct, has been well received by a faculty and student body that wants strong leadership, provided that their own prerogatives are also respected. At Brooklyn College strong faculty leadership and strong administrative leadership have found a way to work together. New programs have been introduced despite budgetary cutbacks. While new courses have been added, literally hundreds of other courses have been pruned from the college bulletin by a faculty that takes its responsibilities with great seriousness. Student pride in the institution, carefully cultivated by the administration, is a new factor in the recent history of this commuter campus.

Program development, improvement in academic quality, restored physical appearances, renewed student life, a fiftieth anniversary celebration, even a National Collegiate Athletic Association Division I athletics program, and opportunity in adversity do not automatically lead to budgetary and enrollment stability. But Brooklyn College is now determined to be the master of its own destiny to the greatest extent possible. The sense of mission in the liberal arts is heightened. Secure in this mission, we can now feel reasonably comfortable with the development of undergraduate programs in preengineering, business, health sciences, and the performing arts as long as they have the sound foundation and strong underpinnings of our core curriculum. Indeed, so heightened is the sense of mission that faculty who have participated in our core curriculum faculty development workshops have described themselves as "born-again professors." Visitors to the campus have characterized the provost and myself—we both, by the way, teach courses in the core—as having almost a missionary zeal for curriculum reform. Certainly, presidential involvement in that kind of reform is most unusual, to judge from Clark Kerr's interviews of some four hundred college presidents. Perhaps the experience of Brooklyn College— institutional renewal through curriculum renewal, faculty re- development, and the determination to forge ahead whatever the budgetary circumstances—can prove to be helpful to other colleges and universities that have undergone the kinds of dis- orientation and dislocation that we experienced.

Epilogue: Opportunity in Adversity

Janice S. Green

In recent years, we have all been bombarded with advice on how to handle stress. We are told to exercise regularly, change our life-styles, practice yoga or biofeedback, meditate, improve our personal relationships, take up a hobby, and so on without end. Indeed, "coping with stress" has become a catchphrase of the eighties and a sure trigger of conversation, no matter what the setting. But the phrase is applied almost exclusively to techniques adopted by individuals seeking to relieve the pressures of daily life. Rarely is it applied to measures taken by groups and organizations, although we know that organizations are not immune to stressful circumstances. Chrysler and AT&T come immediately to mind as corporate examples, and it is clear from the preceding chapters of this book that American colleges and universities for more than a decade have been prey to stressful conditions.

Again, not all responses that individuals make to stress produce long-term salutary results. Someone who begins a strenuous exercise program can expect to feel an initial glow of well-being and exhilaration. As time goes on, however, the glow may fade, stress may increase once again, and, if inappropriate to its user, the exercise program may even result in bodily injury. This same pattern can be observed at many colleges attempting to respond to the stresses of recent years; ill-considered coping strategies can send an institution into a downhill slide difficult to halt. Some of the less fruitful modes of coping with adverse conditions will first be examined in this chapter, followed by a look at more rewarding ones.

Desperate Remedies for Survival

In Chapter One, Michael O'Keefe describes the range of issues affecting higher education. In fact, the litany of problems has been so often repeated in this volume that our readers can probably recite it flawlessly by now: inflation, fiscal constraints and budget deficits, decline of the traditional applicant pool, reduced funding from all sources, loss of public confidence, rampant vocationalism, and the moribund state of the liberal arts. Relief from these interrelated pressures is obtainable only by continuing to attract students and dollars and by stretching revenues as far and as effectively as possible. This is by and large the prescription for survival for the majority of colleges and universities. The issue at hand, however, is not the validity of this remedy but the choice of ingredients and the mode of their application.

One important ingredient of the survival remedy used by many institutions has been the adult student. For the past several years we have witnessed a steady decrease in the pool of high school graduates and the numbers continue to fall even as this book is being published. But it became evident in the 1970s that a new group of potential students was emerging. Administrators began to realize that men and women between twenty-five and forty-five years of age could be attracted to the campus under the right circumstances. These people were interested in accessible urban or suburban locations, flexible class hours, affordable costs, willingness to interpret and evaluate life experience in terms of academic credit, and programs that would ensure job opportunities and mobility. Thus were born divisions of continuing education, weekend and evening colleges, external degree programs, off-campus instructional sites, continuing education units, certificates of completion, and a legion of related phenomena heretofore viewed as at best peripheral to the central mission and role of most institutions.

While many of these programs for nontraditional students have been quite successful, the wholesale rush to attract new audiences has predictably generated a new set of problems bearing on institutional mission and priorities, resource allocation, academic standards, the faculty's role, campus culture, and many other areas. At the very least we are beginning to recognize two facts of life: The supply of prospective adult students is not unlimited, particularly in smaller cities and less densely populated areas, and the dollars contributed by part-time students do not make up for those lost when the full-time population declines.

A second ingredient of the institutional remedy to alleviate stress derives from the strident demand of students for job preparation. Students of all ages have left no doubt that they expect their investment of time and money in postsecondary education to result in meaningful employment and a steady income. One may ask, of course, if this has not been true since the rise of the medieval university. In any case, young men and women, seconded by anxious parents and prospective employers, have declared the study of the liberal arts a waste of time and now demand a practical education. The response to "the new vocationalism" has been an apparently endless proliferation of new undergraduate degree programs in fields ranging from automotive technology and secretarial science to media production and nursing home management. Programs in business administration, nursing, and computer science have increased and multiplied while less marketable liberal arts programs have been dropped or reduced. Faculties in the arts, humanities, and certain of the social sciences have been left to offer "support" or introductory courses. Nontenured faculty in underenrolled departments are let go and at present constitute a band of roving scholars seeking temporary employment. Tenured faculty are often asked to prepare for teaching in another field or to take early retirement. Dependence on part-time faculty has increased dramatically in response to the need both for highly specialized expertise and for reduced expenditures. In short, the effort to respond to student and labor market demands through new programs has left an indelible mark on many campuses.

A third component of the remedy for academic stress is found in the admissions office. Despite new programs, alternative modes and sites of program delivery, and reductions in underenrolled offerings, student recruitment remains a primary concern of all institutions. Most private colleges and universities are tuition dependent, with the degree of dependency contingent on the size of their endowments and the success of annual fund raising. State appropriations for public institutions are almost without exception based on enrollment. There are good reasons, therefore, why the office of admissions has become a focus of presidential concern and trustee anxiety and why institutions have turned to new and sophisticated recruitment techniques derived from marketing expertise and computer technology. The literature of student recruitment has become a highly specialized art form. And surely no one would question the legitimacy—indeed, the necessity—of strong, state-of-the-art recruitment efforts. However, the warning flag must be raised when there is evidence either of unethical practices or of institutional admission standards that are permitted to decline measurably in order to fill the annual quota of new students. These are the kinds of responses to stress that will bring temporary relief but will, over time, weaken the institution.

No prescription for organizational stress reduction would be complete without the fiscal ingredient, as the spending patterns of colleges and universities reveal. When the buying power of the dollar decreased, energy costs rose, and funding sources contracted, it became necessary either to make spending choices or to announce across-the-board budget cuts. The latter strategy was the easiest and often the most politic. Most institutions found, however, that across-the-board cuts would ease the pressure only temporarily. New science and technology programs were costly and so was student recruitment. Faculty cried out for relief, as their salaries fell steadily behind increases in the cost of living. Additional staff were needed to administer bur-geoning operations in continuing education, admissions, and de-velopment. In short, spending choices had to be made, and such choices involve trade-offs. Robert Atwell and Madeleine Green, in Chapter Nine, have discussed this fact of life thoroughly.

On many campuses the trade-off victim was plant mainte-nance. Dollars could quickly be shifted from facility repair and renovation to more immediately critical areas. Many of us are still being reminded of the consequences of this particular choice, as well as of decisions to reduce funding for libraries, student activities, and foreign language programs, among other familiar options.

The most typical institutional responses to stress have in-cluded in some measure all the ingredients mentioned thus far; they appear as variations on a theme. But there is also a quite opposite approach to the stressful conditions of the day. It is predicated on the belief, espoused by many of us as individuals, that we are either strong and fit enough to tolerate large doses of stress without injury or that prevailing conditions will some-how not affect us. Institutions exhibiting these beliefs can be described as having assumed either the "hunkered-down" or the "ostrich" position. The hunkered-down college calculates that its substantial reputation and resources will permit it to carry on business as usual until happier times return. The ostrich imitator wraps itself tightly in protective ivy-covered walls in the expectation that it will remain untouched by prevailing forces. But both of these positions are apt to become uncom-fortable. The decline in number of highly qualified students of traditional age has already generated strong competition among the most prestigious of our institutions, thereby producing a chain reaction of lowered admission standards that reaches down to much less selective colleges. Endowments are tapped and massive development campaigns mounted to compensate for the shrinking dollar. In cases where an institution cour-ageously opts to admit fewer students in order to maintain stan-dards of excellence, some financial or programmatic trade-offs must be accepted to support the decision. The real fallacy, how-ever, lies in assuming that an institution, whether small or large, selective or nonselective, can somehow remain unaffected in adverse times. In light of the incredibly rapid societal transformations of the recent past, it is doubtful that any college or university can reasonably afford to adopt a do-nothing approach.

Painful Results

But perhaps the most troublesome effect of the responses thus far described is a gradual and often unpremeditated shift of institutional mission and purpose. The rapid introduction of new programs and new populations to a campus can result quite quickly in a glaring discrepancy between mission statements in the catalogue and the actuality of curriculum and campus climate. The college is no longer what it purports to be, and this suggests the existence of serious problems. Immediacy as the driving force has outraced the past and short-circuited longer-range deliberation. Confusion replaces clarity of purpose, and the institutional profile, once readily identifiable, becomes blurred and indistinguishable.

A by-product of this syndrome is a troublesome loss of institutional diversity. Where the United States could boast, even very recently, of an impressive array of institutional types and educational options, our colleges and universities are now beginning to look very much alike. A regrettable number have bit by bit relinquished the distinctiveness of mission and purpose, the particular flavor and character, that made them unique. Warren Bryan Martin affirms in Chapter Three that "the mission is the message." He makes it clear that a well-defined and clearly articulated mission statement is central to institutional success. As incremental or ad hoc departures from long-standing tradition and culture occur, the potential for effective planning and decision making is lessened and the long-range health of the institution endangered.

Still another logical consequence of institutional movement away from familiar goals is likely to be a growing anxiety and loss of confidence on the part of faculty, alumni, and trustees who have served the college over many years. Where there had been the assurance of knowing what the college was about and where it was heading, it is now seen that choices are being made and directions set in order to address immediate pressures and constraints. Faculty worry over job security. Alumni wonder why they should continue to support a college with which they no longer identify. Trustees question, if only mutely, the wisdom of the president. Funding agencies look askance at institutions that appear to be in a chronic "state of transition."

We must conclude, then, that responses to stress that significantly and rapidly alter the mission and character of an institution are apt to engender internal stresses of an equally disturbing nature. For example, a sharp increase in part-time enrollment, coupled with a noticeable loss of full-time students, will quickly alter the dynamics and personality of a campus. This is particularly true at the historically residential college. As the residential students find themselves overshadowed by the part-time commuter population, active campus life begins to fade, and the retention of residential students becomes even more difficult. Again, any significant weakening of admissions criteria can be expected to trigger a damaging chain reaction of falling academic standards, dissatisfaction and attrition among the more able students, lowered faculty morale, increased costs for compensatory education, and, in extreme cases, a degree program of questionable validity.

The scenario sketched here so briefly is a familiar one. It suggests that certain of the more familiar responses to institutional stress may in the long run do serious bodily harm to the patient. Emergency measures will alleviate the symptoms but will rarely effect a lasting cure. Survivalism of this kind suggests recourse to extremist measures, departures from behavioral norms, and, above all, an emphasis on the immediate. It calls to mind tactics utilized to avert the most pressing dangers of the moment, even though the lasting efficacy of such tactics may be debatable.

Establishing Our Priorities

Our goal as educators is surely the perpetuation of colleges and universities marked by excellence, integrity, and distinctiveness. Surely we wish also to offer to students of all ages and backgrounds a spectrum of viable educational options from which to choose. The only real question before us is: Are these worthy goals realistic? The contributors to this book have answered with a resounding and unanimous yes. Not only are the goals realistic, but they are being achieved today by institutions across the country. The strategies employed to achieve these goals—strategies that equate with successful modes of coping with stress—are not held by exclusive patent. They are available to institutional leaders, administrators, and faculty everywhere. None of them can be described as stopgap, thumb-in-the-dike remedies. Nor will they bring total or immediate relief. They may even add an initial measure of pain, for they require institutional consensus; untold hours of discussion, analysis, goal setting, and planning; generous doses of patience and tact; and a pervasive, unwavering spirit of optimism. But these must be tolerated as the substances essential for building institutional *survival* in the finest sense of that word.

If there is one thought writ large in this book, it is that of the primacy of mission. Every lasting edifice rests securely on a solid, deep-seated foundation and the foundation of an enduring institution of higher learning is its mission. The founders of each of our colleges, large or small, had very specific goals in mind. Some wanted to prepare young men for leadership positions in the professions and in the nation, others to prepare young women to assume an active role in society. Some wished to foster learning in the classical tradition, while others concentrated on the emerging fields of science and technology. The students at some of these colleges were farmers, at others they were sons of merchants or scions of wealthy, powerful families. The founders of these colleges may have been clergymen carrying on a sectarian set of values, or they may have been scholars intent on perpetuating an age-old academic tradition.

The successful institution can usually retrace its history and find that, despite many phases of evolution and change, its original purposes continue to provide direction. Bradford College, for example has never deviated from its initial mission of preparation for life by means of a broad-based, liberal arts education. Yet over its long history, the college's structure, curriculum, and populations have undergone radical changes. Birmingham-Southern's affiliation with the Methodist church since the college's inception has been the hallmark of its institutional culture and purpose, and it is noteworthy that Birmingham-Southern was most at risk when its ties with the church were permitted to loosen. Today's curriculum at Hood College would be largely unfamiliar to the college's founders, but they would recognize and appreciate the unchanged Hood mission of educating its students to fill active, productive roles in the contemporary world.

In all three examples—and many others could be cited—the motivating force behind a history of development and change has been a clearly enunciated and firmly established reason for being. Upon this base there has evolved in each instance a particular institutional culture, a uniqueness that sets the college apart. The student who selects Hood College would in all likelihood not even entertain the thought of attending either Birmingham-Southern or Bradford, and that is as it should be. She has selected Hood because the college's distinctive characteristics meet her needs and preferences; the same is true of Bradford and Birmingham-Southern students. It is far less true in the case of students at many other colleges. The denominational college that describes itself as a traditional liberal arts institution but enrolls the majority of its students in training programs has strayed from its original path. The small college or university, once considered special because of the quality of its residential life, is on the path to losing its uniqueness because it has chosen to enroll a disproportionate number of part-time commuting adults. The state-supported institution whose mission was the training of teachers and school administrators now justifies an uneasy existence by proclaiming itself a comprehensive college or regional university.

While the reasons for making these changes are understandable, the problem is that all these institutions, initially very different, now bear a striking resemblance one to the other. Cost factors aside, why would a student select one over the other? And what course of action will these institutions take when societal needs and interests change, as they inevitably will? Must there be yet another dramatic shift of direction, or will the institution be able to return to its traditional point of focus and strength? These are hard and unpleasant questions, and they can only be answered in very tentative fashion. There is one certainty, however. It is never too late to seek out, re-define, and crystallize the essential meaning and purpose of an institution and to set about shaping a strong identity upon which to build a secure and lasting future. If we cannot, by some sleight of hand, make the forces of adversity disappear, we can most assuredly work to combat them in creative ways.

As the campus constituencies gather to take up the good fight, they will need above all else effective leadership. Yet we are given to understand that effective leadership is virtually undefinable and that leadership characteristics that work won-ders at one institution may prove wholly inappropriate at an-other. These truths are made manifest by David Riesman and Sharon Elliott Fuller in their description in Chapter Four of two highly successful but totally dissimilar college presiden-cies. It is therefore incumbent upon presidential search com-mittees to consider not only credentials, experience, and dem-onstrated abilities but also appropriateness and "fit." Are the candidate's educational values and priorities in tune with those of the institution? Will this person bring to the campus a cre-ative vision of the future based on a sound understanding and appreciation of the past? Does he or she possess intellectual depth as well as good management skills? In short, are this per-son's attributes, style, and personality going to promote the long-term health of the institution?

Each of the colleges described in the case studies of Part Three is presently led by such an individual. In each instance there is a felicitous match of institutional need and culture with presidential style, vision, and philosophy. These presidents are as different one from another as the institutions they lead. But they hold in common several vital characteristics. Each one is first and foremost an educator—a teacher-scholar in the fullest sense. Each combines visionary insight with a fully pragmatic understanding of what needs to be done and how to go about doing it. If they are not equally charismatic personalities, they all inspire confidence, hope, and trust. They are all very positive, decisive people who are also good listeners. Most critical, each of these presidents has brought to his or her campus a dream of the possible—a dream founded on standards of excellence and rooted in a sound understanding of the college's history and tradition. In each case, the dream has been translated into thriving, dynamic reality.

Another key ingredient can be loosely labeled planning and decision making. It bears on a multitude of campus activities: data collection and analysis, resource allocation, admissions strategies, curricular and cocurricular goal setting, faculty and faculty-related issues, programming for facility maintenance and use, and grantsmanship and fund raising. It is by now redundant to note that all planning and decision making must begin with the mission statement. But the importance of this message is such that I will risk redundancy. Planners will find that the parameters and principles established by the mission statement will serve them well and faithfully as they work to transform concept into actuality. No matter how many separate groups may be engaged in the planning process, their central point of reference will remain constant.

Some good advice for planners can be extrapolated from the success stories of Part Three. First, establish a realistic but tight calendar for various stages of planning, include projected implementation dates, and stick to the schedule as closely as possible. Nothing is more demoralizing than a planning process that does not produce visible results in timely fashion. In and of itself, a planning document is only a pile of paper, and a pile of paper engenders little confidence.

Second, ensure continuity and cohesiveness through strong leadership and efficient channels of communication. The president or his or her designate must see that groups come together regularly to report and consult. If left alone for too long, groups will go off in all directions, and it will be very difficult to get them back on the desired track. Periodic summaries of progress, both formal and informal, are useful. The more widely they are circulated, the better informed and more enthusiastic will be your campus populations. Equally vital, a strong sense of "ownership" will be generated through widespread communication and discussion of issues, plans, and strategies.

Third, be certain that your plans are affordable or that they will be attractive to funding agencies. Each of the institutions described in Part Three received major funding from public and private agencies. They were able to attain such assistance for two reasons: First, their planning objectives and proposed activities were judged to be sound, exciting, useful, viable, and reflective of institutional history and capability; second, the activities in question could be comfortably maintained by the institution upon expiration of the grant period.

Finally, be very sure that your plans are in tune with the interests, beliefs, and expertise of your faculty and staff. Arthur Levine emphasizes this vital point in his discussion of program development and change in Chapter Six. If, for example, your faculty is rigidly departmentalized, a program featuring team teaching and interdisciplinary study will encounter difficulties worthy of a Sisyphus. Or if you decide that the road to better student retention is by way of improved advising, make certain that your prospective advisers have or can acquire the requisite degree of enthusiasm and know-how.

As the planning and implementation phases procede, an all-important ingredient of the survival prescription must be always at hand, ready to be blended with the other elements. I refer, of course, to quality. This is a much abused word. We talk about "quality" programs, "quality" education, "quality" students. Not only is this usage grammatically incorrect, but as a descriptive term the word has lost its meaning. For our purposes, the term *quality* signifies the highest degree of excellence that it is possible to attain within the context of institutional mission and purpose. The programs we develop should be the best possible programs of their type. They will not all prepare students for graduate study at Stanford or Yale, nor are they meant to. The students we admit should be the best possible students we can attract, even if this means rejecting a few who can bring more dollars than talent to the campus. The faculty we recruit should be the best prepared—in terms of scholarship, experience, motivation, and skill—to deliver our brand of program to our brand of student. Let us not be dazzled, therefore, by the *imprimatur* of highly select academic credentials but rather seek out the individual whose enthusiasm for our developing enterprise matches our own and who will enhance the quality of our students' educational experience.

There is another side to quality well appreciated by builders of successful colleges. Here once again we are compelled to refer to mission and purpose. No college or university can be all things to all people or do everything well. The institution that goes off in all directions at once can neither establish a definable identity nor achieve a consistent level of quality. It is fair to conclude, I think, that our term *quality* denotes not only excellence but harmony and cohesiveness among component parts. The successful institution knows its strengths and insists that those strengths provide the energy and direction for all elements of campus life: academic, cultural, social, and recreational. It is the quality of the whole that sends a lasting message to the world at large.

If there is one final ingredient to add to our survival prescription, it is that of a large measure of tenaciousness. The institutions that have told their success stories here are notable for their determination to move forward. Yet they encountered enough snags and obstacles to deter even the stout of heart. None had comfortable financial cushions to absorb the shock of investment in the future. None had hordes of applicants beating down the doors of the admissions office. None had placid, acquiescent faculties waiting to be led down (or up) the path of salvation. Some had to renew important ties with the local community. Some were burdened with long-deferred maintenance problems, others with years of deficit budgets. All had to convince their various constituencies of the worth and feasibility of their intent, for such support and endorsement were indispensable. And some days were probably not quite so fine as others. But success is like the proverbial snowball—once set in motion, it gathers momentum and substance.

The mood of this book has been one of optimism. Its pages describe and define the reality of institutional success in hard times. They offer a reasonable prescription for coping with stress and legitimizing the expectation of long-term survival. Nowhere, however, do our authors promise you an easy task.

Stressful conditions will persist for some time to come; and when they have finally eased, the contours and configurations of higher education will be markedly different. Trustees, administrators, and faculties will have learned, once again, that the prevailing forces of social and economic change can neither be ignored nor addressed in provisional or piecemeal fashion. As has always been true in hard times, a number of new institutions will rise to prominence and other institutions will founder. Those that succeed will do so because they have seized the opportunity to marshal their strengths and build upon them creatively and forthrightly, bringing to bear all the intelligence and energy and conviction they can muster.

Even the success stories, however, are not fairy tales. It is a given that each new program, each innovative curriculum, each step forward puts new and often unexpected demands upon an institution. The task is unending. But this is only another way of describing the eternal dynamics of the educational enterprise. There can be no stasis in the true learning process, only movement. It is no different for teacher, dean, or president than for student. The only alternative to failure is movement forward. And, as impressed upon us by the fitness experts, movement—both physical and mental—is healthy.

The fact that colleges can learn to thrive in a time of stress has been established. And while there is, happily, no single road to success, there are certain elements common to the quite divergent paths chosen by each of the institutions discussed in Part Three. These elements can be categorized as follows: a solid marriage of well-defined mission and purpose with institutional tradition and culture; creative vision; vigorous and appropriate leadership; sound, realistic planning; and unflagging efforts to maintain and enhance standards of quality in every aspect of institutional life. Those who seek instant cure-alls will choose different alternatives, and in the short run their institutions may benefit. But those who truly believe in the worth of their institutions, in their value and importance, will look beyond the boundaries of the immediate and will conjure up an attainable vision of a college stamped with the marks of excellence, integrity, and uniqueness and enjoying the fullest possible measure of strength and stability.

Index

T

U

V

W